Roses round the door?

LOGASTON PRESS
Little Logaston, Logaston,
Woonton, Almeley, Herefordshire HR3 6QH
www.logastonpress.co.uk

First published by Logaston Press 2009
Copyright © Tim Ward 2009

ISBN 978 1 906663 22 3

Set in Minion by Logaston Press
and printed in Great Britain by
Bell & Bain Ltd., Glasgow

Roses round the door?

Rural images, realities & responses:
Herefordshire, 1830s-1930s

by

Tim Ward

Logaston Press

Contents

Dedicated to Arthur F.J. Brown,
Classics master at Colchester Royal Grammar School
and gifted local historian

Acknowledgements

So many people have given me their time and permission to use their memories, photographs and local knowledge with such generosity that I cannot find words enough to thank them adequately. In some instances I was given more information than could be compressed into these pages. If I have omitted details I should have included or have inadvertently included details or mistakes I should have omitted, my sincere apologies to those concerned. As anyone who has compiled a book knows, it is almost impossible to avoid some mistakes creeping in. I hope I have kept them to a minimum. My especial thanks go to Karen and Andy Johnson of Logaston Press for converting my raw research into readable text. My heartfelt thanks also go to everyone in Herefordshire and beyond who has made the compilation of this book so rewarding. They include:

Colin Smith, Dennis Morgan, Margaret Wilce, Frank Bennett, Derek Foxton, Helen Wallace, Barbara Gwinnoll, Roger Savage, Brian Thomas, Miss D. W Harthill, Ivan Monckton, K & D Leader, Cecil Box and the late Roger Snell.

Thanks also to:

The staff of Hereford Library Reference Section, Hereford Records Office, Warwick Records Office, Warwick Library, Ross on Wye Library, Ross on Wye Heritage Centre, Ledbury Library, Leominster Library and the *Ross Gazette*; Herefordshire Federation of Women's Institutes; the Local History Societies of Bromyard, Kington and Leintwardine; the University of Warwick; the Museum of Country Life, University of Reading.

Many thanks to Hereford Library for permission to use the photographs on pages 2, 6, 65, 67, 105, 109, 124, 142, 134-136, 143, 144 (bottom), 145 and 146; and to Bromyard Local History Society for permission to use the photographs on pages 82, 114, 119, 120, 121 (top), 122 (bottom left and bottom right) and 123.

Bibliography

Books and newspapers consulted include:

Catherine Beale, *Champagne and Shambles*, Sutton 2006

Harold Bonnett, *Farming with Steam*, Shire 1974

Sidney Box, *The Good Old Days, Then and Now*, privately published, Marden, Hereford

A.F.J. Brown, *Meagre Harvest*, Essex Record Office 1990

G.E. Fussell, *The Farmer's Tools*, Bloomsbury 1985

Reg Groves, *Sharpen the Sickle!*, Merlin 1981

Peter Henshaw, *Tractors*, Chartwell 2009

Eric Hobsbawn & George Rude, *Captain Swing*, Phoenix 2001

Pamela Horn, *Joseph Arch*, Roundwood 1971

Fiona Mac, *Ciderlore: Cider in the Three Counties*, Logaston 2003

Nicholas Mansfield, *English Farmworkers and Local Patriotism*, Ashgate 2001

Christabel Orwin & Edith Whetham, *History of British Agriculture 1846-1914*, David & Charles 1974

D.H. Robinson, *Fream's Elements of Agriculture*, John Murray 1951

Nigel Scotland, *Agricultural Trade Unionism in Gloucestershire 1872-1950*, Cheltenham & Gloucester College of Higher Education 1991

William H. Smith, *The Golden Valley Railway*, Wild Swan 1993

Genevieve Tudor, *Herefordshire Voices*, Tempus 1999

Brian Weekes, *The Herefordshire Football League*, Lugg Vale 1999

Michael Williams, *Farm Tractors*, Littlehampton 1974

Philip Wright, *Old Farm Tractors*, A & C Black 1962

Kelly's Directories 1892-1937
Littlebury's Directory 1867

Hereford Times
Hereford Journal
Ross Gazette
Ledbury Reporter
Ledbury Free Post
Leominster News
Labourers' Union Chronicle 1873-77
English Labourer 1876-77
English Labourers' Chronicle 1877-90

Introduction

Although it has changed so much in the last hundred years, Herefordshire, with its rolling green countryside and its pretty 'black and white' villages, still deserves its reputation as a beautiful and peaceful rural county; but of course that is not the whole story, and this book is about the underlying narrative. The images, which are mainly photographs taken in the late 19th and early 20th centuries, show the working life of agricultural Herefordshire as it was before the dramatic changes of the last century or so, and also depict the machines and methods which heralded the mechanisation which was to bring about that change. The text, especially that of Part One, aims to tell the story of the changes in the Herefordshire countryside and especially the lives of its agricultural labourers brought about by the Enclosures of the 19th century and the subsequent development of agricultural trade unions.

Things have continued to change since then, of course – very fast. The people who lived here a century ago would be astonished at today's huge fields, with their crops of oilseed rape, sugar beet, and fruit grown under acres of plastic; and there is much less grassland now that pasture is no longer needed for working farm horses. They would also be amazed, no doubt, at the transformation of living conditions – housing, roads and much else; and our own imaginations must be similarly stretched to imagine life as it must have been for them. All times and places have their own forms of suffering and their own needs for improvement, but theirs were particularly hard times: squeezed between the stability of the past and the comforts of the future, it was a difficult life, and it is not hard to see why early trade unionists found ready supporters for their demands for improved conditions in every aspect of life: employment, housing, medicine, wages and electoral representation. It is against a background of agricultural depression and technological advance, war and unemployment, winter cold and summer harvest, that these photographs should be viewed. Cottages with roses round the door concealed intense poverty, revealed in recollections in local history books of children in mended second-hand clothes and leaky boots walking long distances to icy school classrooms and on their way home collecting sticks or even cabbage stalks for a fire to keep out the winter's cold.

I have drawn on my collection of photographs and ephemera as well as items from friends and Record Offices to illustrate the working life of rural Herefordshire as it was in the early days of photography. It is not intended to be a complete record and only reflects my interpretation of part of Herefordshire's social history – a part that still needs to be more fully explored, especially the background and role of the agricultural trade unions.

Chapter 1
Rural life in 19th-century Herefordshire

It has not been a thing uncommon,
To steal a goose from off the common,
But what should be that man's excuse,
Who steals the common from off the goose?

Even before the Roman occupation of England, a system of land use evolved that gave each household an equal share of the available cultivatable land to produce sufficient food and other necessities for the family with maybe some surplus for barter in the local market. With free access to woods and grazing land villagers created a variety of common rights as the centuries progressed, some of which have persisted to this day. This self-sufficient system, varying as local conditions dictated, was a vital component of village life, which villagers defended from outside interference for as long as they could. From medieval times it was characterised, in the Midland counties especially, by two or three large fields grouped around each village and divided into strips allocated to each villager. One field remained fallow (uncultivated) each year to provide grazing for sheep, cattle and geese, whose droppings replenished the soil's fertility. The strips in the second field were sown with wheat or rye in autumn to utilise the renewed fertility, and the third field's strips were ploughed in the winter ready for sowing in the spring with barley or oats, crops more suited to its lower fertility. The cycle was repeated each year. Although the land belonged to the all-powerful Lord of the Manor, the commoners controlled the system themselves and agreed any questions about management, like setting the dates their animals were allowed in to graze once their crops were harvested. There were, of course, variations to this basic system in different parts of the country. If, for example, plenty of common pasture existed, the animals might be excluded for a time and the fallow field ploughed or cultivated once or twice to reduce weed growth. Of the common fields that survive in Herefordshire the Lugg meadows, lying to the east of Hereford, remain a valued relic of hundreds of years of agreed common use of the rich pasture land bordering the river Lugg. Details of land holding varied from place to place, as family members bought, sold or inherited their field strips.

Above: In the Lugg meadows in the summer of 1890 Alfred Watkins photographed these two lady workers in immaculate bonnets and white aprons over their long skirts raking hay into windrows ready to be carted to the farm, with a waggon already loaded with hay standing in the background. The Lugg Meadows extend over 327 acres of rich grassland stretching nearly four miles beside the river Lugg to the east of Hereford. Following a system that has worked well for centuries, adjacent farmers still preserve their ancient common hay and grazing rights on one of only sixteen such meadows surviving still in England.

Left: A farm worker sharpening his scythe as he mowed the lush grass in the Lugg meadows in June 1890.

For centuries this apparently haphazard system worked well, providing the essentials of everyday living for the self-sufficient populations of pre-industrialisation villages. However, the disadvantages of this seemingly haphazard system, at least from the point of view of the ruling classes, became increasingly obvious as town populations grew, and planned land reform with regular sized and shaped fields grouped around farm buildings was seen as the best way to modernise agriculture and provide adequate food supplies, especially in times of war. It is certain that unrecorded private sales and amalgamations had taken place for centuries. Land was filched from commons and roadsides to build houses. Minor enclosures took place by common agreement, and because many people could not read or write, many of these transactions took place without documentation. All this led to fragmented field strips and holdings in many small and scattered fields quite unsuitable for the modern style of agriculture proposed by men like Townsend in Norfolk. Early newspapers carried numerous advertisements of sales of plots of land of very small acreages, very often the remnants of these field strips. In the 17th, 18th and 19th centuries, to further their aims, expansionist farmers and landowners, realising that land ownership meant power as well as wealth, bombarded Parliament with innumerable Enclosure Acts, which land-owning MPs, in the same class as themselves, were unlikely to reject. Empowered by an Act of Parliament which in practical terms was impossible to overturn, landowners were in a position both to change and to control the appearance of the landscape and the lives of its inhabitants. The enclosure of six million acres, a quarter of England's cultivated land, permanently changed the traditional pattern of rural life.

Enclosures occurred especially during boom times, when a quick profit on the money invested on reallocating the land could be expected. Ordinary commoners and villagers with small strips of land could see that they would derive little if any benefit from these new arrangements, but were not in a position to prevent the unwelcome change. Only the well-off could afford this expense, as the new owners were required to meet all the costs of enclosure. The Commissioners empowered to enact an enclosure award allotted land in proportion to the amount a proprietor held under the old system and might sell a proportion of it to finance the general fund to cover their considerable costs of surveying, map making, meetings, making new access roads and so on. As compensation for losing some of their tithes, the cost of fencing lands awarded to clergymen or the Church was often paid from this general fund. As a final act of exclusion and privatisation, all newly acquired fields were to be 'ring-fenced with good Hawthorn quicksets properly planted and guarded' as detailed in the Stretton Grandison Enclosure Act of 1813. This was intended to prevent animals roaming, to control their breeding and grazing, as well as delineating the new boundaries permanently and accurately, but former commoners found this fencing particularly irksome as, to avoid damage, it was forbidden to graze animals on roads bordered by these new hedges for the next seven years. Instances occurred where farmers ploughed minor roadways to prevent any such grazing, exhibiting a petty-minded display of authority towards animals and their owners. Smallholders soon found that without access to common grazing they were severely limited in the number of animals they could keep and were forced to find work away from their holdings to earn sufficient income. 'Three acres and a cow' was to become a dream for some trade Unionists and a slogan for land reformers later in the century.

At the end of the 18th century, villagers in 21 Herefordshire parishes still farmed some of their land on the open field system. This practice was more common in other Midland counties; in Herefordshire it was never strong and had diminished in an area where weather and soil conditions favoured sheep and cattle husbandry. As happened elsewhere, a potent mix of rich landowners, prosperous farmers and Church of England clergymen were eager to enlarge and consolidate their acreages at the expense of their villagers' potentially productive common land. The 19th century 'land grab' in Herefordshire saw 20,000 acres of common land privatised by widespread and successive Enclosure Acts, legitimising a process which protesters at the time and later in the century found to be irreversible. In the 67 years between 1798 and 1865 over 70 parishes had most or all of their cultivatable common land, open fields or 'waste' enclosed, following 70 Acts of Parliament. 21 of these awards involved the loss of open arable fields, depriving many of their right to grow food crops. Included in the third of Herefordshire's towns and villages directly affected by the 1798-1865 Enclosures were Aston, Aymestrey, Bishop's Frome, Bartestree, Bodenham, Bosbury, Brilley, Bredwardine, Burrington, Byford, Canon Pyon, Clodock, Cradley, Dilwyn, Dormington, Dorstone, Downton, Eardisland, Eardisley, Eastnor, Elton, Evesbatch, Ganarew, Hope Mansell, Holmer, Huntington, Kingstone, King's Pyon, Kingsland, Kington, Kinnersley, Letton, Lingen, Little Birch, Little Hereford, Upper and Lower Lye, Ledbury, Leominster, Leintwardine, Lugwardine, Luston, Madley, Mansell Lacy, Marden, Michaelchurch, Much Birch, Much Cowarne, Mordiford, Norton Canon, Orcop, Orleton, Pembridge, Peterchurch, Pipe and Lyde, Puddlestone, Ross, Shobdon, Stanford Bishop, Staunton on Wye, Stapleton, Stoke Edith, Stoke Prior, Stretton Grandison, Sutton St. Michael, Sutton St. Nicholas, Ullingswick, Walford, Weston Beggard, Willey, Whitney, Withington and Yarkhill.

The extent and impact of the enclosure awards varied from village to village. The 1832 Byford Enclosure Award merely ordered the exchange of strips of arable land between some farmers to consolidate their holdings into larger fields without affecting any other people. The 1839 Peterchurch Enclosure of 63 acres beside the River Dore affected the villagers who exercised their right to graze animals and cut hay there. The enclosure and redistribution of over 2,000 acres following the 1813 Bodenham Act redrew the village map and even created eight stone quarries for the roadstone to construct the required new roads and accesses to the reallocated fields. In 1808 and 1813, 3,638 acres were redistributed in the adjoining parishes of Withington, Sutton St Michael, Sutton St Nicholas and Marden, affecting hundreds of people and forcing many previously independent villagers to become wage earners, often receiving the lowest wages in the country. Seemingly this process involved a relatively small percentage (between 5% and 10%) of Herefordshire's acreage, but a large number of people felt its effects, and resentment simmered among the dispossessed for years, to be revealed when Union activity (of which more later) began. Union branches were more numerous and stronger where the effects of enclosures were most keenly felt, while conversely there was violent opposition to Union organisers in the Longtown area, which was unaffected by nineteenth-century enclosures, and apathy in the villages north of the Leominster-Bromyard road, where only one small area had been enclosed. In neither of these areas were Union branches established until 1914.

The enclosures created a more prosperous class of farmers, but deprived commoners of the resource on which their precarious lives depended, for progress always leaves losers in its wake. Ordinary commoners affected by a proposed Enclosure Act had neither the education nor the money to fight the Act that would deprive them of their land and livelihood. Opposition meant the expense of travelling to London and fighting a costly legal action in a Parliament which was in any case fundamentally opposed to their interests. The result was that needless poverty was created in a fertile and richly productive land, although

There were sighs of heartfelt relief all round when the last load of sheaves was brought safely home and stacked. There was no glamour in this work, despite artists' skill in romanticising happy workers toiling in the sunshine. They glossed over the long hours of monotonous heavy work from six in the morning until dark and sometimes continuing by the light of the harvest moon. Sunday was a day of rest apart from attending to horses and other livestock.

that land had the potential to clothe, house and feed the entire population, not just the lucky few. By 1850 it was claimed that enclosure of common lands, together with more efficient agricultural techniques and the rotation of crops, doubled the output of food, but this failed to take into account the produce that the now dispossessed country people had previously produced for their own consumption and the barter economy. Compensation paid for losing their common rights did not last long and any small reallocated plots were insufficient to graze their animals or grow their own food. At the same time farmers became businessmen, often directing their labourers' work from horseback rather than sweating beside them in the fields as formerly, so that a feeling of division began to strain relationships between masters and men. Where previously commoners had augmented their incomes only with paid seasonal work, now deprived of their land, they were forced to become wage earners, selling their labour where and when they could. In addition they endured the demoralising effects of insecure employment over which they had no control, becoming, as Joseph Arch later described them, 'these white slaves of England'. Excluded from their customary resources and with insufficient money to buy the products of the Industrial Revolution now readily available in shops, the people in rural communities felt a segregation amounting to second class citizenship. As William Cobbett noted earlier in the century, 'When farmers become gentlemen, their labourers become slaves'. Bitterness and resentment over the loss of their common land rights and their treatment as wage slaves grew as they watched farmers and landowners prosper, while their own main concern was to avoid the workhouse.

We get a sense of what had been lost from a description of Aconbury Hill recorded some time after the Enclosures, in the 1885 Woolhope Club *Transactions*: 'The cottagers of Aconbury Hill are a thrifty race, and from their well-cultivated gardens a good store of flowers, vegetables, strawberries and other fruits are produced for Hereford market. The women and children collect (from the common) in their season mosses and wild flowers for decoration, elderberries and cowslips for wine, nuts, chestnuts etc., selling them in Hereford market, thus turning an honest penny to supply household wants.' The 'cottagers of Aconbury Hill' were fortunate in retaining their access to common land; but many were not so lucky. Even the traditional access to woods, heaths and roadside verges was lost. These were the 'wastes' so often mentioned in Enclosure Acts, and they were in fact a valuable means of support, providing people with timber for building and fuel, crops of nuts and berries, an occasional animal or bird for a meal and, in the autumn, food for their foraging pigs.

To add to the general discontent, repressive Game Laws laid down harsh penalties for poaching, reserving the abundant wild animals and birds for landowners' and their friends' sport. Half-starved families watched, angry and powerless, as their landlord's game birds and animals ate the vegetables in their gardens. Poaching became Britain's fastest growing offence, brought about not by criminality but by the economics of hunger and poverty. Magistrates administering the laws were themselves landowners and friends and neighbours of those 'wronged', and had no qualms about sending a man to prison for two or three months for illegally snaring a rabbit to feed his children. The severity of the punishments meted out to men trying to feed their families is startling, and the devastating effects on a family thus deprived of its breadwinner can only be imagined. A man caught picking hazel nuts worth 2d by a gamekeeper at Ledbury in August 1870 was fined 4d with 2d damages and 6 shillings costs, with the alternative of seven days in prison. In October 1872, Maria Pendrey, who worked for a Walford farmer, took home a bundle of hop pole cut-offs for her fire, and for this she was imprisoned for seven days with hard labour. In the same month, two men who stole a turnip from Thomas Haynes of Wythal farm, Walford were each fined 3 shillings plus 10 shillings costs, as an example to others who might think of stealing something to eat. In 1873 Eli Carpenter, aged 12, was charged with stealing 2d worth of walnuts from Mr Abrahall of Aston Ingham. The magistrate said that the

The gamekeeper seated in this shed containing bags of pheasant food is believed to be James Payne, Sir John Cotterell's head gamekeeper in 1909, supervising feeding time in a pheasant rearing enclosure. His assistants are about to feed the growing poults from the trugs heaped with corn and pellets. Then they would resume their patrol of the woods with their 12 bore shotguns ready to shoot any predatory animals or birds that might harm their precious pheasant poults. A grisly gibbet was somewhere nearby hung with the corpses of weasels, stoats, rats, crows, buzzards, kestrels etc. so that their employer could see evidence of their dedication to his young birds and the estate's autumn shoots.

walnuts were of so little value that he would 'only' give Eli one week in prison with hard labour. Even worse was the plight of Emily Davies of Brampton Abbotts, who was found guilty of stealing 5 shillings worth of plums and apples from James Whittingham. Ross magistrates sentenced her to two weeks in prison and four years in a reformatory and decreed that her father was to pay 2 shillings weekly for her maintenance. Correspondence columns in the *Ross Gazette* were filled with letters concerning her plight. Thomas Blake, a wealthy self-made Ross businessman, later to become Ross's greatest benefactor and MP for Leominster 1875-80, came to her defence. He organised meetings and wrote letters to friends in high places, and even the Home Secretary was approached, though he refused to intervene. Emily Davies was eventually released, after two months' pressure, but then her friends and family had to find her railway fare for the journey from Birmingham back home to Brampton Abbotts. Perhaps the worst case of local injustice happened in Ross when Samuel James, aged 80, and his son, also Samuel James, aged 50, were illegally

Robert Pashley was famously generous to his native Walford. In the days when the Wye was full of salmon his favourite hobby was fly fishing for them with a light trout rod. In his younger days he preferred bank fishing or wading after his quarry and only took to using a punt when troubled by arthritis in his later years. His catches were phenomenal; 678 salmon in 1936 and 16 in one day in 1935. On the Courtfield stretch of the Wye, his friend and ghillie, Jack Whittingham, holds up his latest catch for a photograph. He generously sent salmon cutlets to Walford villagers to share in the bounty the river Wye then provided.

summoned by a policeman for taking young salmon 'pinks' (small immature fish which might not have been salmon anyway) and fined £2 and £1 respectively. They appealed as the policeman was not a river bailiff and had no power to summons them. Their appeal was turned down and legal costs of £70 mounted up against the unfortunate men. They could not pay what to them was an exorbitant sum and were consequently sent to prison at a cost of 18 shillings and £1 per week respectively, chargeable to the ratepayers. To pay the legal costs, the court distrained all their possessions, including their homes. All for a handful of small fish. Endless examples of this type of harsh punishment were widely reported and naturally fuelled the countryside's feeling of resentment against the all-powerful ruling classes' ideas of property and justice.

A very rare photograph entitled 'Salmon Poachers on the river Wye 1910' shows eight pairs of hobnailed boots as their wearers peer over the bank to hook unfortunate salmon out of the river. Five murderous gaffs stand behind them. Over twenty salmon, the result of their night's 'work' lie in the foreground. In the days before flashlight photography, a night time scene was illuminated by igniting a flare of magnesium powder. No photographer with his cumbersome apparatus could have approached the gang unseen or set up his equipment unheard. Poachers kept a sharp lookout as the penalties for poaching salmon were severe. Although the scene is certainly posed it is nevertheless real enough to show how the poachers worked. For a water bailiff coming on the scene, it would have been both his dream come true and his worst nightmare.

To make matters worse, England's population was growing rapidly, adding to the number of men available for work in the countryside and the consequent underemployment of many. Before the enclosures, independent villagers could hope to maintain or even improve their position in life, but after the loss of their village's open fields and commons they found themselves condemned to lives of seemingly inescapable servitude. Symbolic of this were the generally detested 'Mop Fairs', the traditional hiring fairs, where men and women found it degrading to stand waiting in the street for prospective employers to look them over like the cattle which often stood in the street nearby, and then to haggle publicly over the coming year's wage. Not everyone found an employer by the end of the day, and nor was it certain how their new master would turn out to behave, although workers are believed to have operated an underground grapevine of information to warn others of bad experiences with harsh employers, to which young women were especially vulnerable.

How could this situation be endured, or changed? Many chose not to try, but instead decided to leave it altogether. The solution favoured by the young, strong and ambitious was to make the momentous decision to move from their homes and families to better job opportunities in the new manufacturing towns, or to take an even bigger chance and emigrate to America or one of the new Dominions. Thousands of farm workers joined the Army where they were needed to garrison 'the Empire on which the sun never sets'. This exodus in turn had its consequences. The thousands who rejected their low pay and servile conditions by leaving the land hastened the mechanisation of farm work. Mowers could cut grass and binders could cut and tie corn at half the cost of a gang of men wielding scythes. A contractor's steam ploughing outfit pulling a five furrow plough could turn over a twenty acre field in a day when the same work would take a team of horses drawing a single furrow plough three weeks. Slowly heavy financial investment in machinery was accepted – and, of course, work for agricultural labourers diminished yet further. The drift from the land to manufacturing towns or abroad was outweighed by the increasing birth rate so that underemployment, though lessened, remained a fact of rural life. Although some people simply accepted their miserable place in life as God's will, taking what little they were given, among others discontent spread. Bad housing exacerbated already bad conditions. Enquiring for the 1867 Royal Agricultural Commission the Rev. James Fraser found cottage accommodation in the Newent Union and Linton in Herefordshire 'generally deficient in both quality and quantity'. He saw cottages 'simply unfit for human habitation, lacking the basic necessities of running water and wash house facilities'.

By the time of Fraser's report, the bitterness caused by the injustice of the fundamental changes taking place in society had been simmering for decades. In the agricultural depression following the Napoleonic Wars, many soldiers returned to their old jobs on the land as labourers where wages continued at around poverty level. During the war years, when labour had become scarcer, from about 1805 some wealthy farmers had invested in horse-driven threshing machines. Constructed by a Ludlow firm, they were installed on

Dust hangs in the evening sunshine at the end of a day's threshing at Chantry Farm. Two men feed the last sheaves into the drum. A man on the right shoulders a truss of straw away to a stack, while another fills bags of chaff for winter feed for cattle. Another leans on a sack barrow waiting for a sack of grain to fill. A large portable steam engine powered the outfit.

Large, expensive pieces of machinery like threshing machines were mainly contractors' tools, hired each autumn when needed, though some arable farmers could afford to buy their own. In this farmer's opinion a cheap thatch of wheat straw was thought adequate to keep the rain out. Note the wooden wheels and the curved shafts for harnessing a team of horses to move this early example round the stackyard.

several Herefordshire arable farms. Machines constructed of oak cost £7 10s, and more affordable ones made of deal cost £6 10s. A team of one man, three boys and three horses could now replace a gang of men threshing corn on a barn floor with flails, thus depriving many of their traditional winter job. After a bad harvest in 1830 added to their woes, acts of violence spread across southern England. These were the long-remembered 'Swing' riots, a short-lived and desperate demonstration for guaranteed winter employment, as well as a gesture against the rural establishment and the insufferable dominance of farmers and landowners supported by the clergy The labourers, led by a fictitious 'Captain Swing', roamed the countryside smashing, burning or, in some cases with farmers' help, dismantling the offending threshing machines, writing threatening letters and demanding money from the wealthy, but always taking care that no-one was injured. In the eyes of both labourers and small farmers, Church of England clergy were a suitable target for their anger and frustration as their tithe demands were apparently designed to keep them in idleness and support religious teaching which was entirely alien to the ideas of those to whom they preached. Tithes were a heavy financial burden on farmers, who were compelled to pay an annual levy of one tenth of their produce to the church. The labourers thought that without this levy the farmers would be able to afford to raise their pay. Some farmers colluded with the men's demands for a reduction in tithes, as success would reduce a farmer's outgoings and some smaller farmers even campaigned vociferously against the clergy in the workers' demonstrations. At Bromsberrow, in Gloucestershire, a threshing machine was smashed. As the disturbances grew nearer, some Herefordshire farmers feared trouble and dismantled their offending machines. By mid-November the influence of the 'Swing' movement had reached western Herefordshire. There were, however, insufficient threshing machines on Herefordshire farms seriously to threaten men's winter employment and the impact of the swing disturbances on the county was only slight.

Nonetheless, the authorities decided to make an example of the one unfortunate man they captured. Henry Williams, a 'Ranter', as early Primitive Methodist preachers were called, was regarded as a dangerous agitator of the impressionable poorer classes. In the first week of January 1831 'the wicked, malicious, seditious and evil disposed Henry Williams', a 20-year-old tailor from Whitney and 'by profession an eminent preacher of the Ranter sect', was found guilty at Hereford Quarter Sessions of the crime:

> that he caused to be published a certain paper containing the wicked, seditious, inflammatory and diabolical matter following: '17 Nov 1830 Mr. Monkhouse, Sir, We as you call rebels determine if you don't pull down your machine witch you do thatch [thresh] your grain with you [we] are come that way and will set you and all that you have with fire remember in Kent they have set all that would not submit and you we will serve the same for we are determined to mak you support the Poor better than they have been supported yet for they are starving at present so pull down your thrashing mashchine or els Bread and Fire without delay for we are 5 Thousand men and will

not be stopt. Leave this where it lies for John Monkhouse that Devile of a farmer of the Stow Herefordshire.

The letter was written on a page cut from a book found in the house in Whitney where Williams lived with his parents, incriminating him without doubt. It was left in the road leading to Stowe Farm, where it was meant to be found. As an example to others he was sentenced to 14 years transportation to New South Wales, though this was not as bad as it might have been, for the crime potentially carried the death penalty. At Radnorshire Assizes the same week, John Taylor, a joiner from Presteigne, was also sentenced to 14 years transportation for sending a threatening letter demanding money. Earlier, on 30 October 1830, probably inspired by the 'Swing' disturbances, 50 men rioted in Kington, trying to set fire to some houses. Six men appeared in court, charged with assaulting a constable but they escaped conviction. Apparently this riot went unreported at the time but it was recorded in the Court Rolls now kept in Hereford Record Office.

Care must be exercised when reading newspaper reports of these activities, as exaggerated and even fictitious accounts of events that never occurred appeared in some

Fire has always been feared as it can spread so quickly and cause such enormous destruction in a short time. Isolated farms were just as vulnerable as big country houses. Before telephones were common, the distance someone had to travel on horseback to the nearest town to raise the alarm and then the time it took for the fire brigade to reach the scene often at night along dark rough country roads, often meant the fire was completely out of control by the time help arrived. Only too often salvage work was all the brigade could offer. This is the scene of just such a devastating farm fire at Aylton, four miles west of Ledbury in November 1906.

London newspapers, reflecting people's fears at the time. Reports from the provinces were subject to sensational editorial exaggeration to make 'a good story' in 1830, just as much as today. More than one edition of the *Hereford Journal* stressed in its reports of a farm fire at Kenchester on 25 November, close to a barn housing a threshing machine which had been in use that day, that although the magistrates said that the fire was started maliciously, everyone present did everything possible to extinguish it; and that the paper considered that it was not part of the 'Swing' campaign, whatever *The Globe*, a London evening paper, might report. The truth of the matter will never be known but the fire may well have been the work of one disgruntled labourer, inspired by rumours he had heard of agitation elsewhere. Alternatively, the Herefordshire authorities may have wished to deny any 'Swing' influence to prevent the trouble spreading further. Countrywide the frightened authorities brutally restored order with 19 judicial hangings and transportation for 480 men and two women.

Though the Swing riots were soon crushed, they were not forgotten, for they had drawn attention to the injustice of the changes taking place in rural society. The Speenhamland system of administering the Poor Law both subsidised farmers and kept farm workers' wages low, and the ill-considered reformed Poor Law of 1834 instituted workhouses, which everyone feared and struggled desperately to avoid, and which did nothing to diminish the widespread poverty. Until 1834 each parish was responsible for administering the Poor Laws and elected their own unpaid officers, who managed the often unpleasant task with varying degrees of efficiency and sympathy for their poverty-stricken parishioners. Many parishes adopted the Speenhamland system for assessing Poor Law relief payments, which were in effect the subsidy of low wages by rate payers. In Speenhamland, a village in Berkshire, magistrates decided in 1795 on a scale of out-relief dependent on the price of bread and the size of the family claiming relief. For want of a better system Hereford's justices evidently followed their example. The *Hereford Journal* announced on 1 November 1809:

Assize Bread for the City of Hereford fixed on Monday October 30 1809, at 14 shillings per bushel:
    One penny loaf Standard Wheaten 4 oz 15 dr
    Two ditto 9 oz 15 dr
    Four ditto 1 lb 3 oz 14 dr
    Six ditto 1 lb 13 oz 13 dr
    Twelve ditto 3 lb 11 oz 9 d

There was continual pressure from rate payers to reduce Poor Rates. Another idea tried in some areas was the Roundsman system, where employers (who of course were also rate payers) were required to take turns in providing employment for able-bodied paupers for up to a year. Under another rule, the Labour Test, unemployed men had to perform some public work, such as road mending or breaking stones, before receiving their dole. Reformers of the chaotic systems which had developed since the first Poor Laws introduced by Elizabeth 1 regarded them as 'bounties on indolence and vice'. Spurred on by memories of the recent 1830 Swing disturbances, they wanted a standard 'workhouse test' applied to all pauper claimants. These regulations were to be strictly applied so that only the completely destitute would consider entering the forbidding new purpose-designed workhouses planned to be built in each Union or collection of parishes. In the drive for efficiency and standardisation the extra cost of setting up and imposing this centralised bureaucracy on often reluctant provincial officials does not seem to have been considered. Although the conditions of the rural and urban unemployed varied considerably, any such differences were not taken into account. It was actually cheaper to give out-relief to paupers living in their own (or rented) cottages than to uproot them to a harsh existence in the Union workhouse. The Reformed Poor Law's effect on country people was seen as another controlling layer of officialdom.

This oppressive legalistic management of the labourers' daily lives diminished their rights and freedoms still further. Seasonal unemployment in agriculture was endemic, leading during the cold winter months to claims for out-relief from the local Board of Guardians, which were usually miserly amounts. In the Forest of Dean, the men's leader was transported to Tasmania for organising hundreds of local foresters in 1831 to destroy miles of woodland enclosure fences so that their animals could graze beneath the growing trees. Powerless in their poverty, the people of the countryside seethed with resentment at the harsh treatment the 'Swing' protesters had received and also at the unjust fate of the Tolpuddle men, who were transported for daring to form a legal trade Union in 1833. After the repeal in 1825 of the Combination Acts men had the right, albeit restricted, to form trade Unions. The Tolpuddle men formed a legal trade Union but, on the word of an informer, they were wrongfully charged and convicted of taking an illegal oath. The magistrates particularly disapproved of their actions as they were agricultural labourers, although this was no legal obstacle to Union membership. The authorities did not make the same mistake again when, only three years later, a regular Trade Union was formed in the Tendring Hundred of Essex, centred on Thorpe le Soken and Great Bentley with over 1,200 men paying subs of 1 shilling per month and promised 1 shilling per day in the event of a strike or lock-out.

Despite this Union's failure after a year, it showed the way forward. The countryside was quiescent, but the spirit of political unrest continued throughout the 1840s as ideas of the mainly urban-based Chartists spread. Chartism was an expression of urban working class awareness and aspirations, defined in their six-point manifesto of demands: manhood suffrage, equal electoral districts, vote by secret ballot, annual Parliaments, payment of MPs and the abolition of property qualifications for Members of Parliament. Despite these various movements, apparently no organised (or riotous) meetings were held in rural Herefordshire but occasional sporadic machine breaking and arson attacks still continued into the 1870s. Occasional wage rises between 1850 and 1870 were interspersed with periods of acute distress when lower seasonal wages, prolonged underemployment, and wet weather lay-offs and unemployment in the cold winter months brought debt to many families. Everywhere

Above: Alfred Watkins photographed these two harvesters near Hereford about 1890 as they paused to sharpen their bagging hooks (fagging hooks). This sickle shape had not changed for two thousand years. Harvesting corn in this fashion was a long slow arduous job often taken on by a gang of men at a price agreed with the farmer at the start of the harvest.

Below: It required two pairs of horses to pull this heavy old wooden swing plough on stiff heavy clay soil. The ploughman cleans the mouldboard on the headland before starting another bout. Constructed of local timber, awkward and heavy in use, this type of wooden plough had hardly changed since the Middle Ages. It was superseded as the more versatile iron ploughs were manufactured in increasing numbers in the nineteenth century. Horses could not work all day long and usually did two stints, 7-11 am and 2-6 pm – less, of course, in the winter, when work had to finish before dark.

they could see the wealthy flaunting their riches. In the view of the poor, money spent on the often unnecessary rebuilding of village churches would have been better spent on new cottages or higher wages for estate employees. People came to hate the Christmas hand-outs they received from the wealthy in the big houses; perhaps they assuaged the gentry's consciences, but they reduced the workers' dignity and independence still further and were no answer to the continual problems of low wages, poverty and Parish Relief.

There was one organisation that working men depended upon to help them; in fact, it was their own attempt to help themselves. Friendly Societies were an important part of the fabric of working men's lives and in many ways their aims overlapped those of early trade Unions in supporting members in times of need. From about 1770 working men started to group together to form Friendly Societies, usually centred in the pub, to provide some sort of medical care and sickness benefit when illness struck either themselves or their neighbours. From 1793 Acts of Parliament regulated their activities as National Societies formed to help people cope in an increasingly hostile world. Despite their somewhat exotic names – Ancient Order of Foresters, Independent Order of Oddfellows, Royal Ancient Order of Buffalos, and so on – they all had the aim of helping their members in cash or kind if trouble struck, and most were open to everyone to join. A few excluded the very poor and agricultural labourers as they were more likely to be a drain on club funds. Societies' rules varied, but for an average fee of 3d or 6d per week men 'bought comfortable relief in case of sickness'. Depending on club funds they could receive 3 to 6 shillings per week while 'on the club' and the free attendance of the club doctor, appointed to provide necessary medical care at a fee of 2s 6d per member per year. A widow's pension and funeral expenses, depending on age and length of membership, were among the advantages on offer.

Club funds were raised in various ways. The 'swear box' was a never-failing source of income at some meetings, as were 'fines for drunkenness and lewd behaviour and singing', whilst men fighting were fined 5 shillings at one society. Raffles, social evenings and whist drives all helped swell the funds. Ross Friendly Society was exceptional in owning property (at Spring Gardens, Poolfield) from which it derived some income. As would be expected, most village societies met in the village inn. Linton, however, did not allow intoxicating liquor to be drunk at their meetings, which they held in members' houses. In Much Marcle and Kington female societies were formed, affiliated to the Girls' Friendly Society. By 1857 at least 47 Herefordshire towns and villages supported Friendly Societies and in some there were several. The highlight of their year was the Club Walk, when a parade round the village, or at least to their meeting room, was followed by a slap-up meal and games and sideshows for the children. One or two clubs still survive, as at Fownhope, but most ceased their activities after the establishment of the NHS in 1948 with the Government's promise to 'look after everyone from the cradle to the grave'.

Clearly, despite men's best efforts to look after themselves and each other, change was needed. Several short-lived agricultural labourers' Unions appeared briefly during the

1860s, only to fade away through lack of funds or poor organisation. A strike in Berkshire in 1868 was resolved when many of the men involved moved to jobs outside the county, so that the resulting shortage of labourers forced farmers to raise wages. But 1871 was a year of real change. It was a year in which conditions became unbearable – the shortage of food after the bad harvest that year soon resulted in higher prices for all commodities and already farm workers' wages were the lowest in the country. But it was a year which also brought cause for hope, in that the Trade Union Act finally legalised registered trade Unions and gave them full security over their funds, though they were still restricted by the 1825 Act which regarded peaceful picketing as intimidation. The political scene altered with the extension of the vote to urban workers, stimulating an atmosphere of hope in rural communities and encouraging the formation of Unions in several counties. Another change was the opening up of other opportunities for agricultural workers. Labourers were in demand in the rapidly growing cities, mill owners in the north of England were desperately short of labour and work was available for women also. Regular advertisements appeared in the *Hereford Times* such as that for: 'Widows with large families wanted for Messrs Townsend's Worsted Manufactures, Cullingworth Mills, Bingley, Yorkshire. Six families wanted immediately.'

Gradually, farm labourers came to realise that the answer lay in their own hands, and after years of apathy, they began to organise themselves. In Vauxhall Street School in Leicester, a Mr Selby commenced his first Union meeting with the men kneeling to pray for success. 'He had thought for years that the down trodden and oppressed needed a Union to enable them to ask for higher wages and to strike if need be.' Gatherings in some Lincolnshire villages were reported where wages of 18 shillings and a nine-hour day were mooted (in place of the standard dawn to dusk in winter and 6 am to 6 pm in summer). The seeds of agricultural trade Unionism germinated first in counties in central and eastern England, but soon took hold in Herefordshire. Men's anxiety about static wages and rising food prices, together with longstanding resentment over the injustices of enclosure, the lack of the vote or MPs who were prepared to voice their grievances in Parliament, and the availability of sympathetic leaders, created a fertile seedbed in which agricultural trade Unions could take root and grow. Recognition of their abysmal living and working conditions, which also affected their wives and deprived their children of a proper education, spurred the men to protest and to hope that Unions could achieve these improvements. Above all they wanted to be recognised as responsible members of society with a vote, free education for their children, the right to manage their own village affairs and access to better housing and better wages. All this appeared to be achievable once the Trade Union Act was finally passed and the first agricultural workers' trade Unions were formed. Their long struggle for better living and working conditions began, fuelled by the aspiration that they would no longer be, in the words of Joseph Arch, who became one of the foremost Union leaders, 'underfed, overworked, uneducated, voiceless, voteless and hopeless'.

Chapter 2
Thomas Strange and the first agricultural Trade Union in Herefordshire

The reflection is forced upon everyone who thinks of the matter, that if a farmer can afford to pay thirty per cent more wages in times of agricultural depression than he paid in times of prosperity, and yet live, and keep a carriage, while the landlord still thrives on the reduced rent which has resulted, the labourer must have been greatly wronged in those prosperous times.

Thomas Hardy, *The Dorsetshire Labourer* 1883

On May 29 1872 an historic meeting took place at Leamington: the formation of a National Agricultural Labourers' Union (NALU). Not all the invited delegates attended. The Essex Union, for example, responded by writing that 'the poor fellows are afraid to appear'. On the platform were Matthew Vincent, a Radical Leamington newspaper proprietor who was prepared to spend his own money to support the farm workers' cause, Henry Taylor, an energetic 28-year-old carpenter and member of Leamington Trades Council, Sir Baldwyn Leighton, a philanthropic owner of large estates in Shropshire, George Dixon, a Liberal MP for Birmingham, who took the chair, Joseph Arch, leader of Warwickshire Agricultural Labourers' Union, and the two men responsible for the beginnings of agricultural trade Unionism in Herefordshire, Thomas Hood Strange and William Gibson Ward. Born in 1826 at Barford, Joseph Arch had founded the Warwickshire ALU in February earlier in the year at Harbury in his home county. A fiery and gifted orator, he soon became famous as the champion of the farm workers, who would walk miles to hear him speak.

At this initial meeting, however, the two elected Union representatives from Herefordshire were the first to make themselves known to the enthusiastic gathering. Never one to shun the limelight, Ward stood up at the start of the conference and told them in no uncertain terms that Strange's North Herefordshire and South Shropshire Agricultural Labourers' Improvement Society (NH&SSALIS), sometimes referred to as 'the Herefordshire Hinds', had been in existence for at least a year before the beginning of Arch's Warwickshire ALU. It was by far the largest Union at that meeting, at which it was represented by seven delegates. Arch, needless to say once one appreciates his character, was not impressed with Ward's lack of diplomacy, but Ward was always a stickler for the truth even at the expense of a friend. George Dixon, who was already well acquainted with Strange and his organisation, gave Strange the honour of proposing the formal motion 'That a National Union of Agricultural Labourers be formed, having districts throughout the kingdom and its centre of management in Leamington' amid the ringing cheers of the delegates. It was Joseph Arch, however, who was elected President of the new National Union at £2 per week salary, a position he retained unopposed every year until NALU was finally dissolved in 1896. Henry Taylor became general secretary and Matthew Vincent was elected treasurer and within a week started publication of the *Labourers' Union Chronicle* to spread the Union's message. Distributed both to members and to the general public, it rapidly achieved a large weekly circulation, (said to be 30,000).

This moment of harmony and hope turned out to be short-lived – unsurprisingly because, while all three men were passionately committed to helping agricultural labourers improve their conditions, Strange, Ward and Arch were three very different personalities. Strange and Arch were both from Primitive Methodist backgrounds but, as we shall see, they had entirely different ideas about how improvements could be achieved. After the inevitable fall-out, Arch and Taylor remained in charge of NALU and so successfully rewrote NALU history that they effectively eradicated any mention of the experience and co-operation Strange and Ward brought to that initial meeting, so that later historians have missed the important contributions the two Herefordshire men made. Distortion of the truth (spin) is no modern phenomenon. The fact that Strange proposed the motion to found NALU shows the widespread respect he then enjoyed. Among the men on the platform at that first meeting, only Strange, Ward and Arch were elected representatives of agricultural workers' trade Unions and only Arch, in his young days, had been a skilled agricultural worker. The following chapters introduce each man and, from the scanty records they left, sketch the development of the Union activities they instigated in Herefordshire and beyond.

The first Herefordshire Union

On 14 February 1871 a joint meeting of the Leintwardine, Brampton Bryan, Presteigne and Lugg Side Agricultural Societies was held at Leintwardine's Swan Inn. Farmers from the surrounding area discussed two issues of great importance to them: local taxation (the Poor Law rate that financed out relief and the workhouse) and tenants' rights (that is, the rights of tenant farmers), in particular a long-running argument concerning the amount of compensation due to farmers for any improvements they had made to the farm buildings or land, payable by their landlord at the expiry of their lease. At this meeting the farmers asserted that their workers were paid £1 per week.

Among those attending the meeting was Thomas Hood Strange, a 30-year-old schoolteacher who originally came from Wootton Bassett in Wiltshire but was now schoolmaster at Adforton and a pillar of the Primitive Methodist community. Finding it hard to equate the farmers' statements about the level of workers' pay with the distress he saw around him every day, Strange became determined to discover the men's true wages and find a way to help alleviate their wretchedness. He enlisted some of them to help him organise a meeting of Leintwardine's agricultural labourers in the club room of the Lion Inn and, on 14 March 1871, 350 men from the surrounding villages turned up. As they could not all squeeze into the room, many stood outside so as not to miss the proceedings completely. Unanimously they voted Strange into the chair. His introductory speech was a model for the diplomatic way he intended to conduct the new society's affairs in the years ahead. 'Let us by all means steer clear of bitterness because that will only block the pathway we want to clear,' he told the men. 'Speak freely but with moderation and this night's meeting will be productive of good.' He enumerated the salient points he thought would improve his listeners' lives, being careful to agree with farmers' wishes for lower local taxation and their claim for tenants' rights, but pointing out that workers had rights too. He spoke of 'agitation', never 'strike', and avoided all mention of a trade Union. He wished to 'consider' the condition of the labourer and how he might rise, 'not wishing to use any phrase that might offend outside'. He finished his address to hearty applause. 'And I do hope this night's meeting is only the beginning of the end.'

Several of the men stood up to tell their workmates of the hardships they endured and the struggle it was to bring up their families on their low wages. One single man said that the 10 shillings he earned was not enough for him to live on and he could not begin to understand how anyone could raise a family on that amount. Another said he had no money left from his 9 shillings wages to send his children to school. The men needed recognition of the hours they were forced to work in the form of higher wages. They voted for a number of proposals which they hoped would improve their conditions:

> 1. We continue to agitate until the labourers' cottages are improved. Labourers should rent their cottages from the landowners and have at least one month's notice to quit or lease them on a twelve month tenancy from Lady Day.
> 2. We continue to agitate until the wages of the labourers be increased to 15 shillings and that they take every possible step to improve the conditions of the labourers.
> 3. That they should act in conjunction with the farmers to reduce local taxation.
> 4. That the system of hiring at Mop Fairs is a nuisance and should be abolished.
> 5. Reduce the annual Poor Rate, as some labourers had to find 9 shillings to pay this charge.
> 6. Large estates and farms should be divided into smaller units to produce more food and give more people a reasonable living.

As chairman of the meeting, Strange proposed the formation of an emigration society, all members to pay 1d per week to provide a fund to assist bona fide agricultural labourers who wished to emigrate, who would be voted for by fellow members. Mr Kinsey proposed that Mr Strange be President of the Society, seconded by Mr Owen. Mr Lawrence was elected secretary and Mr Farmer became treasurer. As the *Hereford Times* had 'always been the friend of the working man', its reporter, Mr Allison, was given a special vote of thanks for attending at that distance to report their meeting.

Thus was formed what became the North Herefordshire and South Shropshire Agricultural Labourers Improvement Society (NH&SSALIS), the first agricultural workers' trade Union in Herefordshire. It was named as such at its second meeting, which took place on 11 April, a rainy Tuesday evening, in a barn belonging to their treasurer, John Farmer, as they were refused use of the local schoolroom. Despite the weather, over 300 men turned up, demonstrating their enthusiasm for a chance to improve their lives. In the chair again, Strange recapitulated the labourers' need for higher wages and better cottages with security of tenure. Reflecting memories of their long-lost common land, a number of men voiced a desire for a few acres to keep a cow to give their families a supply of milk, butter and cheese and perhaps a little surplus for sale. The men said that their wives would be better off doing this dairy work at home than working in a farmer's fields for a pittance. They decided that a series of letters to farmers and landowners would be their best course of action.

As well as the NH&SSALIS, a second society, 'formed out of and grafted onto the first', called the 'North Herefordshire and South Shropshire Emigration Society in connection with the North Herefordshire and South Shropshire Agricultural Labourers' Improvement Society', was formed for those wishing to try their luck abroad. Sub-committees comprising 'two agricultural labourers to one man of every other class' were to be formed in every parish, empowered to send one delegate to the 'grand committee' responsible for running the Society. These rules were agreed and after the usual votes of thanks, the men went quietly home, hopeful that their lives would soon change for the better.

The elements of these first meetings – the choice of a suitable venue, sometimes outdoors, the persuasive appeals of a gifted and impassioned speaker, the opportunity for working men to express their grievances, the enrolment of at least some of the assembled men, and the collection of subscriptions to fund the Union's objectives – were repeated again and again throughout the area by Thomas Strange's fledgling Union as well as the Union begun by William Gibson Ward the following year (1872), the Herefordshire Agricultural Labourers' Union (HALU). The format of the meetings was similar to those that had led to the spread of Nonconformist Christianity in the area in the course of the preceding century, perhaps not surprising as both men, like many instigators of Union activity, were Nonconformists. Indeed, the enthusiasm in Herefordshire for Nonconformism was a key factor in the emergence of Union activity in the county. Life for working men was not lived in separate compartments; poverty, politics and religion blurred the boundaries, and the New Testament could be quoted to sanction most radical opinions. By 1850, for example, a third of Monmouth's population attended Nonconformist chapels, despite the

Bishop of Llandaff's assertion that Nonconformity was 'a conspiracy against the state'. The Establishment's Church of England clergy were criticised for their continued tacit oppression of the poor through their demands for tithes to fund their comfortable lifestyle. Primitive Methodists, at first called 'Ranters', grew out of an early 19th century Methodist revivalist movement, and they believed that their teachings were closer to John Wesley's than the Wesleyans' present hierarchy. In 1808 the Wesleyan Methodist Conference disowned the movement. In 1811 Hugh Bourne, the first Primitive Methodist leader, built a chapel at Tunstall in his native Staffordshire, although the 'Ranters' often held their evangelistic meetings in the open air. They were an important element in the working men's movement

If you were born a farmer's daughter there was no escaping the constant round of seasonal work involved in farming. Sheep had been shorn for centuries using hand sprung clippers. These were slow and tiring and did not cut wool evenly except in expert hands. Hand powered clippers were invented in Australia and introduced to this country in 1893, soon revolutionising the job. As the girl in the photograph steadily turned the handle a flexible drive transferred the power to her father's 'Burman' clippers. The blades reciprocated at between three and four thousand strokes per minute, parting the fleece from the sheep in quick clean strokes. She probably shared the hot, tiring, monotonous job with her sister who was rolling the cut fleeces and stacking them against the barn wall. Their father shows the shepherd's knack of holding the ewe steady for shearing with his knee.

towards Nonconformist worship, believing in a simple direct approach to God, unfettered by the unnecessary intervention of an ecclesiastical hierarchy of priests. With roots among the working classes, the Primitive Methodists were naturally able to speak to and represent both the rural and urban poor. By 1842 their membership numbered nearly 80,000 and more than 1,200 chapels had been built across the country. A generation of teachers and preachers was nurtured who believed that their Christian duty embraced politics as well as religion as a way to improve their followers' physical and religious lives, and this led a considerable number of Primitive Methodist preachers and lay members to become leaders of Unions. This independent Nonconformist religious element was very apparent at many of the early agricultural Union meetings, which involved prayers, hymns, biblical quotations and regular Sunday services.

But all generalisations have their exceptions. One of the few Church of England clergymen to give his support to agricultural Unions was Rev. D. Rodney Murray, rector of Brampton Bryan for 47 years. He needed little persuasion to become the honorary president of Strange's new Union, a development which demoted Strange to vice-president and corresponding secretary, a position in which he could use his developing organisational skills to spread their message far and wide. On June 3 they presented their proposals to the public in a letter to the *Hereford Times*. On 27 June 1871 the NH&SSALIS held its third meeting, in the open air outside the Lion Hotel, Leintwardine. Strange was pleased to announce that several prominent men had written in support of their movement. George Dixon, Birmingham's progressive Liberal MP, had sent them £10. The Earl of Shaftesbury had written saying that their movement was attracting the attention of the outside world and 'was characterised by that temperateness and moderation which seldom fail to secure their reward'. John Farmer, the treasurer, reported that the Union now held £13 12s and hoped to carry on without expenses except for postage and stationery. Again Strange's long address stressed moderation in their approach to farmers. He did not want Society members swayed by the unrest elsewhere in the UK to upset his peaceful campaign. Strikes (not in agriculture) were now such a common occurrence that the *Hereford Times* printed a list of them in a regular weekly column. Strange was convinced that emigration was the answer to the joint problems of low wages and underemployment in the over-populated countryside. In the letter to the *Hereford Times* he had requested donations to the Union's Emigration Club, to help fund members' travel expenses to a new life overseas. Although the majority of jobs were still to be found in agriculture, Great Britain was no longer able to grow enough food to feed its increasing population and was already importing 12% of its wheat from Russia and the USA. For the benefit of the newspaper reporters present, 12 labourers took the opportunity to tell their comrades in poverty how difficult it was to live on their wages of 9 or 10 shillings per week. One had to pay an annual Poor Rate of 9 shillings, a whole week's wage, as well as finding 1s 6d per week rent for his cottage.

As the movement gathered momentum, the *Hereford Times* published a number of letters for and against the labourers' stance, as well as a copy of the Society's rules showing it had nothing to hide. Strange also published a list of the average wages in New Zealand, Australia and Canada, taken from the government's own Colonisation Circular, to demonstrate the financial advantages of emigration to these new Dominions. During the summer of 1871 the county newspapers published a number of enthusiastic letters from local families who had recently emigrated to America, encouraging others to join them. The Society invited J.B. Goode, American Consul in Birmingham, to speak at Leintwardine Congregational Chapel on 26 October. On that occasion so many people wanted to hear what America had to offer that they could not all crowd into the room, and a second talk was held at the Oxford Arms Hotel, Brampton Bryan the following evening with Rev. Murray taking the chair. There was 'a very numerous attendance' to hear Strange read letters from local emigrées 'expressive of their thankfulness' that they had been guided to America, which Goode described in his colourful talk.

Strange's conviction that emigration was a key part of the solution to the problem of rural poverty was thus at the forefront of his work from the beginning. He persisted with it over the years and while the other agricultural workers' Unions that arose initially dismissed the policy, in the end they adopted it themselves, reasoning that by the laws of supply and demand the lower number of remaining farm labourers could command higher wages. In the short term this did indeed happen, but by the mid 1870s the overriding economics of cheaply imported wheat and (later) refrigerated meat to feed the populations of Britain's industrial towns were to depress agricultural prices, lower farmers' incomes and perpetuate labourers' low wages for decades to come. The popularity of emigration therefore remained high. Such was the increase in the numbers of people deciding that emigration would solve their problems that in 1872, 195,776 emigrées had passed through Liverpool, just one of the country's emigration ports. Many dull winter's evenings were enlivened by talks on the attractions of Canada and America where prospects for labourers were described in glowing terms. In North America wages were higher, there was no class distinction, no Poor Law and no workhouses, and grants were available for pioneers to settle vacant areas.

Of course, emigration was not without its perils. On arrival at Auckland, New Zealand, in April 1874, the emigrant ship *Mongol* reported that the hundreds of families on board had been struck with illness during their weeks at sea and 12 people had died. Worse was to follow that December when the *Corpatrick*, a Shaw Saville Line steamer carrying 424 emigrants, made up of domestic servants, artisans, farm workers and their families heading for a new life in Australia, caught fire off South Africa. All the emigrants and 49 of the 52 crew perished. Among the victims were James and Hannah Ivens and their four young children from Ross and Mitcheldean, and the ship's doctor, J. F. Cadle from Newent.

Radical and Liberal politicians began to be attracted to the movement Strange had started. On 15 December 1871 George Dixon MP was invited to chair a meeting at Brampton Bryan to hear the farm workers' complaints for himself. The familiar themes were restated: the men said they needed 15 shillings a week to live reasonably, security of tenure if the cottage they lived in belonged to their employer, and 'a little bit of land for a cow'. (This need was recognised in northern England, where labourers could keep cows and had organised Cow Clubs for mutual self-help.) In reply Dixon said it would be 'kind, generous and just, but wise also on the part of the farmers and landowners if they took the condition of the men into consideration and tried to improve it', and also that 'it was a disgrace that men lived in such habitations when there was wealth enough to provide decent habitations for all'. In response to a vote of thanks, 'he promised liberal aid to a fund it was proposed to raise to enable some of the men to emigrate'.

After his success in Herefordshire, Strange embarked on a series of meetings in nearby Shropshire in January 1872. The vicar, Rev. W. Lellicome, presided at Clunbury schoolroom. Strange advised the men to 'combine, not for others' wrong but for your own right', but he had to admit that the Society's funds were not yet sufficient to finance emigration. In the short term, he proposed relocating men to counties in the north where manufacturing industries kept agricultural wages higher. (Even in northern Scotland agricultural wages

Huddled in the winter sunshine, shawls wrapped around their shoulders against the cold and one supported on crutches, a group of old ladies watch as part of their row of cottages at Titley was demolished. These tiny windowless buildings contained only two dark rooms with maybe a roof space under the thatch. Without windows they were dark and airless, lacking basic necessities we take for granted. With no thought for health and safety, even the man knocking down the rubble walls with a pickaxe was in serious danger if he slipped.

were 16 to 18 shillings per week.) A number of men signed up for the Society and others with employment agents for positions elsewhere.

Strange possessed the knack of persuading prominent men to associate with his policies. Despite their differing backgrounds and beliefs, his Union was one of the few to be supported by local Church of England clergy. Members of both the House of Lords and Commons gave weight to his arguments by attending his meetings in country areas far from their usual haunts. With his Wiltshire connections he was able to persuade Lord Fitzmaurice, MP for Calne, to chair a lecture on America in the Oxford Arms, Brampton Bryan on 22 January. On 29 January Strange spoke to an audience in Stokesay schoolroom. On February 26 he visited Clun Temperance Hall, where several Staffordshire farmers took the opportunity to sign up workers for the coming season. At Strange's request, Mr Morris, a Swindon newspaper proprietor, chaired a meeting in the malthouse of the Royal Oak in Bishop's Castle. They

found themselves in this odd venue when the Town Bailiff refused the Society use of the Town Hall for their 500-strong audience. Strange reiterated his condemnation of strikes as a weapon and, expressing concern for labourers in his native Wiltshire, he reported that 200 men had gone to work in other parts of England (probably organised by employment agents), and 30 had emigrated with another 30 soon to follow. More than 60 joined the Society, while employers from Birmingham and Staffordshire engaged others as the evening closed. At a second meeting in the same venue two months later, numbers were reduced to about 100, as a fee of 3d was charged to defray expenses. As

Sir James Rankin was in many ways typical of the big landowners of the nineteenth century. Born in 1842, he was the son of a wealthy Liverpool merchant who made a fortune in the North Atlantic timber trade. After he left Cambridge University his father gave him the Bryngwyn estate at Much Dewchurch as a wedding gift. His huge mansion was the main source of employment for many local families. In its glasshouses and gardens alone he employed sixteen gardeners. He supported plans for a new library in Hereford's Broad Street, which opened in 1873. He became MP for North Herefordshire from 1880-1906 and again from 1910-12, and in local politics, for years he was a County Councillor and chairman of the Education Committee. In this capacity he promoted the building of several new schools in the county, including Ross Grammar School. As chairman of the Education Committee he lost a battle in Spring 1914 with Herefordshire's teachers who, after nine years of official prevarication, successfully went on strike against his committee's refusal to implement a proper salary scale. Not forgetting his responsibilities to his estate he built some new housing for his workers. Nevertheless as a resolute Conservative he opposed farm workers' efforts to raise their income by forming a Union in 1912. After his death in 1915 his huge estate was soon split up. Although virtually forgotten now he left Hereford a lasting memorial in the Library and the name of the Conservative club in his old Leominster constituency.

the movement spread, the *Hereford Journal*, in a change of policy, castigated Lord Fitzmaurice MP, Mr George Dixon MP and the Hon. Auberon Herbert as 'unsafe and rash agitators' while advocating 'caution and moderation by labourers and a fair settlement in wages from the farmers'.

After his Shropshire successes Strange redoubled his efforts as he came to think that the only way for labourers to escape their long-term poverty was for a regional, if not a national, organisation. With this idea in mind he extended his meetings into Gloucestershire, Worcestershire and probably Wiltshire in the spring of 1872. On 8 March five or six hundred men who met at the Feathers Hotel, Staunton, Gloucestershire, discussed the long-term effects of the Enclosures, land to keep a cow, perquisites and wages, which Strange was surprised to learn were lower even than those in Herefordshire. It was here, as the men formed a branch, that he started talking about a 'combination' for the West of England or even the whole country. By early 1872 the society's name was changed to the West of England Agricultural Labourers' Association (WoEALA), recognizing its development from small branches in the Teme valley into an essentially non-militant organisation spread across six counties, with the apt slogan 'Emigration, Migration but not Strikes'. There were branches in Shropshire, Herefordshire, Radnorshire, Worcestershire, Gloucestershire and Wiltshire, with a membership of 30,000. Even Arch agreed with this startling figure, which was published in the May 1872 *Journal of the Chamber of Agriculture*. (The journal also stated that Warwickshire ALU had 4,000 Union members, Leicestershire Union 4,000 and the Cambridgeshire Union 3,000.) As a result of its policy of relocation, the WoEALA sent 'surplus' labour to jobs in Yorkshire, Staffordshire and Lancashire, where men were paid 16 to 17 shillings per week instead of the 10 to 11 shillings paid in their home counties. Some men emigrated to America, Canada, Australia and New Zealand under Union auspices, with the majority favouring America, which was then booming after the conclusion of the Civil War. This relocation of agricultural labourers was widespread. Throughout the autumn of 1872, farming in the Dengie Hundred of Essex was in turmoil as hundreds of labourers' families moved to better-paid jobs in Northumberland and County Durham.

Now confident of his abilities and the strength of the Herefordshire Unions, Strange attended a conference at the Willis Rooms in London on 30 April to discuss the possibilities of forming an umbrella organisation or national federation of agricultural workers. This came to nothing, but a month later Strange accepted an invitation to the WoEALA to send a delegation to the inaugural meeting in Leamington on 29 May of a proposed National Agricultural Labourers' Union (NALU), and as we have seen, it was Strange himself who was invited to propose the formation of that Union, thus fulfilling his vision of the creation of a national organisation. He was quickly disillusioned, however. It seems that, swept along by the excitement of the times, he had not realised that his policy of finding a peaceful solution to workers' problems was not in step with the confrontational policies adopted by the newly formed NALU in line with the beliefs of Joseph Arch, its elected president.

Quickly realising his mistake, once he found that Arch was more interested in confronting farmers with strike threats than negotiating ways round problems, by September Strange had withdrawn the WoEALA from NALU, and his speeches at meetings that autumn were all in favour of finding a happy medium on the basis that 'we must all work together' rather than NALU's 'them or us' approach. Despite their huge membership, Strange and Rev. Murray appealed for more new members in a September edition of the *Labourers' Union Chronicle*. Arch's retort came in a long editorial on 5 October. Ignoring the fact that wages had risen under Strange's guidance, Arch derided his peaceable way of negotiating increased wages and improved conditions, widening still further the growing rift between the two men and their organisations.

On his return from his euphoric meeting in Leamington, Strange resumed his work in Herefordshire. But all did not go his way. At a meeting at Kington not long after his return from Leamington his West of England colleagues made a bad error of judgement when they tried to organise a meeting on the evening of the May Fair. The town was crowded with fairgoers out for a laugh and well primed with drink. In the confined space of the cramped yard next to the Talbot Inn, four or five hundred townspeople, farm workers, holidaymakers, farmers and noisy spectators jostled and pushed for places and climbed on carts. Strange's first reaction on seeing the number of people and the confusion was to postpone the meeting, but farmers' taunts of 'Coward' persuaded him to continue against his better judgement. As he started his speech by saying he had been warned of a disturbance, 'the inglorious upsetting of a cart load of enthusiasts interrupted the proceedings'. Strange tried to continue his speech but a farmer approached the platform, heckling loudly. To cries of 'Turn him out', the crowd surged forward, and all order was lost as the meeting became 'an ungovernable mob' oblivious to Strange's calls for order. A free fight followed for ten minutes until the arrival of the police to rescue the farmer restored peace of a sort. Another half an hour of confusion followed as Strange tried to make himself heard, and then the ejected farmer returned with some friends and began another fight. Two speakers – their names were Perry and Waters – tried and failed to persuade anyone to enrol in the society, and the meeting broke up at 9 pm after providing two and a half hours' entertainment for the crowd. Strange afterwards regretted trying to hold this meeting as there was no possibility of forming a branch in such an atmosphere.

He met with more success further afield, although he appears to have had very little help in his single-handed efforts to enlarge the WoEALA in the six counties where he had influence. A farm wagon formed the rostrum in Mr Miles' field at Shirlheath, Kingsland on April 15 for a gathering of over 200, including many more women than were usually present at such meetings. The Rev G.A. Blakely of Stretford had helped organise the event and offered Strange the chair. C.M. Blackwell, a Leominster printer, spoke first. When Strange asked the men to tell the audience about their conditions, 14 'repeated the oft-told tale of poverty', and said they needed a wage of 15 shillings a week to live a decent life.

From experience Strange was able to tell them that these meetings were often followed by a rise of 1 or 2 shillings, so that there was no necessity to strike. But then he departed from his usual non-strike stance, recommending that the women present should strike at once, his argument being that their wages were half those of the men, that they glutted the labour market and that they should really be at home attending to their domestic duties. He continued by calling for 'one massive association for the advocacy of their rights' i.e. a National Union, a policy he was to repeat many times.

Four days later at Hanley Castle, spreading the Union message into Worcestershire, he told the gathered men that self-help was the best remedy for their troubles. If they could enrol 50 men they could run their own Union branch. Cautioning the men not to strike, he again suggested that the women should do so to increase the demand for their men's labour. He said that he himself had been a farm labourer and had risen to be a schoolmaster but had left that job to promote the cause of the farm labourer. Later he strenuously denied ever having been a farm labourer, but his listeners at Hanley Castle must have taken his words to heart, as they formed a strong branch which was to last for years.

In June he addressed 200 men and women outside the Crown and Anchor in Marlborough, Wiltshire, condemning 'the rickety cottages and cider made of two crabs in a bucket', where their pay was 10 shillings and 'the cottages were a disgrace to the proprietors', and organising the movement of 50 men from the area to better employment in the north. Later in the month in Ramsbury he had no difficulty in forming a branch, for people's memories there ran deep as it had been heavily involved in the 1830 Swing riots. (When NALU later penetrated the area it became a Union stronghold and with a reconstructed branch survived there until at least 1886.) Back in Herefordshire, on 26 June Strange expounded the rules and aims of the WoEALA to a gathering on Stoke Prior village green, only to be met with another frequent difficulty: repeated interruption, on this occasion from Mr S.W. Johnson, a Leominster accountant, who endeavoured to put the farmers' position. But the men refused to listen to the accountant, preferring to hear the grievances of 14 of their fellow labourers instead.

It is not easy to interpret events that happened over a hundred years ago when the complex relationships between employers, employees, clergymen and landowners were disturbed by a Union organiser of Strange's calibre. Imagine the scene on 28 June in Pencombe schoolroom as Rev. George Arkwright, whose brother John owned the 10,500-acre Hampton Court estate, was asked to chair a meeting of disaffected estate workers intent on forming a Union. Perhaps, to take the sting out of their labourers' demands, the Arkwrights wanted to try a subtler approach than the farmers' abuse and violence. Perhaps they genuinely wanted to hear the men's grievances at first hand, or possibly Strange's diplomacy had persuaded George to relay their complaints to his brother. Perhaps the men respected their vicar and did not wish to appear too antagonistic towards him or his family. Whatever the reasons, they accepted Arkwright's wish to take the chair, and whether there was concealed intimidation or not, ten determined labourers from the estate found the courage to tell Strange that their wages averaged just 11 shillings a week. One old man was given just 8 shillings, while a waggoner earned 12 shillings for working 14 to 16 hours a day. Others could not afford to send their children to the village school. The contrast between them and their landlord, John Arkwright and his family, who lived a life of leisure on the rents of 10,500 acres of the best agricultural land in the county, could not have been starker. 'In deference to the chairman, the starting of a branch was not pressed for a few weeks', but one was eventually formed and John Arkwright succumbed to Union pressure, raising the lowest paid workers' wages to at least 11 shillings later in 1872, and a shilling more the following year. The strong religious element in the WoEALA revealed itself on Sunday 7 July when 300 members attended a service they had specially requested in Brampton Bryan church to hear Rev. Murray, their president, preach a sermon on the text: 'But one thing is needful'.

Stung by the injustices they endured, the labourers themselves could be equally eloquent. Edward Mills, a labourer living in Luston, organised a meeting at Yarpole which

At the top of the social ladder these thirty pupils at the Elms boy's boarding school at Colwall Green attend their lessons in the single classroom. Headmaster, Charles Black, and four teachers ensure they study their books while John Tilley, the photographer, was at work on publicity photographs.
Note the uncomfortable bench seats attached to the long desks and the traditional tall chair so the teacher could see what was happening at the back of the class and make sure the boys got as good an education as their parents could afford.

he hoped would become a centre for the WoEALA for all the villages around Luston, Eye, Orleton and Eyton. He was disgusted to be earning a mere 8¼d a day at timber work in the winter. Rent for his tools alone cost that amount, he said, and he maintained that it cost £1 per week to keep a family in the workhouse, twice as much as a labourer earned, and that convicted felons received meat two or three times a week in prison – a diet he could not afford to buy for his family. Enrolling 30 men, Blackwell (voicing a difference between the existing Unions that would become an increasingly heated issue) explained that the national Union, NALU, took 1½d out of every 2d for their central office use in Leamington, whereas the WoEALA used the whole 2d subscription as local requirements necessitated. The meeting's decision to elect officers at a private meeting at the New Inn in a fortnight's time was meant to preserve anonymity and prevent persecution and harassment. Mills ended his speech: 'The luminary of this county is Mr Strange. He is scintillating about the neighbourhood with unfailing zeal, always trying to elevate his fellow beings.'

Thomas Strange realised that there were several possible ways to improve conditions both for farm workers and for everyone else in the area. Migration and emigration provided one solution, but Strange ideally wanted to keep men near their own villages with a real stake in the land where they grew up, and to redress some of the wrongs committed as a result of the Enclosures. With this in mind he developed an interest in the Co-operative Movement. Co-operative stores had been established in Knighton in Radnorshire in 1868 and Eastnor in 1869 and another was proposed at Walford near Ross in 1873. A meeting on 23 November 1872 in Brampton Bryan schoolroom, presided over by Sir Baldwyn Leighton MP, marked the start of the co-operative movement in Leintwardine. As a first move the Western Pioneers' Agricultural Labourers' Association was formed. This was part and parcel of the parent West of England Agricultural Labourers' Association and was formed to finance the proposed co-operative stores and farming ventures. Present at the Brampton Bryan meeting was William Morrison, MP for Plymouth, who explained co-operative ideals and gave a short history of the movement which 28 poor weavers had started in Rochdale in 1844 and which was now worth £120,000. He concluded by eloquently outlining a plan for starting a village store, and as a result a decision was immediately taken to establish a store in the area. The Leintwardine Co-operative and Industrial Society came into being the next year, with premises in Watling Street (probably where Batts Store is now). Its incorporation certificate bears the signatures of Thomas Strange (secretary), D. Rodney Murray, Edward Meredith, Hugh Hughes, Joseph Humphries, James Allen and John Burgwin.

At the same meeting it was announced that, through Mr Morrison's efforts, Hicks Farm of 142 acres had been purchased anonymously, with plans to let it at Lady Day, 25 March 1873 to 30 labourers at £20 per share, half of which was to be paid up front. Because of the men's low wages, shares could be purchased at 2 shillings per week until fully paid off. The capital already subscribed only amounted to £300 or £2 per acre. The usual working capital a tenant needed to stock a farm was generally reckoned to be £10 per acre, but, somewhat optimistically, the organisers hoped that the skill and hard work the men would put into the farm would compensate for the deficiency in their funds. Later subscriptions more than doubled this starting capital. Such was the men's enthusiasm for the project locally that some shares had already been taken in November, even before Morrison and Strange had inspected the farm, which was, the meeting was informed, half arable and half pasture. It was planned to acquire other farms for co-operative farming in the future. Mr Morrison's experience was used in formulating the detailed rules for the administration of the venture.

As chairman of their meeting, Sir Baldwyn Leighton promised to lend what practical support he could to the development of these cooperative schemes and also their trade Union. He promised to publicise among the county's landowners their ideas about cooperative farms and stores, and allotments or small pieces of land for labourers' use and cowruns (three or four acres of grazing land for their cows). A similar farm at Assington in Suffolk (which some members had inspected) had been started in the 1840s and had run successfully for many years, abolishing pauperism in the village and increasing the value of its shares from £3 to £65. Two months before, the Speaker of the House of Commons, Mr Brand, had advocated co-operative farming, giving further encouragement to the Leintwardine men's endeavours. In October 1873 the Brampton Bryan Co-operative Farming Society (Limited) was officially registered with aims to 'carry on in common the trades of farmers, gardeners, quarryers and planters and setters of trees and to purchase and sell land'. It had £612 capital and Strange was its secretary. The farm manager was a genuine working man who had subscribed his £50 savings, earned 18s 6d per week and lived in the farmhouse rent-free with a labourer who earned 16 shillings. He encouraged piece work and worked alongside the men, who were mainly society members. By the autumn of 1873 wages in the Leintwardine area had risen to 17 shillings from their 1871 level of between 10 and 12 shillings. In answer to the venture's critics, Strange wrote in November that 'the men were never in a more prosperous position' and 'were waiting to take another farm'. In 1876, despite ill-health, Strange remained secretary and the co-operative farm had accumulated £900 capital. However in December 1879 it was wound up, leaving only its name in local memory. Lack of capital and inexperienced management contributed to its demise, undermined by the fall in prices obtained for farm produce year on year as a deepening depression affected farming.

Whilst pursuing the co-operative ideal, Strange continued to work to expand the WoEALA, often in the most spartan of venues; he once vividly described an open air meeting in January in an unnamed quarry where the men built him a stone rostrum and lit faggots so they could see each other. He was not able to keep up his exhausting schedule for long, however. On Whit Monday, 26 May 1873, labourers and their wives filled the Little Stretton Wesleyan Chapel to hear an address from Strange, by now a popular and well-known speaker in the area. Imagine their disappointment when Mr

Blackwell arrived to apologise for Strange's unavoidable absence, 'as he had suffered an epileptic fit and sunstroke two days earlier' and 'Home was the best place for him in the circumstances'.

Unfortunately, Strange was never again strong enough to continue his self-imposed task. Like many men before and since, he ignored his doctor's advice and returned to work as soon as he felt a little better, though he really needed a long convalescence. It is typical of him that in early June, although scarcely recovered from his illness, he held a meeting in Eardisley, where several men had been sacked for joining the WoEALA. Placing their welfare before his own he told a crowd of 200, 'It was my duty to ascertain the truth and provide for the men unfairly dealt with.' Armed with details of better paid jobs in Yorkshire woollen mills for the men and women affected and a letter for anyone wishing to emigrate to Canada, he found an immediate solution to their problems. In return his WoEALA was rewarded with the enrolment of forty new members. In due course, Strange's subsequent years of ill health forced his retirement from Union activities. A modern diagnosis might say that he had suffered a slight stroke brought on by stress and overwork. This may, in part, have been brought on by the continued antagonism of NALU's president, Joseph Arch, who believed that his ideas were always right and that anyone who thought differently was his enemy. The continual double-dealing and taunts Strange endured from local NALU officials and their head office were completely foreign to his way of behaving. 'Notwithstanding all the jibes and insults I have received from the Arch party, I have never offered to return it either in private or public', he later wrote. Realising that a public slanging match would do neither Unions nor men any good, Strange refrained from refuting Arch's attacks, but in October 1876 he finally felt obliged to write to the *Labourers' Union Chronicle*: 'It is a gross falsehood to say that my energies are being directed against NALU, nor have I ever denounced the Union. I have only ever denounced strikes.'

Before he had to give up Union work, however, Strange made further efforts to create links with other regions. He called a conference on 30 September 1873 in the Moravian New School room in South Street, Leominster, to discuss extending its activities into more counties. Committees were set up in Hay (Breconshire), Shropshire, Eardisley, Kington, west and north Herefordshire, Radnorshire and Wiltshire. The following month, Strange announced that the Lincoln Amalgamated Labour League and the WoEALA were to be combined into one organisation, each branch to have its own funds and to pay an equal share towards management costs and the support of oppressed members. Plans were also made for fuller organisation of the six counties in which the WoEALA operated and to push further into neighbouring Somerset, Devon, Brecon and Monmouth. Attending this conference with other Wiltshire delegates was Strange's father, Edward, from Wootton Bassett, where the Wiltshire members decided to hold their county conference.

By this time Thomas Strange's Union was not the only one that was independent of NALU, the national Union. There were many locally strong county Unions led by tough independently-minded men who were opposed to NALU's doctrine of centralisation in Leamington, and who intensely disliked the perceived misuse of NALU funds (of which more later) and its advisory committee of well-meaning but middle class gentlemen. Unblinkered by central domination, they wished to pursue their own way forward under an umbrella national organisation, where each Union could respond to its members' demands with support, if needed, from other members of the federation. Some saw the wisdom in Strange's relocation and emigration policies, which succeeded in raising wages without the expense and adverse publicity of strikes, and followed his lead. Many of these Unions decided to come together and on 19 November 1873 a conference at the Rose Tavern, Old Bailey, London adopted the rules of the Federal Union of Agricultural and General Labourers, under which each district was allowed to frame its own rules, retain and manage its own funds and conduct its own business. But despite initial high hopes, this federation of agricultural and general labourers only managed to survive until 1875. It appears that Strange was not well enough to attend the inaugural meeting and from this date he faded out of the Union scene, although echoes of his years as a teacher appear occasionally in the records. In a long letter in the *Labour News* in May 1876 he stressed the need for universal village reading rooms, open to everyone, to prepare people for change and counter ignorance in all its forms. Despite accusations to the contrary, he carefully avoided setting class against class, men against employers, or any form of hostility against farmers and landowners.

It is known that some WoEALA branches in Herefordshire and the neighbouring counties subsequently became part of the NALU district organisation run from Hereford, but not all would accept NALU's rules. Others, like the branch at Lingen, accepted NALU guidance, saying Strange had neglected them, apparently ignoring his illness. But Strange wrote in a letter to the *Labourers' Union Chronicle*, published on 12 December 1876: 'No one can regret more than I do the collapse of my health just when it required a more arduous struggle [against the disunity sown by Arch's clique]. When I fell – I had a partial stroke – this Union gradually fell to pieces.' Without Thomas Strange's direction, the Union he had inspired gradually disappeared from the record. It is not clear how much longer it survived, but it was certainly finished by 1876. It continued its emigration policy for a while, with Mr Potts, Commissioner for Emigration for the Dominion of Canada, speaking at Bucknell, Brandhill, Wigmore, Newcastle, Clun and Leintwardine in October 1873, attracting the usual large audiences. In December, C.M. Blackwell, now the secretary of the West of England branch of the Federal Union of Agricultural and General Labourers, published a letter from the Queensland Government offering free passages to Australia for farm workers and railway navvies. Strange's calls for land reform were echoed too late by J.H. Wait, a Baptist minister in Bucknell, in August 1874, calling for up to four acres of land for labourers to help alleviate rural decline but at no charge to farmers, clergy or the Poor Law authorities. Unlike Strange in nearby Leintwardine, he was an idealist and had no realistic plans to cost and fund a scheme like the cooperative farm at Boresford.

Ironically, Thomas Strange himself apparently became a farmer for a while. The effects of agricultural depression were just beginning to be felt so it was a bad time to enter farming, but by December 1876 Thomas and Maria and their growing family were living at Bicton's Pool, Yarpole, where directories list him as a farmer. He made a last appearance in Union history befriending a NFLU delegate in Yarpole in the rain (the NFLU was another Union, set up later by William Gibson Ward, see page 44). Compelled to give up the Union work he so obviously enjoyed, in August 1877 some of his influential friends appealed for a £250 subscription fund to help his recovery to full health. By 1880 he himself had taken the advice he had given to thousands of other men, and relocated to a better paid job in a city. With his growing family he moved to Aston, Birmingham, where he spent the rest of his working life employed by the School Board as a Visiting Officer to investigate truancy.

Chapter 3
William Gibson Ward and his Unions

In the sweat of thy brow shalt thou eat bread
Book of Genesis

Contemporary descriptions of William Gibson Ward vary. In 1872 he described himself as a retired businessman with property in four counties, living at Perristone Towers, Yatton, Much Marcle. The *Hereford Journal*'s description was 'Once a grocer at Hereford, a retired English merchant, a landed proprietor and country gentleman and a man of cultivation of six acres, where he had built a small home and cottages of very inferior class' (or 7 acres of £63 rentable value, according to the *New Domesday Book* 1876). Modern writers have also attempted to describe his character. In her book on Joseph Arch, Pamela Horn says that Ward was 'a somewhat unbalanced gentleman of passionate views', and in *Sharpen the Sickle*, Reg Groves calls him 'an advocate of the labourers' cause and a humanitarian thirsting for the blood of the farmers'. Among his varied interests Ward was a vegetarian (very unusual at the time), giving occasional lectures on the subject, and a member of the Royal Horticultural Society.

His outspoken attitude can perhaps be traced to an occasion he spoke of more than once when he had chanced upon a labourer's family who were eating a meal of bread and boiled stinging nettles, and told him they could afford nothing better. This incident reinforced his views on the inherent injustice of the Enclosure Acts, affecting his perception so deeply that for the rest of his life he was completely opposed to farmers as a class. A tall, imposing, belligerent figure with a voice to match, for a time he proved to be the right man to project the labourers' demands, but his later inflammatory remarks, argumentative disposition and conviction that he was always right blurred his vision of Unionism and led to unnecessary conflicts with his friends. The recurring theme of his many speeches and articles in trade Union papers was to lay much of the blame for the labourer's state on the unfair bias of land distribution towards the rich and the consequent low wages of the poor. In areas that had been affected by the Enclosures one, two or even three generations previously, Ward found thousands of ready listeners. During his campaigns for NALU and for the National Farm

Labourers' Union between 1872 and 1877 his articles and speeches on the iniquities of land ownership, the Enclosures and their adverse effects on country people aroused considerable interest and support.

It is evident that Ward and Joseph Arch were in correspondence soon after Arch formed the Warwickshire ALU in March 1872, as Ward's first Union branch meeting was a close copy of the Warwickshire model. On 5 April one hundred men from villages as far away as Ballingham walked miles after work to the Old Gore Inn at Yatton, three miles from Ross, in south-east Herefordshire to hear Ward's speech, in which he detailed the historical and economic background of their situation. At least 14 men, who knew the pinch of hunger on a cold morning with no money in their pockets to feed themselves or their families, had the courage to stand up and recount their pitiable experiences as agricultural labourers. Ward told the gathering that men in Birmingham and Warwickshire were ready to offer them their assistance (to strike) and after a calm and orderly meeting the men formed a Union, believed to have been called the Herefordshire Agricultural Labourers' Union. On Ward's suggestion they decided on a similar structure to the Warwickshire ALU: 6d entry fee and 2d per week subscription, payable at their fortnightly meetings. Ward became their secretary and treasurer. With his enthusiasm fired by the men's keen response, Ward persuaded Arch to visit him and address their second meeting on 19 April again held at the Old Gore Inn. This is believed to have been Arch's first Union speech outside Warwickshire. The 300 men who had walked from miles around to hear him spilled outside onto the road where they gave him a tremendous ovation as he addressed them from the mounting block beside the inn wall. Following the success of the first official farm labourers' strike at Wellesbourne, Warwickshire, as a result of which the labourers' request for 2s 8d per day, 4d overtime pay and a shorter working day (6 am to 5 pm) was eventually agreed, Arch was the labourers' hero, the man of the hour. His charisma and the simple language of his crowd-pleasing

Wellesbourne, Warwickshire, where the first farm labourers' strike began

oratory endeared him to many more than just his Union members. An editorial in the *Ross Gazette* wrote of him on 4 April 1872: 'Spring is come and the sap is rising in the most astonishing manner in the sap and manhood of our agricultural labourers. It is amusing to find our Hodge, the ploughman, an agitator and public speaker. And what speakers they have turned out. The man Arch, the leader of the Warwickshire Labourers' Union, is a Demosthenes in a ploughman's garb. For cool commanding eloquence he would ensure attention in the House of Commons, says a London paper.'

On 3 May it was Thomas Strange's turn to visit Old Gore Inn and persuade still more men to join the Union, though its strike policy ran counter to his own 'Combination and Co-operation' ideals. The next day, outside the Three Horse Shoes at Llangarron, a rowdy gathering of farm labourers and Forest of Dean miners from the Amalgamated Association of Miners, who had pledged to help 'their agricultural brethren', heard Ward proudly announce that he had sent men to work at 3s 9d per day in the Abertillery Tin works, where there were still vacancies. Much to the men's delight Ward exchanged angry words with John Scudamore, a farmer at Pengethley, and the Rev. J.H. Potts, Llangarron's parson, but no Union branch was formed there that evening. In early May, as the movement gathered momentum, a branch was formed in Ledbury. In a change of editorial direction the *Ross Gazette* described Ward as 'the labourers' guide and friend' instead of its previously disparaging epithet 'an itinerant agitator', when he successfully chaired a second meeting at Llangarron on 15 May. He told farmers intent on breaking up the meeting 'I have come because you don't pay your men proper wages and they have asked me to come'. Ward was accompanied by Strange, who told his audience that conditions were the same all over Herefordshire and the surrounding counties. 100 men enrolled in the new branch after a vote against 'crab juice', the inferior cider farmers often foisted on their men.

Farmers' opposition grew as HALU spread and someone, presumably a farmer, mischievously circulated printed handbills advertising non-existent meetings at Harewood End and also a 'monster' meeting at Hoarwithy, where no Union meetings were planned. When they realised the game the farmers were playing, the local men were naturally outraged, but the ploy backfired when Ward heard of the deception and turned up at Hoarwithy Timber Yard where he spoke off the cuff on his reasons for supporting the labourers so wholeheartedly. Farmers' organised attempts to intervene at a Union meeting held at the Harewood End Inn on 16 May failed. On a cold windy evening a group of farmers who had met that afternoon in Ross revealed their true intentions towards HALU's growing strength. In an attempt to stop the spread of Unionism and to break up the meeting they liberally distributed free drink and money for beer among the assorted groups of men gathered outside the inn where Ward and Strange were scheduled to speak. In the dusk, reporters and their assistants huddled in the doorway of the smithy opposite the inn, trying to shield their candles from the wind so they could see to record the confused scene. The farmers had imported a group of rowdies from Ross led 'by a sweep of the most begrimed character' who 'brandished his stick in the most defiant manner'. Well primed with drink, they were prepared to do the farmers' dirty work as they 'were not prepared to hear themselves disparaged'. The mood of the labourers also 'would not brook contradiction'. In this volatile atmosphere a confrontation was almost inevitable, and a group of police constables stood nearby expecting trouble. Repeatedly farmers and their lackeys disrupted proceedings as Ward's loud voice announced that there was £800 at Leamington promised 'to support Herefordshire farm workers if they were compelled to strike'. The farmers claimed they were paying 17 shillings to £1 a week so vociferously that the labourers retaliated by threatening to duck one particularly obnoxious farmer in the pond beside the blacksmith's forge. There was no answer to Thomas Strange's direct question: 'Why are the men demanding more pay if the farmers' claims are correct?' To rebut the farmers' remarks, James Gibbons, who worked for Mr Hent of Strangford, found the courage to assert he only earned 10 shillings per week out of which he had to find £5 annual rent for his cottage. During one of the fights that erupted, 'a sweep named Downing of Ross struck a labourer on the head with his stick and was attacked by the crowd'. The police had to intervene to rescue him from the labourers' anger. (Downing had recently arrived in Ross from London claiming to have swept Queen Victoria's palace chimneys.) Strange addressed the confused gathering amid constant interruptions 'by a running fire of comments in not very choice terms' until he was forced to give up the unequal contest. Unexpectedly, at the end of the evening a group of respectable farmers, embarrassed by the others' behaviour, offered to raise their men's wages to 15 shillings. In addition 40 or 50 men enrolled in the Union. Realising the extent of their failure, local farmers quietly conceded the men's ability to organise their own Unions and did not attempt further public demonstrations against them, although individual farmers continued their sporadic harassment.

In an unexpected way Ward's argumentative character eventually let him down, establishing him as a hypocrite, as local farmers had maintained for months. Unwisely he had claimed in several public debates with farmers that he paid his workman, Gladwin, 25 shillings per week. After her latest confinement in May, Mrs Gladwin applied to Ross Guardians of the Poor for the usual 5 shilling fee for her midwife. Before agreeing to the payment the Guardians diligently questioned Gladwin about his wages and by his answers were convinced he only had a rent-free house and 13 shillings for his seven days' work every week – proof enough that Ward paid his employee as badly as the farmers he so despised and castigated and that poor Mrs Gladwin qualified for the 5 shilling payment for her midwife.

Nonetheless, Ward's popularity among south Herefordshire's labourers was high after the encouraging progress the Union had made so far. He was able to report to the fortnightly meeting at Old Gore next evening that after just two months' activity 'their men were now in comfort' (i.e. their wages had risen). Samuel Perkins proposed and John Roberts seconded the motion 'That William Gibson Ward be the delegate to represent us at the forthcoming conference at Leamington'. This was the conference called to establish a national Union. Every hand went up for it. At midnight, after taking subs, enrolling new members and giving tickets (presumably railway and steamer tickets) to men wanting to emigrate, the men dispersed quietly to avoid disturbing local inhabitants already asleep. His characteristically undiplomatic remarks at the start of proceedings (see pages 19-20) were typical of his unthinking approach to those around him and foreshadowed future events; but as reward for his services to NALU's cause, he was elected to their advisory committee with three other gentlemen well wishers and also became a financial trustee – both positions of influence in NALU's future growth.

Meanwhile in Herefordshire, the men's pressure began to bear fruit. An influential group of clergymen, landowners and farmers met at Bredenbury Court near Bromyard on 25 May and agreed a statement to send to Parliament in support of a Bill restricting payment in goods: 'The undersigned agree that the payment of agricultural labourers should be entirely in money and not in kind'. Ward and Strange joined forces again at Bosbury Wake on 26 May, forming a Union branch at an orderly meeting in the street outside the Bull Hotel, where the men demanded wages of 14 shillings per week in winter and 15 shillings in summer, reflecting the longer hours worked. Since Strange's previous visits wages had already risen to 10 or 11 shillings. Mr Watts, already secretary of the Colwall branch of the WoEALA, agreed to be joint secretary and treasurer of Bosbury also.

On 8 June, the men and farmers of Garway met with Ward to discuss the contentious issue of paying part of the men's wages in cider. By a small majority the men voted to continue to accept cider as part of their wages, while for their part the farmers promised to pay cash to those who preferred ready money. (The later Truck Act of 1878 banned payment of wages in goods but the practice continued illegally in Herefordshire for over 50 years. In 1935 one of the next generation of Scudamore farmers was fined and had to reimburse his labourers cash for the cider he had illegally paid them. As retaliation he sacked the man who had reported him to the authorities.) At Linton on 12 June the men met behind the Alma Inn, as many feared dismissal if they were even seen at a Union meeting. To allay their fears, Ward told them that as soon as their contribution was received at Head Office they would be entitled to strike or lock-out relief from Union funds. In an attempt to raise their very low wages of 8 or 10 shillings they formed a branch on 3 September. At Old Gore on 14 June George Tombs told the meeting that he had been discharged for joining the Union. Ward found him a better job at 18 shillings plus perks, where his wife could earn 1s 6d per day if she wanted the work. Ward was delighted to distribute 120 membership cards at the meeting.

That summer Ward worked closely with Joseph Arch, who stayed with him and spoke at many Herefordshire meetings. In Gloucestershire also, Union activity grew with a large gathering at the Glasshouse, Huntley on 19 June and the formation of a branch at Taynton with Ward its treasurer. Ward organised, and apparently financed, a rally on 5 August in George Shaw's orchard at Pendock Cross, where 900 people sat down to tea. The nearby pubs did a roaring trade all day, but the orderly crowd was there to enjoy a free day out, not troubling the two police constables sent to keep the peace. Arch failed to arrive, but Ward gave a stirring speech to the crowd's delight. A drum and fife band from Gloucester provided entertainment in the evening.

In recognition of his efforts, Ward was asked to preside at the conference held in Leamington in December 1872, when the Warwickshire ALU's 70 branches and 6,200

At the end of a day carting hay a farmer's wife offers a jug of cider to the thirsty workers. Note the ladders attached to the front and back of the cart to increase its capacity. Not all farmers approved of free cider because of its side effects. On some farms tea was the usual beverage on offer.

members formally affiliated with NALU. Ward happily read the report of WALU's first ten months' existence. 350 men had been sent to more remunerative employment elsewhere, whilst several had been helped to emigrate. This had helped the Union's efforts to raise wages by 1 to 3 shillings per week, leaving only a few to manage on 11 shillings. Ward gave a lengthy address exhorting the men to remain true to their Union cause (some independently minded Union leaders had already broken away from NALU) and said that 'it would benefit everyone if the upper classes emigrated'.

A year after their first branch formed, Herefordshire ALU met at the Lecture Hall in Bridge Street, Hereford, on 17 April formally to affiliate to the National Agricultural Labourers' Union. Russell, an early Union friend of Arch, reported that there were 42 branches in the county with 2,653 members. He was reappointed district secretary and was asked to move to Hereford permanently. Comprising the new executive committee were C. Williams of Bromyard, G. Cross of Orcop, T. Trumper of Weston Beggard, H. Whiting of Much Birch, W. Thomas of Hereford, Hughes of Madley and Hill of Sutton. Their business concluded, they adjourned to Barr's Court Station to welcome Joseph Arch. After conducting him back to the Lecture Hall, 300 sat down to a celebratory tea. At 6.30 pm they formed a procession and marched along Broad Street and Eign Street to Widemarsh Common where 5,000 people crowded excitedly round a farm wagon pressed into service as a rostrum. Arch gave the crowd what they had come to hear, a typically rousing speech on Union solidarity and the need for the extension of the vote. Ward also spoke as the dusk gathered around. The day following their huge Hereford rally and a year after their first meeting at Old Gore, Ward must have derived great pleasure from presenting Arch as President of NALU and Henry Taylor, its general secretary, to an enthusiastic gathering of farm labourers that completely filled Ross Corn Exchange.

However, by autumn 1873 cracks in the Union's organisation began to appear as disagreements over finances arose. The leadership decided it needed to impose its will on determined and locally popular district officials. The ensuing difficulties were mainly the result of Joseph Arch's inability to settle petty or personal differences within NALU or with other Unions amicably (see page 56), but on at least one occasion Ward's involvement only served to make matters worse. In early October the National Executive decided to dismiss Yeates, the Gloucestershire district secretary, for alleged misuse of Union funds and then divide the administration of Gloucestershire's branches between surrounding county districts. Without hesitation the county executive committee backed Yeates' handling of their affairs, threatening to leave NALU and re-form their own Gloucestershire Union. They stated that they could administer their own finances, that their books were in order and their accounts properly audited before affiliation to NALU and that they had never received a penny from Leamington anyway. This was like a red rag to a bull to Arch. Three weeks later he sent Taylor, the general secretary and Ward, as a member of the consultative committee, to Gloucester, where they barged unannounced into an executive committee meeting. Without full knowledge of the facts Ward ranted and raved at Yeates, accusing him of misappropriating both Union and Sick Benefit funds, his boorish behaviour destroying any chance of a reconciliation and hastening the now inevitable split. Even when it was eventually explained to him that any supposed irregularities predated Leamington's control, Ward made no apology and confirmed with a shrug of his shoulders the unnecessary loss of an important county. NALU administration moved to Cirencester, centre of the Cotswold district where it remained strong and active under Primitive Methodist leadership for many years, but its influence was never to return to the Vale of Gloucester. One of Ward's apologists said, 'Allowances should be made for the mannerisms of Mr Ward, whose ordinary way of saying "Hear, Hear" is quite sufficient to terrify some speakers'. On 25 November 1873 the Federal Union of Agricultural and General Labourers was formed at the Rose Tavern, Old Bailey, London (see page 35), the delegates including Gloucester's Mr Yeates.

In the autumn of 1873 Arch was persuaded that a visit to Canada was necessary to assess its possibilities as a destination for men seeking to emigrate to a better life. Instead of taking an agricultural worker as an assistant, he was accompanied by Arthur Clayden, a Berkshire gentleman who had supported the labourers' cause from the beginning. Clayden intended to write reports of their progress and findings to the English press, particularly the *Daily News*. In December at the Union executive meeting called on their return to hear their report on conditions in Canada, Ward directed a torrent of abuse at Clayden for writing critical letters about Canada and for describing some Union officials as pig-headed and blatant demagogues. Arch said nothing to support Clayden, who walked out. The 300 hundred men from the Market Drayton area of Shropshire who had been unable to find work in Canada and had returned in November would probably have agreed with Clayden's assessment of conditions there. We can only speculate on his reasons, but in his usual undiplomatic way Ward had found a convenient way of attacking Arch and would not leave the topic of the Canadian visit alone, but continued to attack Arch for spending NALU funds on clothes, insurance policies and annuities in case of accidents while on his travels. As Arch's £2 per week salary as President of NALU was his only income, it does not seem unreasonable for NALU to fund some financial arrangements for his family while he was abroad on Union business. The argument between the two men degenerated into personal abuse on both sides and dragged on for months, to the detriment of Union business.

At a meeting in August 1874 tempers frayed, and there were angry recriminations over the collapse of the Union's promises to protect its members involved in the Eastern Counties' strike. Ward's frequent, violent and vitriolic remarks about the 'Leamington Union Monarchs' became too much for his former friends to stomach, and he was removed from the Union's advisory committee. For the next four months Ward sent a steady stream of letters to the *Times* and the *Labourers' Union Chronicle* justifying his position, the letters becoming increasingly wild and intemperate, gaining him a widespread reputation as a firebrand. Although Ward was not directly involved, matters came to a head at NALU's annual conference in Birmingham in May 1875 when serious mismanagement errors and discrepancies in Head Office's accounting for Union funds were revealed. Arch and Taylor were never able to explain the loss of Union funds satisfactorily. Additionally such a furious row erupted between Vincent and Taylor, who was trying to shift the blame away from himself, that Vincent, who was treasurer and should have been aware of any discrepancies, resigned. As proprietor of the Union paper, the *Labourers' Union Chronicle*, Vincent was immediately able to reverse its policies and launched a bitter attack on NALU's leaders. Without explanation or apology Arch and Taylor remained in control, apparently heedless of the utter dismay and confusion the affair had aroused in the minds of the membership.

This confusion proved to become a major contributory factor in NALU's subsequent decline, but also gave Ward his opportunity to continue his campaign to improve conditions for agricultural workers by the redistribution of land. The shared antipathy Ward and Vincent felt towards landowners and especially farmers was reawakened, leading them to found the National Farm Labourers' Union (NFLU) on 20 July 1875, by means of which they hoped to redistribute land to landless farm labourers. (Thomas Strange had the same objective in mind when he established the Co-operative farm at Lingen, where he took a more business-like approach to the problems involved.) In Vincent, Ward found a ready ally in his arguments with Arch, and Vincent's ideas for another farm workers' Union gave Ward a renewed outlet for his energies, helping maintain his fading place in the limelight for a short time longer. The NLFU's aims were to provide smallholdings for farm labourers from a Land Fund, to encourage co-operative stores and co-operative farming, to set up a National Sick and Benefit Society, and to establish a strike fund to finance any strike activity. Like NALU its entry fee was 6d with a weekly subscription of 2d. A halfpenny of this went to the management fund, a halfpenny to the lock-out fund and a penny towards the all-important Land Fund. Founded by well-meaning middle class men with no grass roots foundations, from the very start the NFLU lacked popular appeal to farm labourers, who were sensible enough to see that their pennies would never be sufficient to buy enough land for their needs. Neither was the Union likely to be strong enough to challenge the farmers intent on lowering wages still further while Union strength was divided. Vincent gave the NFLU as much publicity as possible from its purchase of 146 acres of land at Avebury early in 1876. 23 shareholders were present at their first annual meeting to hear that 100 acres had been allocated to 60 men, in plots ranging from ¼ acre to 4 acres in size. Optimistically their leaders estimated a profit of £1,300 for NFLU, but further plans for 50 acres at Newent to cultivate market garden produce came to nothing. A second land purchase in Hampshire was of a mere three acres.

NFLU membership figures are not available but were probably in the hundreds rather than the tens of thousands that Arch could still count on. Ward nevertheless concentrated on creating branches of the NFLU in Herefordshire where he had campaigned so vocally and effectively for NALU four years previously. On 19 October he organised a public meeting at Hereford Corn Exchange and the next day at Ross, in an effort to promote the NFLU and its Land Scheme. The Ross Corn Exchange was only half full, with a disappointingly sparse sprinkling of farm labourers, for whom the meeting was really intended. Local man Thomas Blake, MP for Leominster, took the chair as Ward and the Rev. Lake, the NFLU's secretary, spoke, stressing that the old Union had done its work and more contributions to its funds would be of no further benefit to the men, whereas by contributing to the new scheme, they would raise a big enough fund to buy or rent land for smallholdings and allotments. Ward wrote long articles for the *Labourers' Union Chronicle* on the historical background to and the reasons for land reform, and became a patron of the National Farm Labourers' Union Co-operative Land Company Ltd., which was incorporated on 31 May 1876 and chaired by Vincent, with the purpose was to carry out any land purchases.

With excruciatingly bad timing, Edward Haines, an NFLU speaker, attempted to organise the 'New Union's' publicity campaign in Herefordshire's scattered villages in the first fortnight of January 1876, the worst possible time of year. He was faced by the county's bad roads, floods, rain and snow and a lack of adequate publicity. He could find no one he could trust to distribute the handbills advertising his meetings. Numbers were very low. In rain-soaked Luston he met Thomas Strange, who took him to a friend's house. A promise to start a branch in the village came to nothing. From all his planned meetings at Pembridge, Lyonshall, Luston, Hereford, King's Caple, Mansell Lacy, Ledbury, Cradley, Ewyas Harold, Bosbury and Ballingham, only at Ballingham was he successful in starting a small branch. George Smith, who had already fallen out with his fellow members in the Ballingham NALU branch, volunteered to be secretary and collect subs at his own home at the end of each month.

On 4 April, Ward held a meeting at Old Gore (scene of the first enthusiastic HALU meeting four years earlier), to explain his new ideas for dealing with the land question and improving the men's conditions at the same time. The men listened quietly and then, not convinced, they held a private meeting among themselves and decided not to act, remaining a staunch NALU branch. Ward was more successful on 6 April when 'all were in favour of the New Union' at King's Caple. The next day many ladies were present at the Three Horse Shoes at Llangarron where 22 men joined and John Tummey, landlord of the inn, promised his help. Encouraged by reports of the Pembridge men's divided attitude to NALU see page 59), on April 8 Ward hired a brass band to play outside the Congregational Church to attract attention to his new Union. In this he had little success, for despite their dislike of Arch and Taylor's mismanagement of NALU, the Pembridge men were wary of putting their trust in Ward's promises for his untried infant NFLU. His attempt at a meeting in a picturesque setting under an old chestnut tree beside the blacksmith's shop at Lyonshall misfired 'as they were prejudiced for the old Union'. NALU was also not slow to respond to these threats to its Union monopoly and sent Johnson, their new district secretary, to thwart meetings at Mansell Lacy and Pembridge, where he held meetings the day before NFLU's advertised dates. In an odd item in the *English Labourer* dated 14 February 1877 Johnson reported that although the Tillington men's wages had dropped to 10 or 12 shillings they still favoured the NFLU land scheme. It is quite possible that an NFLU branch existed (perhaps alongside NALU) in Tillington, where for years a NALU branch had flourished.

By April 1877 Vincent had become disillusioned with NFLU's lack of progress. Without sufficient NFLU members the *Labourers' Union Chronicle* was a continual financial drain on his resources, and he decided to sell the paper to NALU for £800 before emigrating to Australia. Without his support the Union and its land scheme soon collapsed and by September 1879 NFLU was 'virtually obsolete'. As a vehicle for its policies NALU republished the now renamed *English Labourers' Chronicle* from 14 April 1877, continuing to print it at a loss until 5 September 1892 when it finally ceased publication. Meanwhile the NFLU slid into obscurity. By September 1880 the Land Company had no funds to continue and the NFLU was wound up on 19 July 1881. The land was sold and any remaining money distributed among the shareholders. Aged 63, William Gibson Ward died in the autumn of 1882 at Perristone Towers, where his widow continued to live a quiet life for the next 20 years.

Fired with personal feelings of spite and animosity, Ward and Vincent founded the NFLU in a spirit of revenge against their rejection by Arch and Taylor. Despite all their bravado and propaganda, they achieved nothing for the agricultural labourers but sowed disunity, increased the existing divisions in NALU with more doubts and confusion, dissipated funds and further weakened the men's chances of success in their struggle for improved conditions. In a worsening economic climate and lacking the agricultural labourers' support, the NFLU was doomed to failure from its inception, a complete waste of effort on the part of all concerned.

Chapter 4
Joseph Arch and the
National Agricultural Labourers' Union

I live
For the cause that needs assistance
For the wrongs that need resistance
For the future in the distance
For the good that I can do.

Joseph Arch's diary, 1876

Thomas Strange and William Gibson Ward may have been the pioneers of agricultural trade Unions in Herefordshire, but it was Joseph Arch, a charismatic but abrasive man, who became nationally famous, and after the decline of Strange's WoEALA, his National Agricultural Labourers' Union (NALU) was the largest and most influential Union in the area. Having become President of NALU, Arch resolutely declared 'We want no outsider; we know our business and will manage our way' – but despite this declaration, NALU set up a consultative committee of favourably minded *gentlemen* (my italics), including Ward, to advise but without voting powers. Indeed, so far as records show, only Arch, of all the officials at Head Office and their appointed district organisers, had been a farm labourer. The new Union's aims were 'to improve conditions for agricultural labourers in the UK, to encourage formation of branch and district Unions and to promote co-operation and communication with existing Unions'. The entry fee was 6d and subs 2d per week.

As President, Arch was determined to do what he did best and travelled the country, especially the counties of the Midlands, south and east England to spread NALU's message of strength through unity. His usual speech lasted 90 minutes, with farmers, squires, landowners and clergy his particular targets. Frequently they retaliated by using their influence to refuse permission for meetings in church halls or schools, forcing the men to meet outdoors. This was no problem for men accustomed to spending most of their lives in the open air but was yet another example of the irritating power of the ruling class. In the early days Arch visited south Herefordshire repeatedly, staying at Perristone Towers with his ally, Ward. On 19 June 1872, as part of a week-long tour of the area, he spoke at a gathering of 400 men outside Ledbury Town Hall (1,000, according to the *Labourers' Union Chronicle*). Joseph Smith, a local farm labourer, proposed that Ward should take the chair. In turn Ward then introduced Edwin Russell, NALU's corresponding secretary, destined later to become Herefordshire's district secretary. Later, amid much cheering, Arch stressed the strength of their organisation and praised the recently formed branches in Bosbury and Dymock (in Gloucestershire). Employers or their agents often attended such meetings to help men relocate to areas of England offering higher wages and at the end of the evening, hoping for better conditions, several agreed to move to jobs on farms in Leicestershire.

In the following days Arch addressed 600 men at Harewood End and more at the Green Man, Fownhope and the Three Horse Shoes, Llangarron. Having been a dedicated Primitive Methodist preacher in his native Warwickshire for many years, Arch's speeches were sprinkled with Biblical and religious references, making strong connections with people of similar outlook in his audiences. Many of this first generation of agricultural trade Union leaders came from Nonconformist or Primitive Methodist backgrounds, and enjoyed holding Sunday services wherever they could, attracting large congregations of like-minded trade Unionists, their families, friends and neighbours. Indeed, Edwin Russell soon became an accredited preacher on the Hereford Primitive Methodist circuit. So it was no surprise that on Sunday 23 June, Arch advertised a service under Ross Market Hall, where he arrived promptly at 3 o'clock with Ward, Russell and other friends. Though other preachers had previously used the same venue he was greeted by the news that the Town Commissioners would not allow him to preach there 'in case of trouble from the large crowd his name had attracted'. To avoid any ill-feeling or disturbance, he suggested that a move to the then open ground between Henry Street and Cantilupe Road would serve him equally well. (This was to become the site of the school and is now occupied by Ross Library.) Here he preached a sermon on the text 'Be not afraid, only believe' to 1,800 or 2,000 people in a voice clearly audible 100 yards away in Henry Street. Next day he addressed 400 men at Much Marcle and finished his tour at Much Birch on Tuesday. All these villages were within easy travelling distance of Perristone Towers, where Ward enjoyed entertaining his Union allies. After Arch's visit, thriving NALU branches developed in all these villages, except for Much Marcle where the branch always struggled to survive.

Arch returned to Herefordshire on 5 September when Ward drove him and Russell the 14 miles to Garway. The upheavals following the enclosure of hundreds of acres of common land in Garway and nearby Orcop in 1826 had provided fertile ground for the Mormon faith to flourish here in the 1840s, and after the Mormons' departure to America the Primitive Methodists became well established. 800 members of this independent-minded community welcomed Arch and Russell on Garway common, forming a new branch 'in the hope set before them in the Gospel of Unions'. Continuing their work the next day, Ward and Arch walked from Perristone Hill to address a crowd of 500 people at Kingsthorne, Much Birch, where the village branch soon became another substantial Union stronghold.

Just five years later, Arch spoke again at Ross but received a very different response. The excitement and euphoria of 1872 had given way to a sullen atmosphere of apathy and despair. Union morale was low. On 7 May at Ross Arch failed to receive the customary hero-worship, unable to find the words to rouse the men's enthusiasm as he addressed a reasonably well attended meeting in Ross Corn Exchange. There was however a noticeable lack of agricultural labourers among the crowd. J.V. Lenthall, who presided, promised to advance their social and political power locally if the men would remain united and work together. Arch spoke in 'a measured prosy style', contrasting unfavourably with the manner so well remembered from his earlier visits, although he 'spoke against the Game Laws in terms to make country magistrates' hair stand on end.' He also advocated an extension of the right to vote, exhorting the men to keep united and faithful to their cause. But his speech lacked its old vigour. He must have contrasted the apathetic scene with his excited visit five years before. The following day a disappointing 240 people took tea with him at the Comet Inn, Madley, where the crowd was entertained for the rest of the evening by the music of a brass band in the adjoining orchard. Whiting, a member of the county executive committee from Kingstone, with Tattum and Johnson, two NALU organisers, accompanied Arch to the last speech of his tour at the Tram Inn, Eardisley, on May 9. Arch was not impressed by the size or the faint welcome from the 300 strong crowd, who stood in silence, unimpressed in their turn by his message and his oratory.

So what had happened in the intervening five years to change things so dramatically? To begin with, all went well. In the autumn of 1872 Edwin Russell, a friend of Arch's and a founder member of NALU's executive committee, became Herefordshire district organiser (delegate) with offices at 52 Cotterell Street. Walking in all weather conditions from towns to villages across most of Herefordshire giving talks and starting Union branches, he built on Ward's work and the success of Arch's earlier tour. Fortunately the reports he wrote for the *Labourers' Union Chronicle* have survived to give us a vivid and moving impression of the determination of farm labourers to attend meetings despite farmer's opposition. Sometimes in dreadful weather, when the difficulty of finding suitable meeting places proved too great they were forced to hold their meetings in the open air. Experience soon taught them it was wise to utilise a heap of convenient roadstone as a rostrum as at Bishop's Frome to deprive trouble-makers of painful ammunition. At Eardisley local farmers frequented the New Inn, while their labourers used the Tram Inn opposite. The open space between the two was the scene of several stone-throwing encounters between farmers and labourers gathered outside the Tram Inn after Union meetings. Both sides, of course, blamed the other when a labourer's wife and child were injured by a stone. At Bromyard Russell reported that 'only one or two out of ten here can read or write and but few what are cider drinkers', declaring that money spent on missionary work abroad would be better spent here.

Heavy rain in late November caused the usual flooding of the rivers Wye and Lugg, preventing Russell from reaching Withington for a planned meeting. The following day, 27 November, he was able to walk to the toll gate at Burley Gate cross roads. 500 people listened to his speech from a wagon 'lit by four candles stuck in the mud at each corner and a lantern a boy hung on the finger post'. 'Many of the fair sex enjoyed the evening', where 15 enrolled in a new branch. It is noticeable everywhere that many women were attracted to listen to the Union speakers' message, as naturally their own welfare depended on their men's wages. Russell was at Dilwyn on November 29, when 25 new men brought the numbers in the existing branch up to 50. He showed the secretary how to keep the books and organised future meetings in the Primitive Methodist Chapel. At Pembridge the next day, John Thomas, the chairman, asked a local man, Mr Bedford, to speak. He voiced a recurring theme in many villages, complaining bitterly that the charities that had distributed bread, meat and coal to the poor were under the parson's close control and their distribution to the working classes who needed them most had almost dried up. He went on

Eight men stooking sheaves of wheat to dry thoroughly. Farmers needed a long spell of fine weather for a successful harvest. There were no grain drying machines and moisture content meters a hundred years ago. Farmers and foremen drew on years of experience to judge by rubbing the corn from the ears, biting it and feeling its texture whether to proceed or leave it another day. Traditionally oats had to stand for three weeks in the field before carting to the stackyard, but this could be shortened if bad weather seemed to be approaching. Harvest work would now be called 'labour intensive' as every able-bodied person was required to help get the job finished before autumn rain wetted the sheaves. Harvesting was dusty, back-straining work, hard on hands and rough on clothes. Barley was the worst cereal to stook, cart and stack as its long rough awns penetrated everywhere.

to complain that the schoolmaster ridiculed labourers' children with names like 'spragfoot, thickhead, snottynose and the like'.

In January 1873 men had to use boats or wade through cold floods to get to the meeting outside the blacksmith's shop in Mordiford. At Madley, among 100 men who belonged to the Union was 'one woman who insists on paying her monthly contributions saying she is determined to have a share in the conflict and strife so she may have a share in the victory'. At Peterchurch Russell was shocked by the gathering of labourers he met:

> We had made this meeting well known and expected to meet a considerable opposition. About thirty Union men from Madley marched into the village two by two with one at their head playing the concertina. At the sight of these men all opposition vanished, preparing the way for a quiet meeting. But, Oh, the poverty, wretchedness and misery existing in this village and all along the Golden Valley is something terrible to contemplate, for the best workmen among the labourers are but now having but 10s a week, while hundreds are working for 9s, 8s, or even 7s and as a consequence their wives, their children, as well as themselves, are in a state of semi-starvation. The gaunt frames of the men with their thin long faces, their sunken eyes and pale cheeks all speak of the down-trodden condition and position of these serfs of the soil. There would not be less than 500 people present, but no manliness, courage or independence seemed to possess them, for when invited to join the Union, only four out of all that number had the boldness to come forward. The men seem frightened out of their wits, but what told against the men forming a branch was the fact they had no money to pay their entrance fee (sixpence). We intend to visit more of the parishes along the Golden Valley, which is one of the finest tracts of country for fertility and beautiful scenery in the whole of England – and yet all this poverty and suffering. Alas, for poor humanity.

At Kingstone, the landlady of the Mason's Arms was Mrs Morgan, 'whose heart and soul were in the good cause, opened her house when others closed theirs'. 400 men listened as one of their comrades complained he had earned just 31 shillings for seven weeks' work cleaning swedes. 'What a good thing I have found you something to do' were the patronising farmer's thoughtless words of thanks for the labourer's long, wet, cold, dirty winter job bent over heaps of roots heavy with soil for just 11d per day. His complaints helped persuade 20 new members to join, bringing Kingstone's numbers up to 50. A thousand people attended a Sunday service on the village green.

On 27 February a mixture of 'mechanics, town labourers, agricultural labourers and their wives, tradesmen, shop assistants, gentlemen and boys' gathered in the Lecture Hall in Broad Street, Hereford to hear a 90 minute speech from Russell attacking farmers for their double standards. He told the story of how in December at the Withington Ploughing Match evening dinner, a farmer had cited his employee, Mr Exall as an example of a man's thrift and ability to raise a family on the adequate wages he had paid him during the 18 years of his employment. Now, just two months later, Exall with his family of five, all under 12 years old, were in the workhouse, destitute. The evening came to an unsuccessful and confused end with a mouse hunt under the chairs as Russell called for new members and the audience headed for the doors. Only half a dozen men ignored the hubbub to enrol.

Despite a local farmer's noisy interruptions, 22 men joined the Union at the Kite's Nest, Stretton Sugwas on 1 April. The farmer was so infuriated that men had dared ignore his threats that he plied some of his own workmen with drink and persuaded them to help him waylay and beat up three of the Union members on their way home. 'He enjoyed the fun of kicking and cuffing all who dared to think or say different to him.' Though known to his victims he was not prosecuted for his assault.

Everywhere it was the same story: help from some sympathetic landlords and innkeepers, opposition from others, attempts by farmers to disrupt proceedings, evidence of dreadful poverty and hardship, and great hope and enthusiasm for the possibilities offered by the new Union. 'Help one another' was among NALU's mottoes, and small collections were made for sick members and for emigrants. Sellack, Harewood End and Walford became well known for their quick responses with collections when needed. Their spirit was revealed as they stood cheering in the rain at Sellack Marsh as several more joined the Union and made a collection of 23 shillings for Mrs Shaw, whose husband had been a member and was accidentally killed when returning from the Forest of Dean with a wagon load of coal. Hereford branch chipped in with 5 shillings.

With inspiring leadership to encourage them, the men proved they could organise their own events at branch level. On August 1 Broad Oak branch laid on a monster tea. 500 members with their wives and friends met Russell and Jordan at St. Weonards and marched back to Broad Oak, to the music of Fownhope Brass Band, passing through a ceremonial arch onto the village green. It must have made a colourful sight with the ladies wearing blue dresses (NALU's colour) while the men carried blue ribbons and sported 6d blue hatbands emblazoned with the Union's gold wheat sheaf emblem. After the usual speeches a thousand people sat down to tea in three sittings, while people waiting their turn sang Union songs, danced or listened to the music. 'It was a day and a time to be long remembered by the people who had come from miles around for the festive occasion.' At Kingsthorne, 'a spot of noted fame and now consecrated to a noble purpose', a thousand people gathered for speeches from Waite and Whiting, two local Union stalwarts. Fownhope Brass Band played dance tunes for the 'hundreds of couples who joined the giddy maze – elderly fathers and mothers enjoying it quite as much as their children and reeling about as fast as the music for the rest of the evening'. By the summer of 1873 the Comet branch at Madley had grown to an astonishing 500 members, said to include every farm worker in the parish. It was so numerous that the membership was divided to start a very successful separate branch at Shenmore at the other end of the village.

Changing social and political conditions produced natural leaders from among Union members. Ordinary labourers with little education, who would not previously have dared voice an opinion, found the confidence to come forward to help themselves and their Union's paid organisers. When 26 men reformed their branch in the street beside Bosbury's church yard wall, they elected a Mr Foster from Wellington Heath as their temporary secretary. Although he had worked steadily for the same farmer for 18 years he was promptly sacked for daring to join the Union. The farmer's loss was the Union's gain as Foster helped Russell organise meetings in the area around Ledbury and Withington on a regular basis. A week after a group of particularly boisterous noisy farmers had disrupted a meeting of a thousand people beside Ledbury Market House, amid scenes the Union speakers had never before witnessed, Foster quietly returned, when the excitement had died down, and formed a thriving branch. In the large branch at Kingsthorne, Whiting was prominent for many years and served on the county executive committee. Many others, whose names are now lost, were convinced NALU was their hope of a better future and followed his example in working for the Union and their fellow villagers. In some villages, however, labourers decided that discretion was the best course of action. 24 labourers at Stoke Edith, fearing Lady Foley's power and wrath, formed their Union branch in neighbouring Weston Beggard. Wages there were eight to ten shillings per week, and women earned three or four pence a day pulling roots.

As the months passed NALU's growth continued despite occasional upsets. Russell claimed over 70 branches in the county, with over 3,000 members, and was unimpressed by the local papers' failure to report on NALU's popularity. In truth, apart from small wage rises (which of course were important to the men who received them), the labourers' conditions were as bad as ever but had lost their newsworthiness simply through repetition. It was no real surprise that other news took prominence. In time Russell was confident and experienced enough to spread NALU's activities into the Shropshire villages of Bucknell, Aston, Culmington and Lydbury North and also into the Presteigne area of Radnorshire. This was all West of England Association territory where Thomas Strange had sown the seed of Unionism two or three years previously, but with which, because of his illness, he had not had any recent contact, a fact distorted by NALU into 'neglect'. After several visits Russell was even able to form a branch in Strange's village of Leintwardine. He was never able, however, to Unionise the scattered villages in the area north-east of the Leominster to Bromyard road. Though Arch was never completely in favour of it, the *Labourers' Union Chronicle* reflected an increasing emphasis on emigration. Advertisements and letters from successful emigrées encouraged men to move to the Dominions, though America was the greater magnet. There were also innumerable evening lectures on the subject in schools and in church and village halls.

Herefordshire's executive committee decided to start a Sick and Benefit Society in 1873 as an added inducement to men to enrol in the Union. In the short term this was successful in attracting new members. However the scheme's long term effect had not been thought through, and it proved to be ruinous to NALU as no proper actuarial assessment of the men's age and health, essential to calculate rates of contribution and benefit, was made before the

Thanks to the long memories of older Allensmoor residents this cottage has been identified as Goose Pool Cottage. It was demolished in 1980 after falling into a ruinous state, as its last use was for housing chickens. A smart new red brick bungalow occupies the site. In 1910 Goose Pool Cottage, surrounded by its quarter acre garden, was a tied cottage belonging to Henry Millichamp's Courtland farm, which he rented from the Pateshall estate. It was the home of one of his labourers. At this distance in time it has been impossible to establish who lived there in 1910 and what led to his eviction. The Electoral Register did not record the occupier and County Court records for the period no longer exist. In Herefordshire in 1910 farm labourers earned 12 shillings for a 54 hour week in winter and over 60 hours in summer. Their tied cottages were not always rent free and they had no security of tenure as the cottage went with the job. Losing his job, for whatever cause, illness, old age, or just a disagreement with the farmer meant losing his home as well. A major demand of all the agricultural workers' Unions since 1871 was for a revision of the whole system, wanting, wherever possible, cottages to be removed from the farmers' to the landlords' control, for proper leases and for reasonable notice to quit. They also campaigned for proper repairs and more new housing for rural workers to overcome the ever present squalor and overcrowding. Surrounded by his two dogs and his meagre possessions, the fate of this unfortunate victim is not known. Thomas Morton, a photographer at 1 East Street, Hereford, photographed the dismal scene on 6 September 1910, but to avoid controversy in a sensitive subject he published this postcard anonymously. He might have feared losing customers and upsetting powerful landowners and farmers with pictures of the harsh reality of rural life. For similar reasons local newspapers did not report these regular evictions that were a constant background threat to farm workers' families.

scheme was started. Eventually NALU's reserve funds were drained away as Head Office was forced to subsidise the Sick and Benefit Society which had to pay out more money than an ageing and declining membership contributed. (This financial commitment was a significant factor in NALU's eventual collapse in 1896.) The low rates of NALU's benefit scheme attracted agricultural labourers who were generally regarded as a poor risk and not welcomed into village friendly societies. At the same Hereford meeting the executive committee also invited subscriptions towards emigrants' expenses, spurred on by Ward's advertisement earlier in the year, because by then they had come to realise that Strange's emigration policy was the best way to proceed towards higher wages for their men.

Money became an issue again in 1874. For five months in the spring and summer of that year a bitter strike and lock-out raged in the Eastern Counties between farmers and members of several agricultural Unions including NALU. Arch toured the country using his talents as an orator in a non-stop series of speeches and demonstrations to raise the thousands of pounds required to enable the Union's strike funds to fulfil NALU's promise to pay all the locked-out or striking labourers 10 shillings per week plus 1 shilling for each dependent child. Herefordshire was not directly affected by the prolonged dispute, although the Amalgamated Labour League of Lincolnshire (a branch of the Federal Union), attempting to widen its influence, published a circular demanding wage increases in a number of counties – demands which everyone ignored. As the strike spread into Dorset the non-militant men of Herefordshire watched events there with concern. There were the inevitable evictions from tied cottages as farmers used their usual bullying tactics to enforce compliance to their terms. The *Labourers' Union Chronicle* report on the evictions of three labourers from their homes in Milton Abbas, Dorset show the strength of the men's convictions. Bowing to the overwhelming forces of law, one sang Union songs as the bailiffs threw his possessions into the road, another played Union tunes on his fiddle, and with great amusement the third watched as the bailiffs tried to evict 'his stock of bees, which were not easy to eject'.

At the height of the strike Ward and Russell attended NALU's annual conference at Leamington on June 13, where its effects were fully discussed. A membership of 86,214 in 37 districts was announced and in its first year NALU had spent £2,500 on migration and emigration and over 25,000 men had left agricultural districts. The following week Ward joined other speakers at a huge Union rally in Manchester, where 12 or 15 thousand gathered in support of the agricultural labourers' struggle. Some men's wages did rise slightly and some were able to return to their jobs, but the Union lacked sufficient funds to continue strike pay through the harvest. Justifiably, many Norfolk and Suffolk men felt betrayed when NALU abruptly stopped their strike pay at the end of July and their former employers refused to re-employ them. After this disastrously expensive episode, NALU policy was modified to a reluctant acceptance of emigration, although the leadership recognised that both they and the farmers lost their best men abroad and that it was very disruptive to village life.

Unrealistic financial commitments were thus one factor in the failure of NALU, and money became a bone of contention in many of the disputes that sprang up between those involved in the Union. The difficulty was compounded by the effects of the selfish personality of the Union's President. Arch possessed many qualities needed to make him a popular Union leader, but his egoistic self-aggrandisement and triumphant bragging were at times excessive. Whenever possible he loved to boast about the defeat of his 'enemies' and to flaunt NALU's supremacy, even at the expense of those who had helped him in its success. For example, in 1875, when Strange had moved from Adforton to Yarpole after his enforced retirement from Union work due to continuing ill-health, Arch made a special journey to Leintwardine to address a meeting of three or four hundred men to sing his own praises in Strange's former stronghold. He made no acknowledgement of Strange's help in forming NALU or his work for the labourers in the area. Two years before, Strange had helped form the loose Federal Union of Agricultural and General Labourers which, to Arch's delight, had soon collapsed through lack of cohesion and firm direction. Although NALU's strength was in slow decline, it was still the dominant Union, a point which Arch loved to emphasise whenever possible, regarding all other agricultural trade Unions as rivals or even opponents rather than comrades in the struggle for better wages and conditions. It is believed that Arch was always jealous that Strange had been able to form a large and viable Union extending across six counties a year before his own part in the formation of the Warwickshire ALU. With Taylor's help he certainly did his utmost to rewrite NALU's story and to obliterate any part that Strange had played in early agricultural trade Union history. Arch's attitude was 'If you are not with me you are against me'; differences were allowed to fester and divide members of the Union from their common cause. Arch's dealings with Ward, Strange and Vincent are all examples of this flaw in his character. Of course, he was by no means alone in this failing. The misplaced pride and lack of diplomacy

Joseph Arch sketched during his visit to Canada in 1873, from the Canadian Illustrated News

of many agricultural Union leaders led to serious arguments that could have been prevented and unbridgeable divisions were caused when unity in the face of the farmers' persistent opposition was of paramount importance. NALU lost the support of many men for this reason.

Given the temperaments of the two men, it was perhaps inevitable that, after a co-operative beginning, the relationship between Arch and William Gibson Ward would deteriorate to a point at which the two men were in a state of feud, within an atmosphere of general acrimony. As has been mentioned (see pages 43-44), Arch's visit to Canada in 1873 provoked Ward into a series of attacks which brought matters to a head. Dogmatic and self-assured as usual, Arch embarked on a speaking tour of Herefordshire to show that he was unwilling to back down before Ward's accusations and to present his version of events in Ward's Herefordshire stronghold. He started the tour on 15 September 1874 in Presteigne, where 465 people sat down to tea with him. Afterwards, carrying Union banners and singing Union songs, they processed to Broad Heath, where 5,000 people had assembled to hear Arch speak, coming from the villages around and from up to 15 miles away in the Radnorshire hills. Arch did not disappoint, and spoke defiantly of Ward's efforts to embarrass him, denying all his allegations. He poured scorn on the farmers' recent failure to pass a Tenants' Rights Bill through Parliament, and went on to demand the vote for rural workers to effect a basic alteration in the composition of the House of Commons permanently and radically. He asked for the men's unity with the Union by which they had obtained their wage rises, and spoke of his view that the Eastern Counties' strike and lock-out was not a defeat. Taking Suffolk as his example, he said that 400 men had emigrated and another 400 had moved to jobs in the north with wages between 20 and 30 shillings. Farmers had taken back 870 men who retained their Union cards and some had had a slight wage rise.

Of course, this was not the whole story. In a bitter drawn-out strike of this sort, an assessment of winners and losers inevitably depends on how the dispute is viewed. In Arch's view, the outcome of the strike in Suffolk was that some farmers had lost by conceding wage increases (albeit low ones) to 870 men, who had retained their Union cards. On the winning side were the 400 men, who had migrated to better paid jobs in the north and the men who had emigrated. The farmers were only victorious in refusing to re-employ the remaining 350 men, who had to find other employment. These 350 men had opposed the farmers' conditions for the long months of the strike. However, when NALU and the other Unions involved had finally exhausted their funds and could afford only one more week's strike pay, Arch suddenly ended the strike against the men's wishes and without consulting them, so that they lost their jobs and with them any respect they had felt for Arch and NALU. Rather than getting the support they expected, they felt completely abandoned by the Union. Their disillusionment spread as others came to realise that NALU had been unable to protect its members and that it was not as powerful as they had imagined. Arch failed to mention or perhaps failed even to realise, that the struggle these men had endured for months had led to nothing except abandonment to their fate, for which many held him to blame. His repeated calls for Union solidarity were not matched by appropriate leadership or unity of purpose when his members most needed it. By a slight margin the farmers had gained the initiative and even 40 years later claimed to have defeated Arch. Repercussions of the outcome of the strike were felt around the country, and NALU never again supported a large-scale strike.

Not that, for the time being, any of this seems to have troubled Arch. At Withington the day after the Presteigne meeting, undaunted by the wet weather (a public tea was rained off), Arch addressed 400 people under a clump of trees on the common. Union stalwarts cheered as he repeated his previous day's speech. Thursday saw a repeat performance at

Garway and on Friday he took tea with the members and their wives at Much Birch where he repeated his message 'Stick to the Union'. Surprisingly, his presence on Ward's old stamping ground failed to provoke any response from his adversary except for a letter from Ward in the *Hereford Times* severing his connection with the *Labourers' Union Chronicle*; ironically, this appeared on the same page as reports of Arch's speeches.

For the time being Herefordshire's support for Arch and NALU remained firm. Accompanied by Edwin Russell and James Airey, Arch returned to a quiet corner of Bosbury on the last day of October to enjoy a NALU tea in a marquee at Pow Green with 300 members and their wives. Five or six hundred people listened to speeches afterwards, danced to the melodies of the Fownhope Brass Band and watched a firework display to close the day's festivities. But even though the Union had been instrumental in raising the men's wages, a general falling off of support was noted from about this time. In spite of all the speakers could say, the men could not maintain their initial enthusiasm to keep pressure on their employers for better conditions. These became more and more difficult to achieve as the deepening agricultural depression started to affect farmers' incomes, and NALU began its long slow decline, with only occasional flickerings of the old spirit. It appears that many of the labourers believed that just belonging to the Union would solve their employment problems, and disillusionment set in rapidly when their expectations of better times failed to materialise at once. Month by month, reports in the *Labourers' Union Chronicle* became increasingly despondent. The unsatisfactory conclusion of the Eastern Counties' strike marked the end of NALU's successes. A year later this was followed by a dramatic downturn in fortune, brought about by the major personality clashes and fundamental disagreements highlighted at its 1875 conference.

As Edwin Russell and Thomas Whiting, Herefordshire's delegates, prepared for NALU's annual conference in Birmingham on 25 May 1875 they could never have dreamed of its disastrous outcome. Russell proudly reported 1,536 members whose subscriptions amounted to £374 1s 8d and donations of £197 4s 7d. They had received £35 in grants for emigration expenses. It must have been painful for him, as one of the original Warwickshire ALU officials, to query some inaccuracies in the Head Office version of Herefordshire's accounts, which were explained away the next day. Much more serious discrepancies were however revealed in Head Office accounting and bitter recriminations broke out among members of the executive committee and especially between Taylor, the general secretary and Matthew Vincent, the treasurer, whose prompt resignation immediately deprived NALU of the *Labourers' Union Chronicle*, its newspaper. As proprietor, Vincent at once reversed editorial policy and, 'supporting all other oppressed agricultural workers', mounted a spirited attack on the whole NALU leadership, including Arch. The resulting confusion dismayed ordinary members and became a major contributory factor in NALU's subsequent decline, especially when Vincent and Ward added to the turmoil by founding the rival National Farm Labourers' Union in July. Union solidarity is easily derided, but unity is fundamental to morale and without a united national leadership members' spirits everywhere fell. Herefordshire's NALU members were just as perplexed as those everywhere else and its membership declined further.

The reaction of the Pembridge branch of NALU could be seen as a typical response to the divisions at Head Office. Pembridge members passed a resolution of no confidence in its leaders, determining no longer to support them and agreeing to return branch funds to its members. Russell responded with threatening letters demanding that their funds be sent to district office, where £24 was needed to pay the rent. Pembridge's membership were further disgusted when Arch and the meek Herefordshire executive committee agreed to maintain Russell's wages at £2, which Arch unguardedly described as 'starvation point', although it was well over double the average agricultural labourer's wage they were both supposed to be trying to improve. Widespread mistrust of Head Office and the leadership's motives was to undermine all their organisers' strenuous efforts to revive Union fortunes in the years ahead. Similar reactions occurred throughout Herefordshire. The loss of their popular county leader, Ward, meant that all later attempts to revive NALU's membership were short-lived. Letters of support for Ward from members and ex-members of Herefordshire ALU appeared in the press, especially after he was shouted down, violently assaulted and literally kicked out of a meeting Arch was addressing at Ashorne in Warwickshire. In any case, there was widespread and general distrust of NALU's leaders, whose arguments and mismanagement were clearly apparent. A thousand branches passed resolutions deploring Union extravagances from which they gained no benefit, and Herefordshire followed suit.

The *English Labourer*, edited by Howard Evans, began publication on 26 June 1875 as NALU's replacement newspaper. News of Union activity in Herefordshire recommenced on 13 September with Russell's report of an executive committee meeting's motion of confidence in Arch and NALU and the recommendation to Herefordshire labourers to read the *English Labourer* for the truth. Routine reports resumed, though Russell found that enthusiasm was lacking and that work often took precedence over Union activity. The damage had been done; stories of financial mismanagement now dogged NALU and were used to undermine the Union. For example, at a Union meeting in Lyonshall on 17 April 1876, a farmer claimed that Arch had run off with all the men's money; spreading this sort of rumour was a tactic frequently used by farmers to denigrate Arch and his colleagues. At the end of 1875, disillusioned by continuing arguments and falling membership, the county's hard-working and hitherto popular secretary, Russell, resigned after a row with Taylor, who literally tried to snatch Herefordshire's Sick and Benefit Society's bank book, containing £200, to use for his own account at Leamington. Russell's replacement, William Johnson, was faced with an uphill struggle against apathy and dissension aggravated by the threat of a rival Union's appearance as Ward tried to establish the NFLU.

Meanwhile, the struggle continued, with or without the help of Unions. A report in the *English Labourer* on 10 October 1876 described a serious agricultural labourers' strike in the county, although it was small, local and not supported by the Union. 'Many men were out of work and wages were going down. The harvest was still out in the fields as the labourers were standing out for their wage of 10 shillings per acre for butting and stacking. Many acres [of corn] have gone down the river on account of the floods.' Such conditions gave the labourers a perfect opportunity to bargain, if not to strike, for higher wages, especially as farmers started reducing wages from about this date in response to falling prices for farm produce.

By 1878, Arch's involvement in the Liberal Party and his ambition to enter Parliament prevailed over any Union aims to improve members' wages and conditions. Shortsightedly, he directed all available funds to Head Office, leaving the numerically smaller districts to manage as best they could. Drained of resources and deprived of assistance from Leamington, like the Eastern Counties strikers five years earlier, members and their officials felt abandoned by Arch. In January 1879 Arch called a Union conference in London, attended by W. Tombs, who had become Worcestershire and Herefordshire district secretary the previous year, after another Union reorganisation. In his usual dogmatic way Arch insisted that everyone who did not agree with his policies was against him, leaving no room for discussion. Arch went on to accuse district secretaries of betraying both him and the Union by not working hard enough. To cut costs from now on, Arch wanted only to employ delegates in real Union strongholds. Tombs felt that instead of being left to fend for themselves, a fairer way to fund weaker districts could have been found. For counties with smaller numbers of members, like Herefordshire, Arch's policy would prove disastrous as resources would be stretched too thinly. Personally, Tombs felt insulted as he had worked hard for his combined district, and he also objected to Arch taking the control of NALU into his own hands without any consultation. Tombs' objections made him an enemy of Arch, who was well

Joseph Arch MP 1879

placed to obtain his revenge. Just two months later, at the annual meeting of the combined Worcestershire and Herefordshire district, the blow fell. Arch sent a delegate to announce, without any advance notice, the news that NALU's Executive Committee, which was completely under Arch's thumb, had decided to amalgamate Worcestershire with Warwickshire and Herefordshire with Cirencester district (the Cotswold half of Gloucestershire that still flourished under NALU control 40 miles from Herefordshire). This decision was taken without any discussion or regard to the wishes of the members or the officials affected. Tombs resigned as agent for the Union newspaper, the *English Labourer*, on which he had lost £7 he could ill afford. By 7 June he was sacked from his post as Herefordshire and Worcestershire organising secretary. This further blow to local Unionism still further reduced any chance of revitalising NALU's fortunes in Herefordshire. Tomb's dismissal was just one of a long list of organised dismissals of hard-working district officials throughout the country. These experienced men were the backbone on whom NALU organisation really depended. Their dismissal for cost-cutting or personal reasons proved to be short-sighted in the extreme. By uncaringly discarding such men, Arch and Taylor, seemingly unaware of the unnecessary tensions and weaknesses they created within NALU, both in Herefordshire and in the country at large, were the architects of their Union's eventual downfall.

Arch was becoming more involved in Liberal Party politics when he paid Herefordshire a rare visit on 5 June 1880 to address a meeting on Much Birch common, but despite a large crowd, just eight men were persuaded to enrol. This was the last of his 27 speeches in the county. Just three months later, Collins and his colleague Boulton tried to revive Herefordshire's old Union spirit with the first of a promised series of meetings at the Axe and Cleaver, Much Birch, deep in old Union territory. Opening the meeting with well known Union songs, they explained the advantages of belonging to the Union and to the Sick and Benefit Society, and promised that it was just the land question that remained to be solved to bring the men everything they had campaigned for. The sombre truth was, however, that the men knew they were in the middle of a serious agricultural depression and had heard all the Union promises many times before. No one enrolled and no one even bothered to ask the speakers a question.

It appears that NALU support simply withered away as no reports of any Union activity in Herefordshire for the next eight years have appeared. The agricultural depression meant that by 1881 land had become nearly impossible to sell. When a farm fell vacant, the new rent was at least 5 to 10 shillings per acre less than five years previously, provided a willing tenant could be found. The depression affected farms in the north of Herefordshire worse than the mixed farms on lighter land in the south. Arable land fell out of use and weeds flourished as the acreage of grassland increased significantly. Until July 1888, a few stalwarts at Staunton on Wye, Bishopstone, Norton Canon and Shenmore continued their contributions, mainly for the benefits they received from the Sick and Benefit Society. Affiliated with NALU, two branches of the WoEALA formed by Thomas Strange in 1872, Hanley Castle in Worcestershire and Ramsbury in Wiltshire, were both active up to this date also. As NALU had never found the correct actuarial balance for its members' contributions to the Sick and Benefit Society, by 1888 it was in deep financial trouble, paying out double its income in sickness benefit. To balance the accounts Arch demanded a special 1s 6d levy on all its branches. The few remaining Herefordshire branches withdrew, although they had done well from the scheme. It had finally dawned on people that Arch and NALU were unable to achieve as much as he claimed and that increasingly they were on their own. At the 1891 annual NALU conference held in Woodbridge, Suffolk, Arch claimed to represent the Herefordshire and Worcestershire branches, though he had not set foot in Herefordshire for 11 years. His mind was now entirely given to national politics, and he spent much of his time speaking on behalf of the Liberal Party and as an MP for Wilton in Hampshire and later for North West Norfolk, proudly representing the Prince of Wales as a constituent as well as the crowds of Norfolk labourers who still flocked to his meetings. Without any warning the *English Labourer* published its last edition on 8 September 1894 and the last of NALU's Norfolk branches finally disintegrated after the 1896 election.

We must not take from all this, however, any idea that the efforts of Thomas Strange, William Gibson Ward, Joseph Arch and many others were in vain. Despite all the difficulties and personality clashes, NALU lasted in Herefordshire for 24 years due to the dogged tenacity of a handful of stalwarts in the county's scattered villages. Before 1871, Hodge, the Victorians' nickname for the agricultural labourer, was the most downtrodden member of society, underpaid, badly housed, neglected and without a vote to give him a voice in local or national government. Once his voice was joined with others in a Union chorus loud enough to be heard and strong enough to take on the farmers and win wage awards, his conditions were recognised and promises were given to improve them. Membership of trade Unions gained him respect and in 1885 the right to vote was granted to rural workers. Arch became the first MP to come from the agricultural working class. Bills for setting up allotments for urban as well as rural workers were passed into law. Royal Commissions investigating workers' conditions reported the appalling state of rural housing and though it took another 60 years for major improvements, some landowners were stung into building decent estate cottages for their men. The Parish Council Act finally gave ordinary villagers the chance to have their say on matters which had previously been the domain of the village's farmers, squire and parson. The administration of the Poor Law to the old and infirm was made fairer and more humane. In the 25 years from the founding of agricultural Unions in 1871, the status of agricultural labourers advanced to equal that of urban workers, though their working and living conditions remained as abysmal as ever.

That no official strikes, lockouts or other industrial action are recorded in Herefordshire during the years of NALU's existence is not a sign of Union weakness or inactivity. Rather, the mere presence of a Union branch, with a national organisation in the background, pushed wages up and kept them at the higher level. It was not until membership of branches declined that serious wage cuts were inflicted on the then isolated and powerless labourers. Many examples can be found of NALU members receiving higher wages than non-Union labourers, though in some cases they all benefited. Combination with their mates gave men a strength they lacked as individuals. This was the reason farmers so detested NALU's growth and continued their vehement opposition to its spread. Another reason for the lack of strikes was that it was extremely difficult to organise co-ordinated strike action on scattered farms where only a few men worked, only some of whom were in the Union and where conditions of employment varied greatly. Many years later, Sidney Box, organiser of the Workers' Union, encountered these difficulties during their short-lived strike of July 1914 (see pages 80-81), and even now (in 2008) the farm workers' Union maintains that quietly working to maintain and improve its members' wages and the conditions of work of the mainly foreign workforce is preferable to a more militant stance in obtaining higher wages – vindication indeed of Strange's policy of diplomacy over Arch's blustering, dogmatic posturings.

Chapter 5
The Bogus Union 1892

The end of the National Agricultural Labourers' Union did not mean the end of Union activity in Herefordshire, and the next development was not long in coming. During the political excitement leading up to the general election in June 1892, the English Land Restoration League (ELRL) announced its intention of sending one of its fleet of 'Red Vans' on a tour of north Herefordshire villages. In the 1890s and 1900s, long before the days of wireless, television and the telephone, it had become common practice for organisations to send these gypsy-style caravans from village to village to spread their own particular message. Missionary Vans for Hop Pickers, the Bishop of Herefordshire's Church Vans and the Herefordshire Beekeepers' Van all made use of this effective method of reaching new audiences in the county's scattered villages. The ELRL's Red Vans were well known at the time as they carried their speakers around the counties of southern England to publicise the League's land reform policies. From late June to September, during 1892's particularly bad harvest, ELRL's Red Van no.4 meandered through north Herefordshire festooned with the slogans 'The Land for All', 'Fair Rents' and 'Fair Wages'. A halt in a different village each evening gave its idealistic middle-class speakers a fresh audience, attracted to hear their ideas of breaking down 'the accursed system of landlordism and land monopoly' under which the villagers had suffered all their lives.

One member of the ELRL's General Committee was the Rev. Arthur Compton Auchmuty, vicar of Lucton since 1873, who for 11 years had also been headmaster of Lucton Free School. He had also founded the Herefordshire Agricultural and General Workers Union (HA&GWU) on 5 May 1892, according to reports in the *Leominster News*, at a meeting at Kington Market Hall. This appears to have been in anticipation of the Red Van's visit, which he seems to have used as a way of gaining members of his Union. Indeed the two organisations were so closely entwined that HA&GWU became a vehicle for ELRL's policies. No reports appear of HA&GWU branches behaving as we would expect, with demands for shorter working hours, better housing and higher wages for its members, though amongst the Union's aims were 'a more adequate remuneration for labour and improvement generally of condition for workers'. Instead of representing men in their attempts to improve their wages and conditions, Auchmuty simply used the Union to promote the ELRL's message of land reform.

Like Ward and Vincent and their NFLU 16 years earlier, the leaders of both the ELRL and HA&GWU believed that the Enclosures had been fundamentally detrimental to country people. They wanted to see large estates divided into small farms, smallholdings and allotments so that ordinary countrymen could enjoy the benefits of working their own piece of land, and believed that the Enclosures had left a resentment among Herefordshire's rural poor that they could harness for popular support. Auchmuty refused to countenance strikes in support of the Union's limited aims of improving farm workers wages and conditions, saying they would damage fellow members' interests. This was undoubtedly the case as membership was open to all men and women living in Herefordshire, 'except only those few (if any) who do not labour truly to get their own living and have no intention or desire to do so'. He regarded everyone, including employers, as workers and said they

Church Army caravans were a regular sight around the county and beyond, appearing in many hopyards during the six to eight week long season. Their missionaries took their role seriously, travelling to crowded hop pickers' camps to bring the Bible to people far from home who might be missing their Sunday church services. To counter the boredom of dark autumn evenings (and to keep the men from the pubs) they entertained children and adults with magic lantern shows screened on whitewashed barn walls. The Church Army was on hand with practical help and advice if an accident, illness or bereavement occurred.

should all receive just reward for their endeavours, which, he hoped, 'they would attain by due process of law'. Seemingly he dreamed that improvements in living standards, wages and conditions generally would follow the process of political agitation for land reform.

And so the Red Van toured the county in the summer of 1892, Auchmuty accompanying Henry Anckehill, general secretary of the ELRL and a personal friend, and Benjamin Riley, their permanent speaker, for most of their tour through north Herefordshire. On its arrival in a village a few sweets or coppers soon persuaded local children to distribute handbills advertising the evening's lecture. From June to September Anckehill claimed to have held 92 meetings throughout Herefordshire at 62 locations, mostly in the evenings. These meetings were not part of the election campaign, but in the excitement of the moment many HA&GWU branches were formed – there was no entrance fee to join and the subscription was only 1d per week, with 2d per quarter for branch working expenses, a total of 5 shillings per year – but without the real and sustained grassroots support of the majority of agricultural workers the Union could not last.

Demonstrating the latest 1890s beekeeping equipment and techniques to sceptical villagers from the back of the Herefordshire Bee Van.

On 6 May a receptive audience gathered at the Croase room in Kingsland, where Henry Anckehill's stirring address persuaded 28 people to enrol in the Union. The new branch voted Arnold Stephens, a local coal merchant, their temporary secretary and Rev. Auchmuty, who lived in the village, their treasurer. Auchmuty later wrote that it was the successful formation of this large branch at Kingsland that was the foundation on which he was able to establish another 35 branches with 553 members by the end of the year. Yarpole, Monkland, Kingsland, Kington, Pembridge and Eardisland branches were among the first he established. Where traceable, HA&GWU officials appear to have been businessmen.

As an avowed Conservative, Lord Bateman, who owned the greater part of the village of Shobdon, would not allow even the Liberal Party candidate permission to use Shobdon school room for an election meeting, and he had no intention of allowing a Red Van meeting anywhere on his estate. Supported and encouraged by his brother, the rector, he wanted nothing to disturb Shobdon's rural calm. He exerted such a powerful hold over tenants and workers alike that he could instruct them all not to allow the Red Van speakers on their land or premises. As landlord of the Bateman Arms, Fred Biddle was one of Lord Bateman's tenants and despite a previously arranged booking, he was easily persuaded that it was not in his interests to allow his pub to be used by the 'agitators'. Making full use of his position as Lord Lieutenant of Herefordshire, Lord Bateman instructed the Inspector of Police, backed up by a constable, to inform Anckehill and Auchmuty that any meeting in the village street was unlawful. To their credit they refused to be permanently excluded from Shobdon and returned a few weeks later, when both the rector and Lord Bateman were away on holiday and held their meeting in the road outside the gates of Shobdon Court. Though absent, Lord Bateman's grip was absolute and 'So great was the terror inspired by the tyrannous privileges of the feudal lord' that none of the villagers timidly peeping from their doors dared to join the Union. To emphasise the ELRL's views on the question of land reform, from August 24-27 the Red Van speakers also visited John Arkwright's huge Hampton Court estate, holding unopposed meetings at Hope under Dinmore, Humber, Stoke Prior and Bodenham.

The *Leominster News* reported that

> In the course of its perambulations the ELRL's Red Van reached Kington on 1 August, Bank Holiday Monday. The town seemed deserted, various holiday attractions having taken off a large portion of the inhabitants. Nevertheless at 8pm a large number of persons had assembled to hear the address, which Benjamin Riley, the van lecturer, opened with a lucid presentation of the objects and tenets of the league, advocating the formation throughout the county of a general association for the purpose of studying political questions. He was followed in the same strain by the Rev. A.C. Auchmuty in his capacity of general secretary of the HA&GWU and a member of the ELRL. The treat of the evening was the fervent and eloquent address of Mr P. Wilson Raffan, proprietor of the *South Wales Gazette*, a powerful and trenchant arraignment of landlordism, which

was listened to with marked attention for nearly one hour by the 200 persons present. At the close hearty cheers were given for the Union and some fresh names were added to the local branch.'

At the final meeting of their tour, in Leominster's Corn Square on 16 September, Anckehill repeated his thesis that 'the principal cause of the poverty of the workers in the agricultural districts, as well as in the towns, is the monopoly by the few of the land, which is the common property of all. This meeting therefore pledges itself to use its best endeavours to send to Parliament representatives, who will demand that those that hold the land shall pay for the privilege to its rightful owners, the people, and so make possible the abolition of taxation which now presses upon labour and its products.

A Government enquiry into the state of Agriculture met at Bromyard on 17 September 1892 and at Hereford the following day. Average wages were reported to be 2s 6d for day work or 12 shillings per week, plus a cottage for permanently employed men, who were usually hired from May to May. On behalf of the men Mr Gwynne stated: 'One might search through a good many counties before finding a place where the cottages were in worse repair than in Herefordshire, especially if they were in the hands of the farmer. The cottages were a disgrace to civilisation and, in some districts, should not be allowed to

This row of poor cottages beside the road at Kingsthorne was sufficiently noteworthy for Alfred Watkins to photograph for posterity in circa 1910. *For the unfortunate inhabitants social housing with proper facilities at reasonable rents and owned by the local authority was only a distant dream that slowly materialised in the next fifty years.*

stand.' He went on to describe labourers' conditions as unsatisfactory, with low wages, no power in their villages, no voice in local affairs or in the education of their children, which was in the clergy's hands. Recent efforts had been made to provide allotments in Garway, Bryngwyn, Ross and Hereford at Holmer Within and Tupsley. Efforts to acquire a suitable field at Upton Bishop in 1892 were unsuccessful. It was stated that there were no agricultural trade Unions in the county, despite the formation of HA&GWU that May. (It is possible also that there were still a few diehard NALU members.) The enquiry also heard that there had been no strikes or lock-outs in the past ten years and that young labourers frequently found work in the coal mines and iron works in south Wales, returning to farm work in their native Herefordshire if work in south Wales declined.

Instead of improving, conditions grew worse. The long-lasting depression forced wages lower and farm profits to fall remorselessly, with a consequent fall in land values. Added to this, the wet weather caused such a bad harvest in 1892 that farmers were hard pushed to find the money to pay their rents. Rather than lose all their estate incomes, landowners were forced to concede rent reductions. Sir Charles Rouse-Boughton of Downton Hall, blaming the depression, issued a circular to all his tenants with rents over £50, offering to reduce them by 20%. At the same time Lord Bateman offered a miserly 5% reduction. This loss of income affected landowners across the country and, coupled with the introduction of death duties in 1894, saw the start of the process which gradually deprived the landed gentry of their estates in the following decades. (Death duties were in fact introduced for political not social reasons, to finance the Royal Navy's expansion to counter German aggrandisement.)

How the rural poor coped with their conditions can only be imagined. A very cold spell of winter weather in January 1893 added to the misery of the many unemployed in towns and countryside alike. Leominster businessmen and landowners subscribed £110 to fund a soup kitchen where an average of 418 people received a measured quart of mainly vegetable soup daily and free bread and coal were distributed to the most needy. With their Red Van in use in another county, Union activity in Herefordshire was at a low ebb in 1893. Only one speech in September by Auchmuty was reported for the whole year. In February he had announced his intention to publish a monthly newspaper entitled *The Herefordshire Beacon* to promote HA&GWU's views. What became of this publishing venture is not known, for the bogus Union soon disappeared from the record.

Unlike the spontaneous agricultural labourers' movements that sprang up in the 1870s and later in 1912-20, the HA&GWU had no solid grass roots foundation, but was entirely the brainchild of the Rev. Auchmuty, whose real interest was the redistribution of land on a fairer basis and whose creation of HA&GWU was simply a means to advance the aims of the ELRL. In contrast to earlier or subsequent Unions, he had no intention or desire directly to agitate to try to improve the pay and conditions of the poor.

Chapter 6
Sidney Box and the Workers' Union in Herefordshire 1912-1929

Sidney Box in 1930

At first sight the Workers' Union, founded by Tom Mann on May Day 1898, seems an unlikely movement for agricultural labourers in Herefordshire to join, as its prime aim was to organise unskilled urban workers in London's docks and building sites. Based in London, its early years were a long struggle to build branches and maintain members as they drifted from one badly paid, unskilled job to another. With no other Union for unskilled workers to turn to for help, two Shropshire farm workers, Beard and Simpson, founded a dozen short-lived branches of the Workers' Union in the Market Drayton area between 1899 and 1901. Without the necessary funds to withstand a lock-out in one village and evictions in another the movement was destined to collapse, but not before the seeds of rural and urban workers' co-operation were sown. Slowly the WU's strength increased as unskilled workers from collieries, quarries, steel works and railways enrolled, and after its initial setbacks it started sending organisers into areas where there was no competition with other Unions. From 1910 to 1914 it was able to capitalise on its increasing funds to Unionize previously neglected agricultural workers in areas like Yorkshire, Shropshire, the Midlands and the West Country. In Herefordshire it found an able and popular organiser in Sidney Box.

One of a family of ten children, Sidney Charles Box's life had been tough since he was orphaned at the age of four, thereafter being brought up by his eldest brother, aged 18. Soon learning to fend for himself, he had a variety of jobs: farm work, delivering milk, railway work at Worcester and in a coal mine in south Wales. He also worked in a quarry at Stanley Hill, Castle Frome, where his brother was killed in an accident. Mostly self-taught and holding strong political opinions, he had acted as a polling agent for the Liberal Party in the 1906 and 1910 elections. Circumstances forced him to live frugally in an isolated cottage on Frome Hill, and had firsthand experience of poor food, low wages, bad working conditions and poor urban and rural housing. Descendants of the family still live in the Frome Hill area and in the 1950s six Box brothers played in the same Frome Valley football team.

By May 1912, a rise in the cost of living led to a mounting current of simmering unrest and outbreaks of strikes and violence in towns and cities, which the government had to use armed soldiers and police to control. In the countryside the same conditions of rising prices and static wages as in 1871-2 led to spontaneous but inconclusive agricultural workers' meetings in Ledbury. W.R. Palmer, a bailiff of Fair Tree, Ledbury with Mr Stanford, a railway

Eight men and two women pause for refreshments of tea and sandwiches on a farm at Lyne Down, Much Marcle, during the hot 1910 harvest. The horses are hitched to a grass mower to cut the crop of oats. Once cut, the stalks were gathered by hand and bound into sheaves with a wisp of straw in the traditional way. Only binders used expensive string. The dog was ready to catch any rabbits sheltering in the decreasing area of standing corn in the centre of the field. As the rabbits scuttled for cover in a distant hedgerow, men, boys and dogs caught as many of these pests as possible, for rabbit pie was a welcome tasty and nutritious addition to country people's diet when butchers' meat was often beyond their budget.

worker and Alfred Ruddell, a cabinet maker and member of the Independent Labour Party held the first farm workers' meeting at Ledbury Market House in May 1912. Because the men were so poor, local shopkeepers clubbed together to give them a little financial support to start their Union. Box addressed their second meeting in Bosbury. Realising that the men needed organising, he found some half-forgotten NALU forms from 40 years before to enrol the Ledbury men into a 'Herefordshire Agricultural Workers' Union'. Branches at Bosbury and Bishop's Frome soon followed. With no supporting organisation, Box realised he needed help and advice, and contacted Charles Duncan, MP for Barrow, the Workers' Union secretary since 1900. Duncan soon formalised the temporary state of the Ledbury branch by incorporating it into the WU as Herefordshire's first WU branch, branch no. 119. (It appears to have lapsed in 1914, reappearing in the 1918 revival as branch no. 1471.) Box was appointed Herefordshire organising secretary in the autumn of 1912 at a wage of

A group of cherry pickers pose for a photograph on J.R. Hill's farm at Orleton Manor in the Summer of 1910. Tall trees like these were a problem to pick and long ladders and platforms were needed to reach the fruit, which was picked into a variety of wicker baskets. Note the dress – despite the hot sunshine there is hardly a bare arm to be seen. As blackbirds, starlings and other birds eat ripe cherries voraciously and spoil many with a single peck, men and boys were paid to patrol the cherry orchards constantly from dawn to dusk, shouting and shaking rattles and tin cans half full of stones to frighten the birds away or shoot any bold enough to eat or spoil the crop.

25 shillings per week plus expenses and moved his family to a more conveniently situated house at 27 Chandos Street, Hereford. His expenses were small as he cycled round the county to organise branches and meetings, often not arriving home until after midnight. In those days Union organisers were regarded as dangerous subversives. As well as verbal abuse at meetings, he was physically attacked several times in Hereford's streets and was shot at from behind a hedge. Robert Owen Hornigold, a veteran East Anglian farm workers' organiser from Fakenham in Norfolk, gave him valuable assistance after coming to live in Worcester in 1913. For his last year's work Hornigold was National Organiser of the agricultural workers in the WU and before his retirement in 1914 he worked closely with Box in north Herefordshire.

The WU soon made an impact. Such was the men's enthusiasm that within a year the Ledbury branch was followed by 50 more. Some farmers, surprised by the rapid growth of a strong farm workers' trade Union in their midst, gave an immediate 2 shilling pay rise, saying that the men had no need to join the Union as they were about to raise their pay anyway. Social and economic conditions favoured the growth of the WU and by 1914 Box claimed to be organising 98 branches in Herefordshire with over 5,000 members and, like his NALU predecessors 40 years earlier, also managed 33 branches in adjoining counties; twelve in Worcestershire, nine in Monmouthshire, and a further twelve across Brecon and Radnorshire (though his totals do not tally with the list of known branches). In January 1914 the WU claimed 150 branches in 14 counties, with another 50 by the end of the year. Nationally WU membership increased from 18,000 in 1911 to 143,000 three years later.

On most Herefordshire farms cider was traditionally given to workers at haysel (hay-making season) and harvest. Cider still made up part of the wages on some farms, the 1878 Truck Act being widely ignored by farmers and men alike. Like the NALU previously, the WU wanted the removal of all perks so that the men had cash in hand to buy whatever they wanted. A frequent complaint from the men was that farmers paid them with 'crab juice', inferior cider that the farmers themselves would not drink and could not sell to anyone else. A few teetotal labourers were against drink anyway. This was one aspect of the wages issue that both sides could quickly agree on, and by mutual consent the practice of giving cider in partial lieu of wages almost disappeared from farms from 1914.

Pampered local clergymen, living in huge vicarages and cushioned from work by a bevy of servants, aroused Box's continuous and vehement condemnation. Enjoying positions of power in village life they often unfairly refused use of village halls or schools for Union meetings, although these same halls were used for election meetings by both the Conservatives and Liberals. Box considered that the clergy's education, religious training and position in society deprived them of the compassion necessary to understand their less fortunate parishioners' plight. Instead of trying to 'keep them in their ordained place' to live out their lives in continual poverty, they should, at the very least, not hinder people's attempts to better themselves in a rapidly changing society. In 1916 the bachelor vicar of

Walford claimed he needed eight servants to look after his needs at a tribunal at which he bitterly opposed the conscription into the Army of his gardener.

Rural WU members benefited from the fact that many urban workers accepted Union branch officials' jobs as they had no fear of reprisals or even evictions by anti-Union farmers, landlords or clergymen. Railway workers were prominent in taking Union officers' positions in village branches. Whilst farmers had been accustomed to rudimentary collective bargaining with their workers to set wages for harvest work, hay making, hop picking, turnip hoeing, hedging and other agricultural piece-work jobs, they felt threatened by the increased bargaining power of Unionised workers. In response many joined the National Farmers' Union, seeking collective support in refusing to recognise the WU as the men's negotiating organisation.

As in the 1870s the *Hereford Times* and the *Hereford Journal* were sympathetic to the men's grievances, reporting their meetings and airing their views. Under the pseudonym Garge Gee Up, Box wrote almost weekly letters to the press, who published frequent letters on both sides of the debate. Few outsiders supported the farm workers' struggle for a decent life, but one exception was Canon Bannister of Hereford, who placed the labourers' cause before the 1913 Diocesan Conference, appealing to the clergy 'to assist in removing the scandalous state of housing and wages paid to country workers'. He also addressed a number of Church organisations on the same theme, but with little apparent success.

Alfred Watkins was another champion of the labourers' cause, his concern being related to his interest in land reform. He wrote an open letter to the South Herefordshire Farmers' Union concerning the men's wages and plight, which was not well received. The farmers said he didn't know what he was talking about, apparently forgetting that he had travelled the county for 40 years representing his father's brewery and flour mills. It is inconceivable that he failed to notice and accurately describe conditions he saw on local farms every day, and his photographs from this period reflect his knowledge of people's working lives and housing. (Some are reproduced in this book.) On Sunday 1 February, the day before the anniversary of the Battle of Mortimer's Cross, he organised a meeting on the site of the battlefield near the inn. He addressed nearly 200 people, mostly farm workers, on the subjects of adequate wages, housing and land reform, and castigated the Enclosure Acts, saying 'In nineteen out of twenty Enclosures the poor were injured'. He repeated this theme at subsequent meetings in Hereford. While the rain held off, Box spoke briefly, thanking Watkins for his courage in championing the farm workers' cause.

Agricultural wages varied widely across the country with the highest in northern England. Along with Norfolk, Herefordshire's farm workers were reported to receive the lowest. Employers blamed the long depression that lasted, with only a short break for the First World War, from the 1870s to 1940. Very gradually machinery replaced men's jobs. Reaping machines in 1851, steam ploughing in the 1860s and milking machines in the 1880s all increased the pressure on the remaining workers to leave agriculture, as their underemployment perpetuated their low wages. As a result hundreds of thousands left the land for better employment in manufacturing towns or abroad. From 1873 to 1904 imports from the New World halved the price of wheat. Refrigerated beef arrived from New Zealand and the Argentine, reducing the price of home-produced food. Townspeople were able to enjoy cheap food at the expense of British farmers and workers, which added to the depression. Despite this cheap food, malnutrition caused by a poor diet was rife in towns and villages alike, as for a generation or two, men's wages had been insufficient to buy enough nourishing food for their families' needs. Many 1914 would-be recruits were rejected for failing to meet the Army's physical standards. Later in the war they were enlisted in 'Bantam' battalions.

In 1901, in return for working a 12 hour day (with an hour and a half for meals) Herefordshire farm workers' take home pay was on average 13s 11d per week. There are examples of a family of 12 living (or more properly existing) on this wage. By 1912 it had crept up to 14s 2d. Waggoners (horsemen) worked two hours a day longer, feeding and caring for the animals in their charge for an extra shilling per week. In the Golden Valley wages remained below the county average at 12 to 14 shillings per week. Depending on the farmer's inclination, perks such as firewood, potatoes, or a pint of milk might add the equivalent of a shilling or two to the family income. It was no wonder that at Christmas the wives of the big landowners assuaged their consciences by giving presents of coal, meat, bread or clothes to the village poor and their workers whose labour kept them in luxury.

On 15 February 1913 the first conference of all the Herefordshire branches of the WU was held in Hereford to draw up a programme to improve their social conditions, especially housing, which had not improved in decades. Two days later Box presided at a meeting in Ross Town Hall to explain WU aims to local Union members. In his address Alderman Robert Morley of Halifax, President of the WU, said their intention was to obtain better conditions for town and rural workers as the cost of living had increased 15% while their wages had not. (Other contemporary figures give an increase of 35% while wages had risen by 12%.) Housing was one of the farm workers' biggest grumbles. The tied cottages were said to be rent-free but in the majority of cases 1s 6d to 2s 6d rent was deducted from the wage packet each week. Sometimes a worker put in more hours in lieu of paying rent; this still happened in Essex in the 1950s. Some farms provided reasonable accommodation, but on others the cottages were hovels, unfit for human habitation. The tied cottage system also created a servitude not known in other industries. It deprived the worker of his independence as he could lose his home and disrupt the life of his whole family if he offended or disagreed with his employer. His position was especially vulnerable as he was not acknowledged as the legal tenant. (Farmers' dictatorial attitudes to workers living in tied accommodation died slowly, lasting at least until the 1980s. To my certain knowledge a Weston under Penyard farmer threatened in the summer of 1981 to remove the roof, under the pretext of repairs, if a worker he had sacked following a disagreement did not leave his tied home.) Sir James Rankin, the Conservative MP for Leominster until 1912, believed that cottage ownership would be an encumbrance for farm workers because of the cost of maintenance. In his opinion tenants were getting a bargain.

On 20 May 1913 the *Ross Gazette* published the WU programme which demanded a 54 hour week for general workmen in winter and 60 hours in summer at 4d per hour (£1 per week) – waggoners, stockmen and shepherds to work 70 hours in winter including Sundays and 63 in summer at 4d per hour; boy labourers aged thirteen to get 6 shillings per week, rising with each birthday by 1s 6d until they reached their 21st birthday. Overtime was to be reckoned at time and a quarter i.e. 5d per hour. If workmen arrived on time they were not to be stood off in wet weather. If dismissed, workers were to be given three months' notice to quit their tied cottages and if they had made any improvements these were to be paid for by the owner before the notice to quit had expired.

South Herefordshire's MP, Captain Clive, said he would welcome an agricultural workers' Union and with foresight suggested on 5 June that a Wages Board should be set up for the industry. The NFU started correspondence with workers on their grievances and a lively exchange of letters began in the *Ross Gazette* between 'a mother of six', a 'cowman's wife' and Sidney Box, then living at 6 Windsor Street, Hereford. During that summer there was more industrial unrest in nearby Forest of Dean coal mines and a strike by building workers in Hereford.

On 18 July 1913, Box spoke at a meeting in Sellack Mission Room chaired by the vicar of Sellack, George Whitehouse. They had been refused use of the village hall by Sellack Parish Hall Committee which was largely composed of farmers who refused to let it be used for Union meetings. On 23 August Box spoke at an open air meeting at Ross Market House on 'A fair day's work for a fair day's pay'. A supporting letter from Thomas Taylor of Chapel Tumps, Hentland was read, calling for workers' candidates in Councils and Parliament. Box himself argued that increased branch membership would help lead to success at council and parliamentary elections. There were a surprising number of stack fires that autumn but they were not proved to be related to the farm workers' discontent.

At the beginning of 1914 Box was satisfied with his work in south Herefordshire and turned his attention to the northern part of the county with Robert Hornigold's help. On 16 January they were refused the use of a public hall so held their meeting in the cold under Pembridge Market Hall, echoing NALU meetings there 40 years earlier. In the years 1912 to 1914 local grievances had provoked the occasional small and successful strike in other counties. One at Southrop and East Leach in Gloucestershire raised wages by 2 shillings in early 1914. Elsewhere, workers in the mines, steel industry, docks and the railways were striking for better wages. In Herefordshire itself, teachers had tried unsuccessfully since 1903 to persuade the Education Committee under its ultra-Conservative chairman, Sir James Rankin MP ('an old fossil' according to Box), to agree a scale of salaries. Their Union again approached the committee in July 1913 only to be told 'this was not the right time'.

The teachers decided that this procrastination had lasted long enough and started to plan a strike in January. Like the county's farm workers their wages were well below the national average. With most schools closed and unexpected supporting strikes by boys in Ross and girls in Ledbury, the Education Committee was forced to grant the teachers a proper salary scale. It is possible that the teachers' success in February 1914 influenced Box and the WU to prepare their men for similar action for higher wages in the summer.

In February 1914, after prolonged farm workers' agitation and some small scale strikes in Norfolk, King George V agreed that his agent, Captain Beck, should give a pay rise and a half day Saturday to his estate workers at Sandringham. (A popular leader, Captain Beck was killed with almost all his 'Pals' battalion of Norfolk men at Gallipoli.) Landowners and farmers in Norfolk followed the king's lead, although, as one ruefully commented, 'The king only farms as a hobby'. With the king's acknowledgment of their grievances, the WU felt it

Ledbury Girls' School in Back Lane was built to accommodate 177 children. In 1909 the average attendance was about 166 girls, supervised by Miss Isabel Hooper, their headmistress, and three assistant teachers. Dressed in their best clothes, there seems to be a full attendance for their 1912 school photograph. Their teachers appear to have been popular with the girls and probably with their parents also for most of these girls were to take part in a most unlikely action two years later to support their teachers against the Education Committee's strike breakers. The Ledbury girls decided not to be taught by strike breakers, preferring their own teachers who lived in the town. It is impossible to say whether their action was spontaneous, or whether there was forward planning involved, but the girls linked arms, crowded round the doors and literally barred the replacement teachers entry into the building. After repeated futile efforts to gain entry into the school the strike breakers had to retire defeated while the girls rejoiced in their unusual victory against unwanted authority. For two days boys at Ross refused to be taught by strike breakers and were bribed into orderly behaviour by the chairman of governors. Disturbances occurred at Ashperton school for the same reason.

had won an important moral victory, giving it encouragement to win similar concessions from employers elsewhere. As winter turned into spring, Herefordshire farmers' attitudes hardened. Despite Box's efforts, they continued to refuse to recognise WU as the men's representative in collective wage bargaining, and fewer were prepared to give their men wage increases. Herefordshire farm workers began to adopt the Norfolk men's slogan: 'The king's pay and the king's conditions'.

On 9 April the Rev. John Powicke, minister of Ross Congregational Church, took the chair as the leaders of the WU, Charles Duncan MP for Barrow in Furness, the general secretary, John Morley from Halifax, the WU President, Sidney Box and 18 delegates from the area around Ross met at Ross Town Hall and discussed how to improve the social conditions of Herefordshire's farm workers. They decided that the time for action had arrived. The WU began to plan for a farm workers' strike across southern England, timed for harvest time when its impact on the farmers would be greatest and would also achieve maximum publicity. Union preparations began in earnest in mid May when 1,500 strike notices were prepared and sent to branch secretaries 'To be delivered by the men themselves to their employers giving them fourteen days to decide what attitude they wanted to take'. When this news reached the farmers, consternation ensued, triggering lengthy correspondence in the press. On 21 May the South Herefordshire branch of the NFU decided 'that their committee had no power, nor authority, neither had they any desire to interfere between the farmers and their men', but a possible conference between both sides, to which the NFU was not opposed, was suggested for 11 June.

A good attendance at Sellack's regular monthly Union meeting on 9 June decided 'Unanimously to hand notices to their employers as soon as they received word in the next few days' (to strike). Some 20 militant branches – Bishop's Frome, Brimfield, Canon Pyon, Fawley, Froomes Hill, Harewood End, Hope under Dinmore, Kilpeck, King's Pyon, Leintwardine, Llangarron, Much Birch, Orleton, Peterstow, St. Weonards, Sellack, Sugwas, Wellington, Wigmore, Withington and Yarkhill – now threatened strike action as their only means of redress. Most of these had been prominent NALU branches 40 years previously. Their vote for strike action was conditional; they would strike unless a mutual arrangement was reached at a proposed conference on 27 June 1914, but at the conference it was announced that no agreement over official recognition of the Union by the farmers had been reached. A further 20 branches had not decided what action to take. In early July Box informed the farmers that 'they intended giving notice to strike on July 10'. The notices were worded:

> I hereby give notice to cease work on . . . . 1914 unless an arrangement has been come to regarding an increase of wages and alterations in conditions asked for by the Workers' Union on my behalf. Signed . . . .

It was customary for some country people to keep a pig in a sty at the end of the back garden. 'Bowling for the Pig' was always a popular competition at village fetes for the chance to win a free piglet to fatten for Christmas. In days when little went to waste, it could be fed on kitchen scraps, spoilt or surplus vegetables, potatoes, harvest field gleanings and a some meal from the local mill. A pig provided so much cheap, tasty meat in the form of pork, sausages, ham, brawn, black pudding etc., for the family that some would be given to friends and relations, who in turn would repay the gifts when their own pig was killed weeks later. Tied to prevent it struggling, the pig was hoisted onto a stout wooden bench, where a semi-professional pig killer or the village butcher would cut its throat. The blood was caught in buckets to be made into black puddings. Tipped off the bench its hair was scorched off with burning straw, taking care not to damage the skin. The carcase was then hoisted up onto a beam, eviscerated (gutted) and left to hang for two or three days, when it was ready to be butchered into joints for curing or for immediate use. Hams, flitches and chines were dry cured with salt and saltpetre and hung from the kitchen rafters, where slices could be cut as needed. There were no deep freezes so everything that could not be preserved had to be eaten or given away. Brains became brawn, the small intestines chitterlings, feet became trotters and odd bits of meat were converted into faggots, sausages and pork pies. Fat was rendered into lard and the residue eaten as pork scratchings. The old story was that every bit of the pig was eaten except its grunt. To help food production during the Second World War village pig clubs were organised to entitle members to rations of pig meal. These clubs soon disappeared after the war as social conditions improved and pig keeping was no longer regarded as necessary to feed the family.

One, two or four weeks notice was to be given, depending on how often the men were paid.

The farmers had more than their usual summertime worries about the state of their crops, as the threatened strike loomed ever closer. This was an almost unheard of event in Herefordshire, where the apparent peaceful rural calm was broken only by the occasional urban migrant hop-pickers' short-lived strike for a higher price per bushel. An NFU meeting on 4 July at the King's Head Hotel in Ross discussed the unusual situation, agreeing to 'recommend each farmer to meet his men individually and treat them fairly and liberally with generous recognition of the needs of the times'. Under no circumstances should they negotiate with the WU.

On 17 July the notices were in branch secretaries' hands ready for delivery, but on the next day the WU reluctantly dropped its demand for recognition in view of the farmers' complete refusal to budge on the issue. Instead the Union concentrated on the pressing need for higher wages, as they claimed the cost of living had increased 25% in two years. However, without formal recognition and signed contracts the farmers could renege on individual agreements at any time. A properly constituted Wages Board, set up by the Government, was needed to make agreements stick. During the following weeks women workers added their voices to those of the men, demanding an increase in their own meagre wages. As deadlines approached, Box arranged extra meetings on Sundays to give men a chance to attend on their day off. For extra encouragement, George Whitehouse, the vicar of Sellack, held a special service for the local branch, who marched to the secluded parish church in the rain.

Their intentions won the men some support, but most letters in the press still favoured the farmers, saying in effect that the men should be content with their lot and enjoy working outside in the healthy sunshine (conveniently forgetting the cold, mud, rain and snow of winter, when in any case they were often laid off). A *Ross Gazette* editorial suggested that a lack of recreational facilities and hobbies and the indifference of the farmers to their employees' social welfare was 'the root cause of the whole evil'.

Instead of finding a way to raise wages from their own pockets, some farmers tried to shift the remedy onto the men themselves, making suggestions that were out of touch with reality, such as that they should lease one of the County Council smallholdings that were now available. Ordinary workers had no capital with which to stock and equip such a holding, of course. Other farmers said that the men were better off than they realised, one suggesting that they could keep a pig to sell or to supplement their diet – which many did in any event.

However, there were signs that public opinion was slowly beginning to swing towards the labourers. Miss Radcliffe Cooke of Much Marcle wrote conciliatory letters in the *Ross Gazette* and *Hereford Times* urging farmers and landowners to improve wages and conditions for their men. Because of Union pressure, wages in Much Marcle rose by 3 shillings to 16 shillings in the month before the 1914 harvest. Official realisation of the farm workers' plight was revealed in unexpected ways. At Leominster County Court, Judge Amplett constantly referred to the low wages in the area and reduced fines and allowed labourers guilty of petty crimes months of 'time to pay' instead of the previous mere seven days.

In line with the WU policy of demanding recognition from the NFU, Sellack farm workers had refused individual offers of wage increases, but after Box accepted that this recognition was not going to be forthcoming, the men accepted the wages on offer, provided they were permanent and not seasonal. After this change the *Hereford Journal* editorial remarked that 'Now this attitude is not to be insisted upon, the strike where notices are tendered will simply be on the question of conditions and can be settled in any locality by conceding better wages and a weekly half holiday'. By 25 July the strike had had the desired effect, for the *Ross Gazette* reported that the largest farmers in the affected Sellack area had given their men a 2 shilling rise, which was as much as the realists could expect. Box stated that over 50 Sellack men had received these pay rises but this figure cannot be verified – different newspaper reports vary slightly on the details of the settlements these men accepted.

Precise details of dates and farms where these strikes were to start do not now exist, if they ever did. We know from newspaper reports that 1500 strike notices were prepared and were in branch secretaries' hands, ready for delivery by Union members if their employers failed to give wage increases. Some strike notices were certainly delivered by Sellack farm workers to their employers, who rapidly met their demands. For maximum impact the strike was timed to commence just before harvest, but even this point was left to branch secretaries' judgement, so its timing was uncoordinated. The fact that the strike notices gave one, two or four weeks' delay before taking effect, depending on how frequently the men were paid, also increased the difficulties of effective co-ordination.

The campaign of strikes did have some impact in Herefordshire. It is believed that farms in at least 18 villages in the county were affected, and Box later wrote that most of the disputes were resolved by a rapid 2-shilling wage rise. (It is believed that Union agitation followed a similar pattern in the parts of southern England targeted by WU in that eventful summer of 1914, but that the unrest did not extend into Wales.) Across Herefordshire in general, however, strike action turned out to be patchy and uncoordinated – hardly surprising given the factors mentioned and also the very limited means of communications then existing and the numbers of Unionists who were scattered on separate farms. Local newspaper reports suggest that between 150 and 200 men were directly involved in Herefordshire, and Box put the figure even lower. A handful of gardeners at Hampton Court whose wages were below even farm labourers' levels struck for a few days. Mrs Burrell, the owner, allowed some to return to work on condition they left the Union, but refused work to two she claimed were 'agitators'. She had bought Hampton Court in 1912 and was reportedly 'very outspoken, highly eccentric, loved by children, animals and the people who worked for her'. On 26 July on Mr Longford's farm at Wellington, 14 men struck but soon returned to work after a few hours picketing. Men on strike at Stretton Sugwas returned to work on 4 August. A maximum of 50 men struck at King's Pyon and held a church parade on Sunday 2 August. Ballingham strikers returned to work after receiving a 3 shillings per week rise but lost their free cider. In the traditional Union stronghold of Leintwardine some 20 or 30 men struck on 31 July and 1 August, and returned to work after four or five days out. In somewhat strange arithmetic the August 1914 Workers' Union Record reported 885 men on strike across the country, with 52 in Herefordshire, 118 in Suffolk, 255 in Wiltshire, 15 in Shropshire, 110 in East Gloucestershire and 200 in Staffordshire and Worcestershire. Sidney Box wrote that 'not more than a hundred men were out for a few days [in the Ross area] and having received an all-round advance, good relations were soon restored. With the declaration of war on 4 August the strike was closed and the rise of wages given to all was to the credit of the employers'. The unexpected European political situation completely disrupted the WU's plans for a widespread agricultural strike when Great Britain declared war on Germany and patriotism replaced Unionism.

On 6 August the *Hereford Times* published this letter from Sidney Box, signalling the end of the strike:

> Now it is imperative that we should all unite. We are advising the whole of our members to return to work and assist in gathering in the foodstuffs of which there is an abundance in this county. This is a fine opportunity for farmers to prove they are willing to meet their men in a conciliatory spirit. May I be allowed on behalf of the workers to thank those employers who have met their employees. It is a proof of the statements I have always made that there were in the county a large number of kind hearted gentlemen among the farmers that were held back by unscrupulous employers. May I also state that where notices were handed in 75% have received clear 2 shilling rises. We hope farmers who have raised wages will induce others to do likewise and that the workers will know how to appreciate the rise by taking a greater interest in their employers' interests. We hope this will be a foundation for future work for the benefit of labourers and the whole of agriculture.

The start of the war, which everyone felt would be over by Christmas, gave farm workers another option – to volunteer for the Army in the tide of patriotism and snub their employers at the same time. Nicholas Mansfield reported one worker's remarks: 'When the farmer stopped my pay because it was raining and we couldn't thresh, I said to my 17-year-old mate "Bugger him. We'll go off and join the Army." For the first time in my life there was no strenuous work. We were all damn glad to get off the farms.' Many Herefordshire farm workers took this route and after the rigours of farm work they found soldiering easy.

Newspapers reported that 500 Herefordshire farm labourers enlisted at the beginning of August, leaving farmers so short of workers that volunteer civilians were organised to gather the harvest. (This was cheap labour for farmers. Reports of children receiving as little as 6d a day were quite common.) The labour shortage persisted into October when boys as young as ten were permanently away from school working on the county's farms. Sir James Rankin, who saw no harm in keeping boys away from school to drive pheasants for his shoots, condoned the practice he should have condemned outright. Men could have been released from the Army for a few months for harvest work. (So many active young men enlisted that the Herefordshire League abandoned football matches for the duration of the war.)

The Workers' Union paper, the *Record*, was soon full of war news and printed a Roll of Honour of members killed in action. Union officials struggled to maintain their organisations. Older members kept the branch structure alive and some were able to gain a premium for their agricultural skills at a time when farmers were short of labour. Box restricted his Union work to evenings and occasional weekends and took a gardening job. Rising prices, Union pressure and shortage of labour forced the wartime Government to pass a Minimum Wage Bill in 1915, greatly benefiting farm workers. 1917 saw the Agricultural Wages Boards

So great was the labour shortage during the First World War that convalescent soldiers from Frome Bank Military Hospital in Bromyard were persuaded to pick hops at Little Frome. Seen here in their distinctive hospital uniforms they probably enjoyed the escape from boredom to a few hours in the open air with an invigorating cup of tea, a joke and the chance to earn a few shillings for cigarettes.

established to ensure fair wages for the depleted rural work force. Although the number of men working on farms had fallen since 1914, rising wartime wages led to increasing Union membership and an expectation of better times as the war came to an end. As men returned from the war they rejoined the WU in large numbers. Box stood unsuccessfully as a Labour Party candidate in the 1918 election, polling 5,000 votes, and developed an interest in local politics, where he felt his influence could benefit labourers and their families. In 1919 Box and members of the WU tried to meet representatives of the NFU and the Agricultural Wages Board to discuss a joint approach to agricultural problems and policy generally but his efforts came to nothing. Later that year he helped organise a huge farm labourers' demonstration in Hereford for a wage of 50 shillings. As a result wages rose from 34 to 46 shillings, but this proved not to be sustainable in the prevailing economic climate.

On large dairy farms milking was usually men's work, but on family farms and in the dairy farmers' wives and daughters made the butter and cheese. Labour shortages in the First World War soon altered people's perception of what constituted men's or women's work. Without any publicity, country women replaced their menfolk in a range of farm jobs as they were accustomed to rural conditions. Despite all their publicity, numbers in the Women's Land Army, drawn mainly from middle class townspeople, never exceeded 16,000 and in Herefordshire in 1917 there were only 32 at work at the height of the drive for more home-grown food. The girls in this photograph were almost certainly farmers' wives or daughters as there is no sign of the uniform or armbands that trainee WLA would have worn. This is said to be a ladies' milking and dairy competition held at Warryfield Farm, Walford under the auspices of the HCC and the Harewood End Agricultural Society on 16 October 1916. The weather was so wet that all the classes except the milking were cancelled. Note the shining white enamel buckets, white aprons and three legged stools the girls used to demonstrate their skills on the placid old dairy shorthorn cow. Miss Yeld, county dairy instructress, stands in the centre of the photograph.

Farmers' pressure on the coalition government forced it to repeal the wartime Wages Boards in 1922. These had been introduced as part of the Corn Production Act of 1917 when food supplies were running dangerously low and extra efforts were needed to boost cereal growing. As one of its priorities the first Labour Government, which came to power (briefly) in 1923, reinstated the Wages Board. Farm workers' wages stayed around the 30 shillings level for most of the inter-war years.

Meanwhile in Herefordshire, Sidney Box's career was taking a new direction. Details are vague, but Box's independent stance on some policy matters did not please Duncan, the WU's general secretary, who engineered his dismissal in the same way that Arch had treated his district secretaries. The WU's executive committee announced that the income from the Hereford district was insufficient to justify a full-time organiser and at the same time assigned the 29 branches in neighbouring counties then administered by the Hereford office to different districts. This reduced the income to Box's carefully constructed Union organisation with disastrous results. After this episode, Box channelled his energies and

In 1917 a farmer in Sellack sold his crop of hay to the Government. Eight privates under a staff sergeant of the Army Service Corps Forage Department operate a Ransome traction engine driving a Ruston baler which rammed 1½ cwt of hay into each wire tied bale. Each hay bale was carefully weighed on a hand operated crane as they were loaded onto waggons destined for France. By 1917 the Army owned nearly a million horses, over four hundred thousand in France carrying the troops' supplies. Fodder was the heaviest material sent there, even heavier than ammunition for the guns. In 1915 the Government was offering £6 per ton for hay, £3 10s for oat straw and £3 per ton for wheat straw. Farmers soon benefited from the rising prices and as all other prices rose, a Wages Board was established in 1917 to ensure farm labourers a fair weekly wage, vindicating the Workers' Union 1914 campaign for better pay and shorter hours. Soldiers on this type of work were usually from agricultural backgrounds, who, through wounds or infirmity, were not fit enough for active service abroad. They earned more than the civilians they worked alongside, often causing resentment.

local knowledge into work for the National Union of General and Municipal Workers and later into local politics. On 13 March 1937 he was elected Herefordshire county councillor for the villages of Marden and Wellington, and for the next 12 years he sat on twenty different committees directing social changes until his last meeting on 19 February 1949.

Box used the strike weapon only when he believed it was the only way to achieve results, and he was diplomatic and persuasive in putting the WU cause when confronting reasoned opposition. His family history says he championed the unemployed casual workers waiting for day work outside Bulmer's factory gates during the cider making months, reflecting Tom Mann's early struggles outside London's docks.

The post-war economic depression saw WU membership fall by half a million nationwide with an accompanying fall of its bank balance from £300,000 in 1920 to £8,000 three years later. It is possible that the National Agricultural Labourers' and Rural Workers' Union (later to become the National Union of Agricultural Workers) penetrated the county before 1914. Details are sketchy, but certainly inter-Union rivalry developed between the WU and the NUAW, which did not help the workers the Unions were supposed to represent. It seriously weakened both Unions as NUAW took root in the county between 1918 and 1921, eclipsing the WU in north Herefordshire and Shropshire, initially with branches in Bishop's Castle, Leintwardine and Brimfield and by 1924 in Pontshill and Weston under Penyard in the south. Just as in the 1880s NALU had abandoned small districts to struggle on unaided, after 1926 the WU abandoned its rural workers to concentrate on its 'more responsive industrial members'. But all its efforts were to no avail as its finances fell so ruinously that it was forced to amalgamate with the Transport and General Workers' Union on 3 August 1929, forming the largest Union in the country. The rise and decline of both NALU between 1876 and 1890 and the WU between 1921 and 1924 bears a close relationship with the economic state of the country and how much money labourers had to spend on non-necessities. When wages fell they had no spare pennies for extras like Union subscriptions, which could have preserved the Unions when they were most needed.

In the continuing agricultural depression in the 1930s, the *Ross Gazette* commented in an editorial which could almost have been written in any of the preceding 60 years:

> Unemployment and distress, less in evidence though they may be in thinly populated country districts than in larger centres, have made their presence felt and the vastly reduced spending power of the population dependent almost entirely upon the agricultural industry has meant a poor business year for most people in South Herefordshire. With wheat quotas and reduced meat imports [we have] hopes for a better 1933.

The legacy of NALU and WU's demands for improvements in rural housing were very slowly realised in south Herefordshire but not throughout the whole county. Ross and Whitchurch Rural District Council slowly took steps to improve the rural slums farm workers were forced to inhabit when the 1926 and 1930 Rural Workers' Housing Acts provided a subsidy to bring some houses up to standard. The council was able to use the provisions of these Acts to grant subsidies of between £50 to £100 for renovating decrepit agricultural workers' houses with improvements to the structure, water supply and drainage, but not for maintenance. The owner was expected to make up the difference in cost, but was not to charge more than 4 shillings rent to his farm workers. Property owners were slow to take up this offer of subsidies as there was no immediate gain in spending money on improvements to houses that could not be sold. By 1933 only 15 out of 99 eligible owners had applied. The position improved in 1934 with the Council spending £2,675 in subsidies on 33 cottages, with another 33 to be considered the next year. Over a six year period Ross and Whitchurch RDC eventually assisted with grants and loans in reconditioning 72 dilapidated cottages, as compared with 46 in Ledbury, 25 in Dore, four in Hereford, one in Weobley and none at all in the Bromyard, Leominster and Kington District Council areas. With wages in the 1930s around 30 shillings and better housing, conditions for the county's farm workers slowly started to improve.

The farm workers' Unions veered between times of considerable strength and times of extreme weakness. When strong, their members benefited from higher wages and better conditions which gave them a comradeship, a wider social life and help in sickness and death. Nearly a hundred years later Box's Union successors are working towards Union recognition and fair wages for the thousands of Eastern European workers picking fruit on Herefordshire farms. Some employers' attitudes never change.

Chapter 7
Crop farming:
from traditional methods to mechanization

Horses

For millennia all farming and food production was organic. It is only in the last fifty years that modern inorganic methods have been adopted to increase production. With improved understanding of plants and animals, new drugs, chemicals and modern technology farmers have found short cuts to producing extra food. In the traditional rotation of crops, every field in turn was given a dressing of farmyard manure. Forked from the cattle yard or a dunghill onto a tumbril (a two-wheeled farm cart that could be tipped up for ease of unloading), the manure was emptied into small tumps on the field. Labourers hated the cold wet dirty winter time job of spreading this manure, which before the days of fertilisers was essential to produce a good crop the following season. The land could then be ploughed ready to sow corn or potatoes in the spring. For best results wheat is sown in the autumn, but less was drilled years ago than now as farmers were hampered by the amount of work their horse teams could manage in a day. The speed of modern farming operations is a world away from what our grandfathers believed possible and would leave them speechless with disbelief.

All the details of his Ransome's plough are clearly visible in this photographic postcard as the ploughman pauses for a chat with the photographer. In ploughing one acre – a day's work – the ploughman would walk between ten and twelve miles behind his team of horses, one of which was trained to walk in the furrow, enabling him to control them more easily and keep his furrow straight. At most these ploughs would penetrate nine inches deep and twelve inches wide – nothing like the draught of their modern tractor equivalents. The larger wheel ran in the furrow whose depth was controlled by the setting of the smaller land wheel. To give a straight clean edge, a knife coulter cut the furrow wall just in front of the mouldboard which turned the soil over, burying weeds and rubbish.

On the way back to the farm after a day drilling peas or beans, an old horseman poses beside his team. The widely spaced seed coulters and empty sacks reveal his day's work. Notice the details of the horses' harness connecting to the wooden whippletree to distribute their pull evenly to the heavy Smyth seed drill.

Ledbury Agricultural Society, formed in 1843 to improve local farm workers' skills, held a ploughing match in October each year within a six mile radius of Ledbury Cross. The 1907 event was held at Tonies Farm, Bromsberrow on October 17. To draw out ruler-straight furrows like these took a great deal of skill; it took particular concentration to plough out the opening and closing furrows. Men took great pride in the accuracy of their work at competitions as well as on their own farms, where their furrows were visible for everyone's comments. Any slight mistakes took a lot of living down in the pub later. Harness and horse brasses gleaming, champion G. Stevens' team draw the closing furrow of their stint.

The Herefordshire and Worcestershire Agricultural Society was formed in 1797 and reformed in 1895, and held a show at a different venue in the two counties each year to stimulate local interest. Hazle Farm on the Ross road just outside Ledbury, was its venue in 1911, attracting entries from all over the country, made possible by England's then extensive railway network. A groom proudly holds 'Bradgate Majestic', winner of the first prize for the heavy horse class, taking the £10 prize home to Leicester, with the prospect of increased stud fees to follow.

Steam Ploughing

Portable steam engines, mounted on a trolley which had to be moved from job to job around the farm by horses, were introduced in the 1840s, to power barn machinery or threshing drums. In ingenious experiments it was found that they could power a windlass and with a series of rope anchors on the further headland and an endless rope they could even pull a plough across a field with moderate success. The idea was too complicated to catch on, especially as the length of wire rope required frequently broke. At the Great Exhibition of 1851 a pair of steam engines with winches using a chain was demonstrated but the chain kept breaking. In the following decade steam became an established part of the farming scene as knowledge and experience grew. In 1856 John Fowler of Leeds demonstrated his first steam-powered winch pulling a plough across a Suffolk field. Two years later he developed this idea by utilising winches mounted beneath two steam engines on each side of a field, an arrangement which found acceptance as the most economical and practical. It was found that steam engines' size and weight made them too awkward and difficult to manoeuvre to pull a directly hitched plough, though on the drier expanses of the prairie provinces of Canada and America this idea was used successfully. To keep costs down, trials of cable ploughing with one engine and a rope anchor on the other side of the field continued but with limited success. The price – up to £1,500 for a pair of ploughing engines – meant that only the richest could afford them, so they became agricultural contractors' machines; farmers paid an agreed price per acre in addition to supplying the coal and water needed. By 1863 there were two agricultural steam engine contracting companies in Herefordshire, both complaining of the difficulty of travel between farms on the county's notoriously bad roads.

These new six furrow one-way implements improved cultivation by ploughing a deeper furrow, and when they finished, the turned earth was left nearly level instead of the wavy undulations characteristic of the ridge and furrow formed by horse ploughing. Much faster, deeper uncompacted work was possible but a disadvantage was that wide headlands were left which had to be ploughed using horses. Rectangular fields of above 30 acres were considered an economic size and some fields were enlarged to facilitate steam cultivation. Field work stopped in the wet winter months for fear of bogging down these 18-ton machines in the mud. Cultivating and improving land drainage by mole ploughing were easily tackled by pairs of these powerful machines. A more unusual task was clearing accumulated silt and rubbish from ornamental lakes, the two engines pulling a mud scoop across the bottom between them. Steam power was the first phase of agricultural mechanisation, lasting for a hundred years until superseded by petrol- and diesel-powered tractors. There were over 600 sets of ploughing engines in use in Great Britain by 1900. In the corn-growing east and south of England, steam had a significant impact, but on the smaller mixed farms of Herefordshire its role was limited, though at least 12 agricultural contractors were using steam engines in 1902.

This 18 horse power Fowler ploughing engine, weighing 18 tons, was one of a pair used to winch a reversible plough across a field between them. A foreman, two engine drivers, a ploughman and sometimes a boy operated a set of this type. The standard wire rope wound on the drum mounted under the engine was a quarter of a mile long, but some models were constructed to take a rope 800 yards long.

This anti-balance plough had a moveable axle to shift the weight distribution when the pull was reversed at each side of the field. Earlier balance ploughs tended sometimes to lift out of the soil, especially on undulating fields. The ploughman had the cold, uncomfortable, demanding job of steering straight across the field between the two engines, moving his seat to the other end of his plough for each pass. A toot on the engine's whistle signalled that all was ready for the return trip. Each engine alternately moved the plough's width along the headland as the other winched it across the field again.

Nine men pause from their work threshing clover seed to watch a local photographer, V. Palin, set about recording this scene at Chanstone Court, near Peterchurch in the Golden Valley in about 1909. The portable steam engine in the centre was an 8 hp Marshall driving a Humphries threshing machine. The engine on the left was a Brown & May driving a Ruston & Proctor clover sheller, unfortunately obscured from view. Portable steam engines had no driving wheels and had to be pulled from site to site by a team of four or five horses, which were also needed for the heavy threshing machines. Neighbouring farmers regularly co-operated in lending teams of horses for these moves. It is believed that these machines belonged to Robert Howard of New House Farm, Peterchurch, who was listed in the directories from 1867 to 1909 as a threshing machine proprietor. Accurate dating is not possible but these machines appear to be early models, mounted on wooden wheels. Their tall chimneys were designed to keep sparks away from the flammable stacks of straw and were hinged down onto the Y brackets for transport. A crew of two men accompanied each outfit – one to tend the engine and the other to cut the sheaves and feed the straw evenly into the drum of the threshing machine. Their hours were longer than those of the regular farm employees as they had to light the fire in the boiler to raise steam before work could start. The men's jackets, tea jugs and food are all piled in the right hand corner of the yard. Threshing was hot, dirty, dusty work and the men needed constant drink. Some farmers supplied beer or cider. A hierarchy of sorts can be seen as the drivers pose beside their engines slightly above and apart from the regular farm labourers. These portable steam engines were popular and at an affordable price found a place on many farms, where they could be pulled to new jobs round the farm by a team of horses. At different seasons they were used for cutting wood, pumping water or driving corn mills and other barn machinery by means of a continuous belt from the flywheel.

Early Farm Tractors

An immediate effect of the outbreak of the 1914-18 war was the loss of the thousands of men from the countryside who volunteered for the army, and from 1916 conscription aggravated the shortage. Not just men but horses were scarce by then. So many horses were requisitioned for military use that as the war dragged on almost anything capable of pulling a plough was saleable, according to the *Ross Gazette* of May 1916. As Britain was by no means self-sufficient in basic food production, new sources of power had to be found to replace the half million horses commandeered by the Army. By mid 1916, in the drive to plough up old grassland, the government was operating a fleet of 600 tractors throughout the UK, with plans to increase this to 6,000 in 1917. Experimental tractors had been demonstrated in England a decade earlier but they were then too expensive for most British farmers, although larger models had become popular with prairie farmers in Canada and the American Mid-West who realised their value. During the war, American factories began shipping increasing numbers across the Atlantic to meet British demand for greater food production. Subject to German submarine attacks, the same vulnerable transatlantic convoys brought supplies of grain to avert the very real risk of a food famine in Great Britain.

The crew of these government tractors consisted of a driver and ploughman. Soldiers unfit for front line duty worked with civilians for 60 hours a week, earning 4 shillings per eight hour shift and 6d per acre bonus. The contract price to the farmer was £1 per acre ploughed or 2 shillings per hour for working a threshing drum. Much time was spent moving from farm to farm, as the spade lugs, essential to get a grip on wet fields, had to be removed from the iron wheels for fear of damaging weak road surfaces. Unbolting these was a two-hour job and replacing them at the next farm took another two hours – a statistic never mentioned amid the manufacturers' extravagant advertising claims. Neither was the fact that a man could walk faster than these early tractors' speed in top gear. All the same, these teams' ploughing achievements attracted considerable publicity in local papers, perhaps to divert people's attention from the dismal war news. The best crew in the Ross area (and in the whole of Herefordshire) ploughed 31 acres in a week in November 1917. The six Ross crews averaged 23 acres each that week, bettering the Hereford and Leominster crews. In a demonstration at Llangarron, a Titan pulling a three furrow Cockshutt plough comfortably turned over a 40-year-old pasture, cutting furrows 12" wide and 6" deep, and the team of seven Ross tractors claimed a British record in March 1918 by ploughing 208 acres in a week. Although these results are tiny by modern standards, they were incredible to a generation accustomed to a team of horses ploughing just one acre in a full day's work.

Two pre-production models of the famous 'Model F' Fordson tractor were demonstrated near Warrington in 1917 but they were not manufactured or exported from the USA until early 1918, too late to make any real impact on wartime food production. Lighter and of a simpler design than the previous models, their main attraction, especially to small farmers, was they were cheap, costing only £250, falling to £156 by 1931. In April 1918 Passey and Hall advertised a Fordson tractor and Oliver plough for £290, 'deliveries from the USA permitting'. 674,467 Fordsons were built in the USA up to 1929, when production of the 'Model N' was moved to Cork in Ireland. The three litre 12/22 hp engine was the first to be bolted onto the gearbox without any chassis, an innovation which became a universally accepted design. Newspaper advertisements in 1917 claimed that an 'Overtime', pulling a four furrow plough, could turn over ten acres in a day, at a cost of 1s 8d per acre for paraffin. Weighing 39 cwt and powered by a 24 hp engine it could plough an acre in 63 minutes. It could also be used for a variety of other jobs around the farm, replacing the work of eight or ten horses without any of their drawbacks. Of course, such advertising claims rarely equated with actual results in ordinary farm conditions and must be taken with the proverbial pinch of salt.

James Fryer Ltd, motor engineers of Aubrey Street and later Widemarsh Street near Hereford Market, and Leominster, was the local agent for 'Overtime' and 'Mogul' tractors, made by the International Harvester Company of Chicago, which was formed by a merger of five different firms and consequently, in its early days, produced several different types of tractors. It exported numbers of their 'Mogul' tractors to Britain during the war years, but despite a nationwide advertising campaign it was never popular, though some contractors liked its robust build. In a sales drive in January 1918 Passey and Hall of the Central Garage, Ross advertised 'Mogul' tractors at £375 with a top speed of 2¾ mph. The Company's Titan 10-20 tractors were more popular; 3,500 were imported to Britain between 1914 and 1920, and 17,000 of this proven design were sold in America in 1918. Higher wartime food prices gave British farmers more capital to invest and although Titans cost £400 they found willing buyers. Like other tractors at the time, the engine was started on petrol and then switched onto cheaper paraffin (kerosene) when the engine was properly warmed up. (Shell introduced TVO, tractor vaporising oil, in the mid 1930s.) The 35-gallon water tank over the front wheels was the radiator. Although it tended to be heavy and awkward for field work, it was a versatile machine with belt pulleys to drive threshing machinery or barn equipment when needed, and a few could still be found in use 20 years later. The old Herefordshire slogan 'God Speed the Plough' was never more appropriate to the county than in 1917 as tractors converted grass land to arable. The inevitably reactionary anti-tractor farmers were soon converted to new ways as tractors proved their capabilities in completing work faster and more efficiently than the remaining horses, even though performances were never quite equal to the manufacturers' claims. The numbers of farm horses recovered quickly after the war, and they were still used for another 30 years, but their days were numbered. Their lack of speed, their need for attention seven days a week and the amount of land they needed for their grazing and a winter supply of hay, oats and straw bedding ultimately led to their replacement, and the release of many acres for cash crops or for pasture to graze cattle or sheep.

Seen at work on an unidentified farm, a Mogul showed it could comfortably pull a four furrow Ransome, Simms and Jefferies plough, albeit at no great depth. This one may have belonged to a contractor, as the cab was an unusual concession to driver comfort, not generally seen on farm tractors until the early 1960s. Experience soon found that it was easier to draw a straight furrow if the tractor's wheels ran in the furrow instead of on the unploughed land and ploughs were redesigned so that the driver could reach to control them from his seat with comparative ease, eliminating the extra expense of a man seated on the plough.

In the tradition of horse ploughing, the first implements were attached to the tractor with a length of chain. A man had to sit on the plough to operate the levers to drop it into or lift it out of the soil at the end of each furrow. With no protection from the weather, the ploughman must have been perished with cold by the end of the day, having completed four times the work his old team of horses could manage. This is a 1918 Model 'F' Fordson pulling a two furrow Oliver plough.

This model 'M' Waterloo Boy, seen ploughing stubble on a local farm in 1917, was the forerunner of the huge green John Deere tractors popular on farms today. Astutely, John Deere bought the Waterloo Gasoline Engine Company in 1914, entering the tractor market as it was about to start its rapid expansion. Their tractors were powered by a sturdy, reliable twin cylinder horizontal engine mounted just in front of the driving wheels, a design they employed for 40 years. It was rated at 12 hp, strong enough to pull the two furrow Oliver plough at a reasonable depth. A girl controls the plough while two men (only one was really needed) drive the tractor. The kerosene fuel was contained in a tank mounted over the front axle. Whether the single acetylene headlamp threw out enough light to work in the dark is debatable.

Not only in Ireland, but in the rest of Britain, potatoes were found to be a cheap, easily grown, nourishing and substantial food for people and animals alike. In 1907, 1,563 acres were grown on Herefordshire farms according to the Agricultural Returns. Potatoes were chitted into growth in early Spring and to economise, larger seed were cut in half. A baulking plough, which turned the soil to both sides, ploughed out furrows for planting. The two men simply dropped the seed potatoes from the chitting tray along the furrows eighteen inches apart, an arm-aching task often given to children. Another pass of the baulking plough covered the seed with soil. This was another long, slow, labour intensive job confined to history by the huge mechanical planters now in use.

Seen hitched to a Standard Fordson tractor on a farm near Ross on Wye in 1940, this potato spinner could lift between five or six acres a day, depending on the size and speed of the gang of pickers working behind it. In comparison a modern potato harvester can manage up to 30 acres depending on how many trailers are available to cart the crop away to store. A hundred years ago itinerant Irishmen were often employed on piece-work to dig the crop up with special three tined forks that had flattened tines to avoid damaging the tubers.

Harvest

Since man's first farming ventures in growing cereals, i.e. wheat, barley, oats, rye, bere etc., a successful harvest has always depended on his ability to cut and store the grain before disease, animals or the weather could spoil his year's work. The Celts of Iron Age Britain used iron sickles to cut their crops from about 700 BC. Sickles were simple heavy blades, curved to cut the straw and very tiring to use for long hours but remained with us until the twentieth century. Most men favoured scythes which had been introduced in the Roman era. They swung easily in accustomed hands but were awkward for the beginner. It was usual for gangs of men to contract to bring in the harvest for a farmer for an agreed price. Cutting corn and grass (for hay) depended entirely on manual labour until the introduction of mowing machines, which were developed about the same time in England and America and shown for the first time at the 1851 Great Exhibition in London. The great advance in these new horse-drawn mowing machines was the set of triangular knife blades attached to a rapidly reciprocating bar, sliding between iron fingers and driven by gearing from a land wheel. Following their 1851 introduction their use spread across the country slowly. Farmers resented spending their limited capital on machines that would stand idle most of the year. (The same argument prevailed about buying combine harvesters in the 1950s until rising wages and falling manpower forced a more businesslike approach.) Farmers and labourers alike did not like change, saying that what was good enough for their fathers was good enough for them. Labourers thought they might be deprived of a job and remembered the 'Swing riots' in 1830, a generation earlier. Disturbances involving the destruction of threshing machines, fires and threats to farmers and clergymen had swept across Southern England as far West as Bromsberrow, Kington and Whitney-on-Wye when farm workers and others protested against low wages and unfair tithes. Whatever the reasons, it was well into Queen Victoria's reign before threshing machines replaced flails for threshing and sickles and scythes continued in use in some districts until the 1900s especially in wet seasons when the corn was laid. (Flattened to the ground by its own weight and bad weather, a wheat field was cut by scythes as late as 1963 on a Cambridgeshire farm.)

Threshing the corn with a flail (a jointed stick about six feet long) had modified the design of barns in corn growing areas. The traditional tall, wide double doors on each side of the barn were built so that waggon loads of sheaves could be driven in and unloaded into the bays on each side. In Winter, with all the doors open, the through draught blew away much of the chaff as the labourers beat the grain from the straw with their flails, leaving a cleaner sample to be shovelled into sacks for storage or later sale. As crop yields increased, overfilling the barns, stacks were built in the open instead, where threshing machines could be easily manoeuvred alongside. Depending on the weather harvest time lasted six or even eight weeks. It was a continuous struggle to cut, stook, cart and stack the crop as quickly as possible, as each stage demanded a huge input of manual labour involving all the men, women and children available. Once the corn was cut, either by hand or mower, women and children bundled the straw into sheaves tied with a wisp twisted from a few straw stems. The invention of the knotter, an ingenious device for tying string, eventually eliminated this boring task when the self binder made its appearance in 1876. In one operation its sails gently pushed the stalks onto a continuous canvas belt behind the cutter bar. The cut stalks then travelled up another belt to the knotter, fed with string from a drum in the front of the binder. Tied round the middle into sheaves, they were dropped at regular intervals onto the stubble. The sheaves then had to be stood in stooks (or traves) of six or eight, resembling rows of little pyramids, to dry out thoroughly. Wet weather was dreaded as damp could spoil the corn, causing it to germinate. Fine weather was essential to dry the sheaves before they could be pitchforked onto waggons and carted off the field to the stackyard. Building stacks required unseen skill as the sheaves were built up regularly round and round, layer upon layer so that they did not slip and could easily be pitched to the threshing machine (drum) when it arrived sometime in the autumn or winter. These stacks were often bigger than a house and were immediately thatched to keep out the rain until threshing time. A fine spell of weather in Winter was ideal for threshing, when land work was completed. The sheaves were cut open and fed smoothly into the top of the threshing drum, where the corn was separated from the straw and chaff and graded for size. The grain descended chutes into sacks which weighed 18 stone (2¼ hundredweight) when full. Labourers had to carry these backbreaking loads away to the grain store on their backs – sometimes up steps. Chaff was collected into bags for feeding cattle. The straw was either compressed into huge bales tied with wire or elevated loose onto a stack for animal fodder or bedding. One man driving a modern combine harvester, supported by two or three tractors with trailers to cart the grain, can clear in hours what his grandfathers took weeks to harvest. The remaining straw is wound into round bales so heavy they can only be moved mechanically. With machines taking over, thousands of men have been released from drudgery to find other work elsewhere, taking the sweat and labour but also some of the fun out of farming.

An 1873 mowing machine made by Samuelson of Banbury and sold by Perkins and Bellamy of Ross. A big land wheel drove a reciprocating knife in the cutter bar, suitable for grass or corn. The cut corn had to be gathered by hand and tied into sheaves with a wisp of straw.

Forty years of development reveal numerous advances in design on this 1916 Climax reaper/binder. Revolving sails push the standing corn over the cutter bar onto canvas rollers which move it up to the knotter mechanism where it is bound into sheaves tied with string. The knotter is clearly visible near the farmer's right elbow. No. 5990 on the mudguard shows this Titan was one of two Government owned tractors in the Ross district in 1916. The drivers were probably soldiers unfit for overseas duty, employed here cutting a crop of oats on contract.

A team of five horses was needed to move this heavy threshing machine at Chantry Farm on the Perrystone estate *circa* 1930.

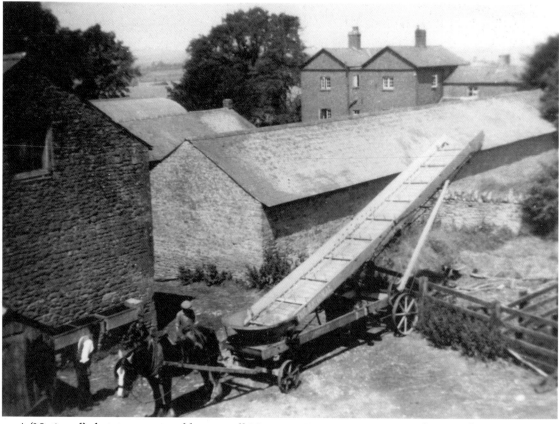

A 'National' elevator, powered by a small Lister stationary engine, was often used to move the threshed straw from the back of the threshing drum onto a stack.

An early Massey Harris combine harvester seen at work at Brampton Abbotts in 1952. A second man, obscured from view, was kept busy filling grain sacks which were dropped on the headland for collection later. Later models incorporated a large grain tank which could discharge its load through an auger into a trailer driven alongside.

Two men stacking straw bales in the evening sunshine at Foy *circa* 1980.

Hay

Dry grass or hay was used in huge quantities as winter feed for horses and cattle and was the fuel that provided the horse power for all transport until mechanisation. Large acreages of permanent and semi-permanent grass were required for the horses kept in towns as well as in the countryside. One of the unmentioned reasons for the decline in bird numbers and the disappearance of wild flowers from the countryside was that after the 1940s, as horse numbers declined, their old pastures were ploughed destroying the natural or semi-natural habitats where birds and flowers had flourished. Sitting on a mower on a warm summer's day behind a pair of well turned out horses was one of the pleasantest of farm jobs ever. Power for the cutter bar was transferred from the land wheel through a simple gearbox to a reciprocating knife blade which cut the stalks close to the ground, releasing the scent of new mown grass. Hay needs thorough drying before carting to the stack. Repeated turning and raking to help the sun and wind dry it was another job demanding every available pair of hands. If it was not dry enough when stacked it could, and often did, self-ignite spontaneously. (During the nineteenth century arsonists took advantage of this, as blame for an arson attack was difficult to prove if a haystack could burst into flames by itself.) With mechanisation in the form of sophisticated mowers, tedders and balers, the modern haymaker hardly needs to get off his tractor seat. Similarly grass or maize preserved as silage in huge clamps or in plastic-covered bales is widely used instead of hay as a nutritious feed for cows or fattening cattle. The contrast with his grandfather's generation is almost unbelievable.

These two photographs, taken on a farm near Leominster show how, if hay was sold off the farm, it was tied into manageable trusses that could be easily handled and weighed. The man on the left cuts sections from the hay stack about three feet square with his two and a half foot long broad bladed hay knife. These squares of hay were carefully placed on the trusser and compacted by the ratchet bar in front of the other man. The strings trailing from the bottom of the press were then tied by hand. Barfords of Peterborough manufactured the trusser, which could be found on most farms, as they could be easily moved from place to place and only required cheap manpower to operate. Forage merchants like George Hinton, whose premises were in Rainbow Street, Leominster supplied the huge demand for hay to feed the thousands of delivery horses in towns and pit ponies, Army horses and the heavy horses used for a multitude of transport and recreational jobs around the country. Eventually stationary or mobile balers replaced these handy little machines with which two men could tie over a hundred trusses a day.

The usual method of lifting hay from a cart onto a stack was to fork it onto an elevator. A cheap ingenious method adopted, especially in confined spaces, was to use a winch operated grab and hoist powered by a continuous belt from a small engine, in this case a trolley mounted 4 hp Victoria. A grab from the jib was dropped onto a load of hay. The engine lifted it to the required height, when a man swung the jib above the stack and released the hay onto the stack. This was a useful arrangement in a small stackyard and cheaper than an elevator. Early versions of these 'Johnny Ball' grabs were powered by a horse walking round a central gearbox turned a shaft linked to the grab. Other simpler systems just relied on the horse pulling it up to the height of the stack directly.

Depending on the angle the machine was set, this side delivery rake either turned the cut grass over to help it dry in the sunshine or combined two swathes into one to make collection and carting easier. The spring-mounted tines scraped gently along the ground and ensured all the grass was turned. Comfortably pulled by a single horse that only needed guiding round the field, hay-turning was another pleasant summer job.

Photographed near Ross on Wye *circa* 1940, a farmer's daughter mows a field of grass for hay. The man with the wooden rake pulls any clumps of grass away that might block the knife on the next pass of the mower round the field.

During the war a few jokes help this cheerful group of ladies gather the 1942 hay harvest near Ross-on-Wye. Sometimes farmers took advantage of volunteer child labour. In 1916 a 12-year-old girl from Lydbrook was given 6d for her 14-hour day's work haymaking. She vowed never to work on a farm again!

Water Mills

In every village where there was a suitable stream there were one or more mills located along its banks on sites in use for centuries. As an essential part of the local economy the miller ground villagers' wheat for bread making and sold feeds for farmers' livestock and cottagers' pigs. Most water wheels were the overshot type, where the flow of water was introduced through a sluice from above so that the descending water using gravity and its own weight drove the wheel round. This was discovered to be more efficient than the undershot type, where the flow of water passed beneath the wheel. At the edge of the waterwheel the speed was between 4-6 feet per second with buckets set twelve to eighteen inches apart. This provided sufficient power to drive the simple massive wooden machinery geared to the millstone and to hoists in the building above. The controls for the water wheel were simplicity itself as water only had to be diverted by a sluice to stop or start the drive to the machinery.

To grind wheat into flour, power generated by the waterwheel turned an upper millstone against a stationary lower one. Usually very hard French Burr stones from the Paris basin were used for flour production. Coarser millstone grit stones from North Derbyshire were used to grind peas, beans, oats and barley for animal feeds. Opposing grooves cut in the stones in segments, called harps because of their triangular shape, ground the wheat into flour as it trickled through the centre of the upper stone from the floor above. The flour was collected in sacks on the floor beneath. Some millers could dress (recut) the grooves themselves as they wore. Others employed travelling dressers who called when necessary. Extreme care and skill was needed to hit the 'millbille' with the right force to cut the gently tapering grooves from the centre to the circumference accurately. The four feet diameter stone weighed 1¾ to 2 tons and took two or three days to dress at 30 shillings a time. This expense and delay was a major reason for the change to steam driven roller mills in late Victorian times. About 30 water mills were still in use in Herefordshire in 1940, continuing a traditional use of water power from Saxon times or maybe earlier. By 1960 they had all ceased commercial work as electricity replaced steam in ever larger factories that became part of national and international companies.

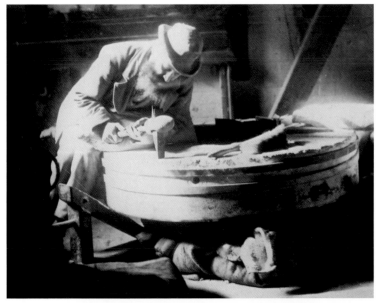

Dressing a millstone by the light of a window in Pontynys Mill, Longtown.

An interior view of the workings of Pontynys Mill, Longtown, where Richard Bridgewater was miller for several decades from 1909.

As a shopkeeper and wheelwright John Pikes was well qualified to take over Trenant Mill in Peterchurch in the early 1900s, where he continued to mill locally grown corn in the traditional way. But as the century progressed, increasing use of steam, oil or electricity put water mills out of business and by 1920 the changing economic climate had forced his antiquated mill to close. Falling water as a source of free, clean, non-polluting power was ignored.

Chapter 8
Cider and Hops

Cider

The Celts are believed to have drunk cider and perry in pre-Roman Britain and the taste for it continues to the present day. Certainly as the river Wye's navigation improved cider was one of the local products shipped down the river to Bristol *en route* by sea for London and beyond. Almost all farmers made cider for their own and their workers' consumption. Any surplus was readily saleable. The best drink is made from traditional varieties of cider apples, the higher sugar content of modern varieties not making such a good drink. Depending on the variety of cider apple grown, the season lasted from August to Christmas and their harvest could be fitted in between other autumn tasks. They were usually grown on standard trees so that sheep and cattle could graze the grass beneath until the fruit was nearly ready. The animals then had to be moved to other grazing as otherwise they could get drunk on apples fermenting in their stomachs. Modern orchards of bush trees give a higher yield but animals are excluded as they would eat foliage within reach. A good autumn storm was welcomed

to shake the ripe fruit to the ground. Failing this, the apples had to be shaken off the branches with a long hooked pole. The fruit was collected in baskets by women and children and then tipped into heaps to mature. After a few weeks it was then sold to a dealer or direct to a large cider maker like Bulmers or Westons, or made into cider on the farm.

Perry (made from pears) was made by the same method as cider. The first process after the fruit was washed was to crush it into pulp in a circular stone trough about eight feet in diameter. A horse walked round the trough harnessed to an overhead beam, which in turn was attached to an inclined heavy stone wheel crushing the apples to pulp as it revolved. The pulp was spread a few inches thick onto hessian sheets called hairs, and a cheese was then built of eight or ten hairs placed one above the other in a press. A heavy board on top evened out the pressure as it was screwed down, slowly squeezing out the raw juice. Collected in wooden buckets, the juice was tipped into large barrels to ferment naturally with its own yeasts and sugars. Three or four men could produce about a hogshead (54 gallons) by this slow, dirty, laborious traditional method in a day. The crushed pulp was fed to farm pigs. (Cider makers still sell their pulp to animal feed mills to be mixed in animal feeds.) Depending on the temperature of the building or cellar used, fermentation varied between three to eight months, at the end of which the cider was ready to drink. In the spring and summer local papers regularly carried advertisements for barrels of cider as farmers sold off their surplus or traded it for something they needed.

The Act of Parliament known as the Truck Act was intended to stop the practice of paying wages in goods, but in Herefordshire for cider often formed part of a farm worker's wages, and although the Unions had some success in changing this, after the decline of the National Agricultural Labourers' Union, the practice was often resumed and taken as a matter of course by farmers and workers alike. It was the 1914 farm workers' strike in Herefordshire and the establishment of the Wages Board that finally put an end to it, and even as late as 1935 a farmer near Ross-on-Wye was fined for continuing to pay his men in part with cider. His response was promptly to sack the man who had dared to inform the authorities. There was nothing to prevent farmers giving their workers cider at hay and harvest time as an extra, and some continued to do so.

Economic factors saw Bulmers become the dominant cider producer in the county as the smaller manufacturers slowly gave up. After the Second World War, Bulmers expanded, replanting orchards ploughed up in the war. While these new orchards grew, Bulmers were forced to import apples in bulk by rail from Normandy. As the biggest cider factory in the world, Bulmers became a large employer in Hereford, and looked after its employees well. Hundreds of casual labourers were taken on in the busy season. It is unfortunate that, forced by the economics of large scale, mechanised production, Bulmers now produce standard ciders lacking the character and individuality of taste of the original drink. As a reaction farmhouse ciders have made a comeback in the last 20 years and are widely available, giving 30 or more small producers in Herefordshire a valuable share of a niche market where quality and taste matter.

An age-old scene in a Herefordshire orchard, as women pick cider apples in one of Ridler's orchards at Clehonger in 1908. The lady on the left is wearing a traditional bonnet to protect her head and neck from the sun. The apples were left for a few weeks in heaps (tumps) to mature.

A photograph by Alfred Watkins showing a horse and tumbril carting a load of cider apples in the snow to the Pomona Works at Withington to be transformed into cider.

All the details of this standard 8-feet diameter one horse cider mill are clearly visible in this 1910 photograph. There were bigger and smaller models. There are stories of travelling cider makers with their own portable scratters (mills) and presses who visited farms without cider making equipment taking their payment in the form of a barrel or two of cider.

John Lewis had a smaller cider mill at Ashley Farm, Rodd. Note the grooved stone wheel the horse pushed round, pulping the apples to extract the juice.

Westons bought their first motor lorry, a three ton Guy, CJ 3059, in 1919 to deliver their cider to cities as far apart as Bristol and Birmingham. Another regular delivery run was to Dymock railway station, from where barrels were sent across the country by train. Driver Harry Probert stands beside his lorry outside the Bounds, Much Marcle, ready to deliver another load.

Henry Weston realised the value of publicity and used this eye-catching tableau on the back of a lorry to visit local shows. In the summer of 1925 it won several awards as it promoted his different brands of cider under the title 'The Wine of the West'.

A scene in the cask filling room in Bulmers in Hereford. The workers were drawing cider from their huge fermentation vats into barrels ready for sale. A modern bottling line has long since replaced this 1925 process. In 1910 Bulmers' price for a 10-gallon cask was 15 shillings and 25 shillings for a 25-gallon cask.

In 1909 there were 28 cider makers, 10 cider merchants, 7 cider retailers and 10 perry makers in the county. In addition there would have been an unknown number of farmers who made small amounts of cider in sheds and cellars on their own farms. Three men and two boys are seen here pressing a cheese to extract the apple juice. Poured into barrels without anything added, it fermented into a delicious drink after a few months' patient waiting.

Bulmers had a railway siding into their factory, and made full use of it after the Second World War, when they had to import apples from Normandy because of the shortage of English fruit. This diesel powered Fowler locomotive was kept busy shunting wagons of apples and cider round the factory.

Some idea of the scale of Bulmers' business in the 1950s can be gathered from this view of their lorry garage. At least eight bulk tankers are lined up on the right and ten 10-ton delivery lorries on the left, with Leyland and ERF the preferred makes.

Fruit Growing

Not all apples were made into cider. Cold stores for keeping apples through the winter until prices were high were a distant invention, but they could be stored on a cool dry barn floor, spaced slightly apart to prevent the rot that could start if they touched. Apples intended for storage like this had to be very carefully picked and handled to avoid bruises.

Herefordshire's climate and soil are of course suitable for growing a variety of fruit besides apples. The recent trend for farmers to diversify and spread polythene tunnels over hundreds of acres of strawberries in an effort to extend the growing season of their ever-popular fruit, is another development in a tradition of commercial strawberry growing extending back over a hundred years. In 1907, 367 acres of strawberries, 35 acres of raspberries and 265 acres of currants and gooseberries were grown in the county, giving employment in June and July to women from surrounding towns and villages. Baskets of the best fruit were sent to south Wales, Birmingham and Midlands markets and the remainder was made into jam.

As well as his fruit and hop farm at Pixley Court, Thomas Davies owned the Ledbury jam factory in Little Marcle Road. It is said that during the First World War the Army bought most of the factory's jam and that the profits helped the factory become an important part of Ledbury's economy. For the next 80 years it gave local men much needed employment.

In 1907 wide-brimmed hats were in fashion. Strawberry picking is a hot uncomfortable job, crouched over the rows of plants to find the ripe berries beneath the leaves. These ladies must have possessed a magic formula to keep their aprons so spotlessly clean during a long morning's work before their break for dinner.

A cheerful group of Women's Land Army girls pause for their lunch (bait) on a fruit farm near Bromyard during the Second World War. Bare arms, serviceable overalls and only two hats between them reveal the next generation's freer attitude to life and work.

Hops

The hop (*Humulus lupulus*), a member of the mulberry family, is a perennial related to hemp and nettles. Each year it grows a long twisting stalk bearing bitter catkin-like fruits used to make beer and some medicines. The deep soils in parts of Herefordshire are excellent for growing hops and it became a widespread farm crop in the nineteenth century as the expanding brewing industry in the Midlands looked for more supplies to flavour its beers. In 1907 hops were grown on 6,143 acres in Herefordshire, giving a nucleus of farm workers, both men and women, regular year round employment. In September thousands of extra people were required for picking the crop. During the winter months the posts and overhead wires were overhauled and repaired prior to next season's growth. In April and May, when the plants started growing, men and women strung them to the 12-feet high overhead wires that spanned the hopyards. Originally hops were grown up tall wooden poles, rather like gigantic runner beans. This method was very labour intensive as the poles had to be removed, creosoted and replaced firmly in the soil beside each plant every spring. On the other hand the 12-15 foot poles were cheap and could be reused for several seasons, so a few hopyards still used them as late as 1939. By this date growers had invested in overhead wires with string for the plants to twine up, a method introduced in Kent in 1863. The expense of sturdy posts and thick wire delayed its acceptance in Herefordshire until 1911, when it became the usual training system. Modern high-yielding, disease-resistant varieties grow only six to eight feet high so don't use such expensive posts and wire.

Left: Winter maintenance of posts and wires continued even with snow on the ground at Canon Frome. Everything had to be ready for tying in the shoots when regrowth started in April.
Right: To prevent wind damage to the tender bines, hedges around hop yards were grown up to 20 feet high. They were so difficult and time-consuming to trim, even using ladders, that one enterprising grower constructed a horse-drawn moveable platform
to enable his workers to cut the highest branches, reached by a tractor-mounted flail.

Wearing gloves on a cold bright April day, women string the emerging hop bines to the wires.

Ready for the start of the busy hop picking season, employees line up for a photograph. In the centre the farmer holds a bushel measure. His foreman is ready with a pencil and notebook to record the amounts as they are tipped into the pokes, the large hessian sacks three of the men carry slung over their shoulders. The poles were used to pull down the hop bines from the wires for the pickers. Note the foreman's leggings, made of strips of sacking.

When the hops were ready to pick, the bines were cut down and carried to a crib, a large canvas tied to a wooden framework which was moved forward to a new site (house) as the picking progressed. The pickers were recruited from surrounding villages and distant towns. A family stood or sat round the crib cheerfully stripping the hops from the bines, not letting leaves fall into the crib. The farmer or his foreman came round regularly during the day to measure the amount of hops picked in a wicker-work basket called a bushel. Each crib was numbered and the amount carefully recorded in the hop picker's account book as well as in the foreman's account book. Originally accounts were recorded on a tally stick, a system that gave way to account books as rural education improved after the 1870s. The simplest system, though not very widespread, was to give pickers a token for every bushel of hops picked, redeemable on pay day. Disputes over amounts were few as people soon realised the foreman would tip the hops back into the crib, then measure them again if there was any doubt. They always measured less the second time, as they had been slightly squashed in the first measuring. Occasional short-lived strikes occurred at the start of picking to establish a fair price for the work involved. The strikers frequently gained a small pay increase, but knowing what was likely to happen, some farmers set a lower rate than they expected to pay, raising it if there was a strike to what they had intended to pay in the first place, so that everyone was happy at the outcome. Once recorded, eight bushels

A family group enjoy a warm day picking in a local hopyard. The rough timber framework of the crib is plainly visible as little children sit on the sides helping their mother work.
Wide brimmed hats protect everyone from the sun, even the baby in the pram.

The seven children and six adults in this well dressed family group show that all the generations were eager to earn some money. The oldest girl was in charge of the picnic basket. Her younger brothers' boots display rows of nails to protect them from wear.

A 1910 scene near Ledbury. In older hopyards the poles supporting the spiralling hop bines were pulled up and taken to the cribs to be picked. All classes of people enjoyed the atmosphere of the work. For the well dressed little girls on the left, it was a chance for a picnic in the sunshine, while for the family of 13 on the right it was essential income.

of hops were bagged in a poke for transport to the oast house for drying in the square coke-heated oast houses that are still a feature of the former hop growing districts.

To accommodate the rush of pickers, railway companies ran special trains, often on Sundays, made up of their oldest carriages to transport hundreds of hop pickers to the nearest station, where farmers provided waggons to take them and their luggage the last few miles to the hop yards. It was estimated that 12,000 'foreign' hop pickers travelled to Herefordshire for the 1907 season. Agents, or gangers, organised pickers' travel arrangements from Birmingham, the Black Country and towns in the south Wales valleys, receiving one or two shillings for each picker who arrived at the right farm. Families treated the hop season as a working holiday to earn some much needed money for Christmas extras, new clothes for the children or just to supplement their meagre dole during the Depression. At weekends friends and families came to visit, swelling the numbers even further. Gypsy caravans' iron-tyred wheels left white trails along the roads as they travelled miles to meet their extended families at traditional farms, where they tended to remain aloof from other pickers. Busloads of women and children travelled every day from Hereford and other towns to take part in the work and at weekends were often joined by their menfolk, eager to earn a few extra shillings from this annual bonanza. Despite a fall in the hop acreage during the 1920s and '30s the population of Bishop's Frome was reckoned to rise from 700 to 5,000 during the hop picking season. Such an influx brought welcome trade to local shops and pubs, but extra unwanted work for the police, doctors and nurses. For the seven or eight week season the Chief Constable thought it necessary to double the police presence in nine rural

beats where there was the greatest influx of casuals by drafting in policemen from other parts of the county. The number of tramps in the Ledbury area increased dramatically. In mid-September 1910, 1,300 'casuals' were given beds in Ledbury Workhouse, compared to the average 250 to 300. (Homelessness was a desperate problem in Edwardian Britain.) Mostly the 'foreigners' did not cause trouble, only wanting some fun while earning a bit of extra cash.

Butchers, bakers and mobile grocers' shops all did a good trade, visiting hopyards and farms where the pickers wanted basic necessities for their stay. Stables, cowsheds, pigsties and farm buildings of all sorts were cleaned out and whitewashed to provide the temporary shelter needed. Accommodation

Hop pickers queue in the evening darkness as Mrs Ethel Waldron sells groceries from her mobile shop sometime in the late 1940s. She owned the Post Office at Burley Gate and drove her mobile shop around local hop yards after Post Office hours.

varied from farm to farm. Some farmers built cheap 'barracks', others lent rough blankets. Mostly, however, pickers brought their own bedding and baggage enough for their six week stay away from home in somewhat spartan rural conditions. Medical health authorities tried to impose regulations and did slowly improve the temporary accommodation, but as the occupation was seasonal, and the pickers migratory and uncomplaining, little in the way of improvements could be enforced. There were occasional reports of pickers being given cowsheds that had not been cleaned out. Mostly, however, farmers looked after their pickers reasonably well as, for six or seven weeks, they were a vital part of the workforce, without whom the hops could not be picked. Some farmers gave them basic farm produce like milk and potatoes, and many families returned to the same farm year after year like migrating swallows.

Church of England missionaries were very concerned for the hop pickers' moral welfare. They toured the hopyards and gave magic lantern shows to the children in the evenings and held services on Sundays for the adults. In Bosbury there was a Hop Club where pickers could relax, write letters, read the newspapers etc. free of the expense and distractions of the pubs. Similarly, generous local families in Bartestree and elsewhere raised money during the year to fund a Hop Pickers' Mission to provide a few comforts for people far from home. When school holidays failed to coincide with the hop picking season, children faced a good telling off when they returned to school. Their parents were sometimes fined but never enough to spoil their working holiday or deter them from going again the next year.

Cribbing was the name given to the age old custom of throwing a man and a woman into a crib at the end of the season. Here a tussle develops as a girl resists a man's attempts to lift her into a crib and onlookers smile and decide whether to watch to see who was going to end up in the crib or whether to join in the fun. Today people might designate this as 'sexual harassment in the workplace', but no doubt those involved saw it as just a bit of high spirits.

Some farmers took an urn of tea to the hopyard, but usually each family brewed their own and cooked a meal on an open fire. Forgetting their scratched arms and hands blackened by the hops, food never tasted so good. Vast quantities of sausages, bacon and eggs, sandwiches, bread and dripping, apple pies and fruit cake were washed down with cups of tea. Some people remember working from six in the morning until dark. Fondly remembered wartime school holidays were extended so that the children 'could do their bit', earn a few shillings and enjoy some fun and games too. Rainy days were horrible but quickly forgotten.

The first Bruff hop picking machine appeared in 1953, replacing about 250 pickers with just 35 men and women needed to operate the new system. By this date there was more regular work available in the towns and it became increasingly difficult to attract enough seasonal labour into the hopyards. It is little surprise that machine picking took over in the following decade, though it was a considerable blow to the local economy with shop keepers, pub landlords and villagers all affected. Old pickers reminisce nostalgically about the scent of the hops mingled with the aroma of bacon cooking over an open fire and the camaraderie enjoyed by all. The era ended in about 1960, leaving many happy memories.

Hops were subject to a number of pests and diseases. Early preventatives included nicotine powder to control aphids, sulphur dust for mould and Bordeaux powder for downy mildew. These powders were blown onto the crop in still weather by horse or tractor drawn dusting machines. This photograph from the 1920s shows one mounted on an early model 'F' Fordson tractor. At this period no protective clothing for the driver was thought necessary, though the unfortunate worker ended his day's work covered in chemical dust.

Spraying young hops with a Fowler FD2 crawler tractor pulling a KEF orchard sprayer. The Y-shaped arrangement of the strings tied to the overhead wires is quite clear in this 1950s photograph. The driver had a filthy cold job without any protective clothing against the hidden dangers in the spray.

Top left: Unloading hop pockets into a kiln near Ledbury; fans blew hot air, heated by coke fires, through the hops. When dried they were stored for despatch to pubs that brewed their own beer, to local breweries, to the Hop Market in Worcester, or to the big breweries in the Midlands. Kilns were kept operating night and day on a two shift system until hop picking was finished.

Top right: A special 2-feet square shovel was the best tool for moving hops on the drying floor. A hop pocket was suspended through a hole in the floor beneath a Drake and Fletcher press. The man on the right shovelled dry hops into the pocket as his mate screwed down the round plate to compress them.

Bottom left: The man on the floor beneath removed the full pocket, made sure it weighed 1¼ cwt and stitched the neck tight.

Bottom right: 'Picking out the leaves' in a modern barn where a Bruff machine has stripped the bines, leaving women the monotonous task of removing the unwanted leaves as the hops are elevated to the drying floor.

Chapter 9
Animal husbandry

Milk and dairy work

Before milking machines were invented, a good cowman – or woman, for milking was often regarded as a girl's job – could milk five or six cows an hour by hand. Experiments in new milking technology in Britain lagged behind the USA and the rest of Europe for many years; labour was cheap, so there was little incentive to find another method. W. Murchis' 1869 attempts were unsuccessful but paved the way for Stewart Nicholson of Kirkcudbright to invent an improved model in 1891. When the technical difficulties of Dr. Alexander Shield's pulsator combined with a vacuum pump were finally overcome in 1910, dairy farmers' dream of mechanised milking was realised. Small stationary engines powering vacuum pumps appeared beside cowsheds, and at last technology made it possible for one person to milk up to 25 cows an hour. De Laval's introduction of the first mechanical cream separator in 1879, copied by many competitors in the next ten years, speeded the butter-making process.

In 1910 Miss Nancy Legge, whose father farmed Shortwood Farm, Little Cowarne, won several milking competitions organised by John Peet, Herefordshire County Agricultural Instructor. Gleaming pail at the ready, she poses beside a placid Dairy Shorthorn cow.

This advertising postcard from about 1911 extols the advantages of installing an Amanco Chore Boy 1¼ hp engine to drive the vacuum pump. These horizontal open crank Amanco engines were found to be robust and reliable and different sizes, up to 10 hp, were imported from the USA in large numbers both before and during the First World War.

Left: The farmer demonstrating this wooden butter churn appears too tall to be comfortable turning the handle for the time needed to transform the milk into butter, a job often reserved for a boy. In fact Alfred Watkins had persuaded a local farmer to carry the butter churn out of the dairy into the sunlight for a clear photograph.

Below: Herefordshire County Council took its responsibilities as the governing body of an agricultural county seriously. In 1890, it started to provide instruction for adults, and by 1905 John Peet had been appointed to inform the farming community of the latest techniques and ideas, and teach basic skills. He gave lectures on subjects as varied as dairy hygiene and the application of artificial manure on crops, and organised poultry and dairy classes to help train women in their traditional occupations in farm dairies. This display of cheeses is believed to be the result of a four week cheese and dairy school held at Huntsham Court, Goodrich in 1910.

Hereford Cattle

Recent imports of foreign breeds of cattle have done little to diminish the popularity of the local breed of Herefords. They are docile, sturdy, do well in poor conditions and are hardy enough for any climate that grows grass, and they have consequently been exported to five continents. Their records are kept at the Herd Book Society in Offa Street. They cross well with other breeds, producing calves with distinctive white faces which fatten into good beef animals. Because of their strength and docility they were found to be good draught animals and, shod with small iron shoes, were used to pull ploughs and waggons before horses came to be preferred for the job. In old photographs Herefords are seen to have horns, but to eliminate the damage horns could inflict a polled strain was introduced in 1955, so that now there are both varieties.

Hereford Bull "Bodenham Leonardo"
First Prize, Royal Agricultural Show, Norwich, 1911
Exhibited by Mrs E. Medlicott, Bodenham S. O, Herefords.
Fed on Thorley's

Depicted on an postcard advertising Thorley's cattle feed is Mrs. Ellen Medlicott's prizewinning Hereford Bull, 'Bodenham Leonardo'. Much to his owner's delight he won this award at the 1911 Royal Show at Norwich, where he is seen displaying his rosettes. Returning with the prize made the long rail journey from Court Farm Bodenham and all the hours the stockman spent preparing for the show worth all the effort.

The Herefordshire and Worcestershire Show moved around to different farms in the two counties for many years before combining with Gloucestershire and settling on its permanent showground at Malvern in the 1960s. In 1911 it was held at Edward Dawes' Hazle Farm, Ledbury. It was always a prestige event, attracting entries from all over the country. Here the prizewinning Hereford bull, the Earl of Coventry's 'Dallemont', leads the parade from the judging ring past rows of corn and seed merchants' tents and John Tilley's ever ready camera.

What a heartbreaking scene for a farmer to find after a summer thunderstorm. Lightning strikes usually go unnoticed but grazing on an open pasture, cattle are vulnerable to them. In 1910 there were no JCBs to dig the deep pit to bury the seven Hereford bullocks. Four farm labourers, given the task, pause while digging their trench as a group of schoolchildren study the results of the storm. A young man on the right holds a stout long pole with which to lever the carcasses into the burial pit. The animals' market value was about £20 each, and as few farmers could afford livestock insurance, the owner probably lost about £150 in a flash.

Mr. Leighton of Wall Hills, Thornbury was so pleased with his 1913 crop of mangolds that he posed with his workers for this Hadfields' advertising post-card to endorse the value of their fertilisers. Mangolds produce a high yield of dry matter and are suitable for stock feeding from January to April when other fodder is scarce. If given generous treatment they can produce up to fifty tons per acre. Harvested in October or November, they were clamped until the New Year to mature as they could cause digestive troubles if fed too soon. Sliced in a root cutter, they were mainly fed to milking cows and fattening beef cattle, though in small amounts they could be fed to sheep and horses if no grass was available. For many years they were the standard winter fodder crop, but the time and effort required to harvest and feed them has made them uneconomic to grow now, and silage made from grass or, increasingly, from maize has replaced them. Up to 50 acres a day of 8-foot high maize can be cut, chopped into pencil thin pieces and carted to a silage clamp with modern machines that would be unbelievable to this group.

Sheep

For hundreds of years there were weekly markets in Kington's streets for farm animals as well as for the usual agricultural produce. Once the Leominster and Kington Railway arrived in August 1856 it gave the town the economic boost its company prospectus had promised. One important benefit was that it enabled the nearby sheep breeding areas in the hills of Wales to develop their sales of the local Clun and Kerry breeds to farmers in distant parts of lowland England where they were found to thrive. Crossed with Suffolk rams, these breeds produced lambs with hybrid vigour that fattened rapidly on the lusher pastures of southern England. Kington's auction sales grew from small beginnings to sales of 20,000 ewes in one day with about half from each breed. The sales were held on a field off Victoria Street opposite the Olde Tavern. It was situated conveniently close to the railway station and goods yard, from where buyers could easily send their purchases all over the country. Similar sales venues developed in the Welsh borders at Knighton and Craven Arms which were both served by the extensive railway system.

On market days flocks of sheep were driven on foot from farms in the surrounding hills through Kington's streets. Gates and hurdles were placed across doors and alleyways to prevent them straying into gardens and shops, not always successfully. To accommodate the crowds of farmers, drovers and buyers the landlord of the Tavern Inn, the twin gabled house in the centre of the photograph below, unscrewed the doors from their frames and laid sacks on the flagstone floor in a vain effort to keep the floors of his pub clean. The following morning Kington Fire Brigade's job was to hose the streets clean of sheep droppings. The auction was very much a social occasion for many of the farmers, meeting relations and renewing old acquaintances on their annual visit, which for many, was a worthwhile pay

day. These markets were an important part of Kington's economy, attracting dealers, farmers and their families to spend money in the town's shops and pubs.

McCartneys continued auctioning sheep on this site until the 1980s when the bypass was constructed across a corner of the field and the cottages standing in its way on the right in the photograph on the previous page were demolished. The railway had closed for passengers in February 1955 and to goods traffic in 1964, after which fleets of lorries transported flocks of Clun and Kerry ewes to farms as far away as Essex. The two little white tents in the far left of the photograph were busy all day as auctioneers clerks did the necessary paperwork, taking buyers' cheques and paying the breeders. A quiet modern housing estate now covers this once busy venue in the sheep breeders' calendar.

A drover takes a mixed flock of sheep from Ledbury market past the Seven Stars towards the railway station, from where they could be transported to abattoirs in south Wales or the Midlands within hours. This common sight disappeared from market towns in the middle of the last century when livestock lorries appeared, providing a quicker, cleaner and more efficient mode of transport. Before then, sheep and cattle would be driven for miles to and from market along quiet country lanes, enlivened occasionally when an animal took a wrong turn through an open gate or entrance. Just rarely there was a tragic accident, as when some boys at Overross threw stones at a herd of bullocks a drover had driven the 12 miles from Ledbury uneventfully. Stung by the stones, the bullocks panicked, and one charged an old man watching by his garden gate with fatal results. Ross magistrates sent the stone-throwing culprits to the reformatory for a year to learn how to behave.

Despite all the shepherd's skill and attention, lambing time always results in a few casualties and orphaned lambs. It was usually the farmer's wife's job to tend them in the kitchen or a warm shed for their first few days. When strong enough they were turned out into a nearby paddock and bottle fed cows' milk until they were weaned. Henry Taylor's wife at the Garlands, Mordiford, helped by her Welsh servant girl, had four such orphaned lambs to feed in May 1913. On the reverse of this photographic postcard, the girl, W.K., tells her family she intends riding her bicycle from Mordiford to Abergavenny then catching a train home to Ebbw Vale. Without letters from her family she was desperate for news of home.

For many years William Holmes lived at Goldhill Farm, Bosbury, where he ran a traditional mixed farm growing hops and fruit and breeding Ryeland sheep. He is seen here posing in the garden with one of his prize-winning rams. The small docile Ryelands originated in south Herefordshire, probably in the fourteenth century. With white legs and faces they yield about five or six pounds of good quality uniform fleece. Like Hereford cattle they can thrive in adverse conditions and became a popular breed for export, transacted through the Ryeland Flock Book Society in Hereford.

The Snell family enjoy feeding mangolds to sheep on winter pasture *circa* 1938 at Chantry Farm, How Caple.

Sheep farmers used to have a legal obligation to dip their animals in a chemical solution to prevent attacks of sheep scab. Flies and other insects were also controlled by these dips. There was a dipping tank on most farms, sunk into the ground with sloping concrete ramps. If sheep numbers did not justify such an outlay of capital it was possible to hire a portable tank. In this example Ellwood & Son, chemists, of 25 Draper's Lane, Leominster hired out their McDougall's dip together with the necessary chemicals. One man holds a ewe ready while another ensures the first one is thoroughly immersed using a T-shaped pole or a soft broom to push it under the surface. Sheep wait in the sloping trailer to drip dry before release so that surplus liquid ran down the metal floor back into the dip tank. The village policeman's job included visits to sheep farms at dipping time to see that the regulations to control sheep scab were obeyed.

Sheep were washed in a stream or river on a warm day in May or June just prior to shearing so their clean fleece would command a higher price. This scene is believed to be in the Bromyard area.

This photograph at Thomas Lewis's Town House Farm at Bredwardine in June 1909 demonstrates again how much manual labour was needed on farms before mechanisation. It was one man's job to turn the handle of the shearing device continuously. The drive was transferred through a flexible cable to the clippers his mate used to shear the wool from the sheep. Another man rolled the fleeces and brought another sheep to the shearers. The old boy in the background appears to be pouring himself a horn of cider. As the century progressed small stationary petrol engines, and later electricity, were eventually to replace this outfit with more efficient machines, as these ended on a scrapheap or in a museum.

In the Edwardian era, advertising postcards were distributed widely to promote firms' products or services. In 1910 Thomas Pedlingham of Chevenham, Colwall used this one of a champion Suffolk ram to attract farmers' custom in the Ledbury and Malvern area for his animal feeds.

Poultry

On many of the county's mixed farms, dairy and poultry products were regarded as the wife's responsibility. Her job was to make some extra money for the family from the sale of butter, cheese, eggs and table birds that were surplus to the family's requirements. Her shopping in the nearby market town was funded by profits from her weekly trips to sell their produce.

This mixed flock of free range turkeys, geese and chickens feed greedily in the summer sunshine as a farmer's wife throws them grain to search for in the grass. Most of these birds were destined for a Christmas dinner table, though some were probably retained for next year's breeding stock. The roof of the farmhouse in the background had been thatched when first built but now supported a corrugated iron roof. With no insulation it would have been unbearably hot in summer, freezing cold in winter and noisy in rainy weather. The cost of thatching a house was comparably as expensive 100 years ago as it is today, and the cottage's iron roof is a mute sign of the shortage of money in farming, even for house maintenance.

Above: A farmer's wife and daughter take a few minutes break to watch their mixed flock of White Sussex and Rhode Island Red chickens and a few ducks feeding in the sunshine. The traditional broody coop in front of them was used to hatch a dozen eggs under a broody hen. During the three week incubation period the broody was released once or twice a day for food and exercise but soon returned clucking to her eggs. In these real free range conditions each hen managed to rear 8-10 chicks.

Right: This magnificent turkey's destiny depended on whether the farmer had spotted him as a potential a breeding bird for next year's flock or if a heavy bird was needed for Christmas dinner in their Orcop farmhouse.

Bee Keeping

Bees have had a long association with man and have been kept since Roman times for their honey to use as a sweetener in food. In medieval Archenfield tenants often paid rent wholly or partly in sesters of honey, believed to weigh about two pounds. Monks used it mixed with water to ferment into mead. Before cheap and plentiful sources of sugar were found in sugar cane in the tropics and sugar beet in Europe, honey was the only available sweetener and was consequently regarded as a valuable commodity. Square wooden hives with extractable frames were a Victorian introduction. Previously bees were kept in thatched straw skeps and destroyed when the honey was collected.

Ownership of a swarm of bees has been a contentious issue for centuries. Often the landowner where the swarm alighted claimed them. The owner of the hive where they originated and the person who caught them might claim them also. It would have been a brave man to dispute this swarm's ownership with the Edwardian lady persuading it to fall from the branches into her straw skep. Apart from her ordinary clothes she was wearing no gloves, veil or other protection to keep her safe if the bees became angry and decided to sting.

Thomas Charles of Caerswell, Much Marcle, was a keen beekeeper and built this ingenious bee house for his ten colonies of bees. He kept them more for their importance in pollinating his apple orchards each spring than for their honey, although he is seen here extracting some from their hives.

A confident beekeeper did not to bother to wear protective clothing as he inspected a frame.

Alfred Watkins and a friend extract honey from a frame. After the beeswax covering was sliced off into a dish, Watkins placed the prepared frames in a galvanised centrifuge, which he spun by a handle at the top, releasing the honey by centrifugal force against the sides of the tank to run down into a collecting tray at the bottom.

Chapter 10
Crafts and craftsmen

Woods and timber

Woods still cover much of Herefordshire's varied geology and undulating terrain. The 1907 Agricultural Returns record over 43,000 acres of different types of woodlands covering 12½% of the county. Directly and indirectly these extensive woods gave employment to thousands of men, extracting and working their timber, with jobs as diverse as tree fellers, bark strippers, carters, sawyers, carpenters, hurdle, pump and furniture makers and charcoal burners. The county's 114 wheelwrights used mostly local timber for different parts of their carriages, waggons and wheels. These woodlands were a source of raw material with many more local uses than today and supported 16 timber merchants and dealers and a chemical works at Pontrilas.

About two thirds of Herefordshire's woodlands, 27,122 acres, were coppiced (cut to ground level) on a regular cycle. Osiers were cut every year for basket weaving. Hazel was coppiced on a seven to ten year rotation for fence panels and thatchers' pegs. Every 20 years sweet chestnut was cut for fence posts and rails and ash for hop poles. Oak and elm were left to grow for about 200 years until mature and were the most valuable trees. For hundreds of years this continuous cycle of regrowth and harvest provided a steady supply of wood both for local use and for the charcoal needed by nearby ironworks. As a side effect this system of opening different areas to direct sunlight benefited the flora and fauna and enhanced the environment. Now only in a few nature reserves is the old cycle of cutting a patch every 20 years continued, not necessarily for the timber, but for the sake of the flora and fauna which need different degrees of open woodland for their very existence. Before the overhead wire system was introduced, the extensive acreage of hops needed a steady supply of poles for support, so that some owners of large estates found it profitable to plant areas of larch quite thickly. This encouraged quick straight growth with 12 to 14 feet poles in eight or ten years. Selling these thinnings at 28 shillings per hundred gave a little income while leaving the remainder to grow on to maturity to provide employment and income over a 40 year period with different sized timber selling for pit props, fencing posts, gates etc.. As the tanning industry developed, large areas of oak were harvested every year for the bark. An advertisement in the *Ross Gazette* in 1870 offered good pay to 'fifty good strippers to strip bark in the Penyard woods'.

Timber for the building trade came from the remainder of Herefordshire's 14,803 acres of old woodland, though some went for chemical extraction and bark for tanning found a ready market. Oak was used for making barrels. Ash and hazel barrel hoops (transported to Bristol by barge for the West Indian sugar trade) were a Wyeside speciality before they were replaced by iron barrel hoops. While many men served in the Army in wartime, the Women's Forestry Corps' vital work in the woods saved the need for much imported timber. When horse power still reigned and chain saws and powerful timber tractors with winches had yet to appear, a large input of manual labour and real horse power was required to extract this valuable resource from the woods. Steel, wire and plastic have replaced many of the traditional uses for wood in homes and farms, eliminating for ever rural jobs that were a vital part of village economy.

From the time of the Iron Age, the traditional method to fell a tree was with an axe, but with improvements in the quality of steel, which held a sharp edge better, cross-cut saws slowly replaced axes for the job. Said to be the last of its kind, this four man team from Clun, led by Reg Preece and Alf Cornfield, travelled the country felling trees on contract. In the winter of 1904 they were at work with their 7 lb Elwell axes, felling oak trees in Ledbury Park. The gamekeeper and estate manager pose with them for the photographer. Note the jar of cider and the enormous heap of wood chips. Skilled as they were, it would have taken several hours to fell a tree of this size.

Horse power did not give way to steam engines immediately and teams of horses continued to pull timber from woods to the roadside. They could still manage the job today without all the damage modern logging machinery causes if the overriding need for speed were not so great. This accident happened when an oak trunk twice fell off its carriage as it failed to negotiate the turn into South Street, Leominster. From August 10 to 12 it blocked the roadway, gathering an appreciative crowd giving much unwanted advice and encouragement to the embarrassed driver and his mate.

Modern machinery in the shape of a Latil timber tractor made easy work of removing this huge oak trunk from the Perrystone estate *circa* 1935.

Seen here in Gloucester Road, Ross with a huge oak trunk on its way to a sawmill, William Price, the driver standing nearest the camera and his brother, Charles, beside the log, were listed in Kelly's 1926 *Directory* as threshing tackle owners at Coughton, Walford, near Ross. Hauling timber was an important part of their business outside the busy threshing months in autumn and winter. 'Stick' was the joking name given to these huge tree trunks by old timber hauliers.

Somewhere in the Golden Valley a steam engine driver stands beside his machine, as a well-dressed estate owner watches a gang of eight men and a boy saw tree trunks into planks. These are stacked behind, with a heap of firewood off-cuts to the right. Circular saws of this type made short work of cutting timber for estate or farm work and soon eliminated the old saw pits where two men slaved all day to produce a few planks for their labours.

Like many other businesses, Kingsland Saw Mills did well from Government contracts during the First World War. The Great Western Railway even laid a new siding into their yard to speed up the transport of the timber products – posts, planks and duckboards – which were urgently needed to combat the mud in the prolonged trench warfare in France

and Flanders. In about 1920 the staff line up beside their gleaming portable steam engine for a souvenir photograph. Mr Wiltshire stands next to the flywheel and his father is on the far left. A modern sawmill stands on the site but the railway connection has long since disappeared.

Two men's experienced hands carefully guide a tree trunk onto the sawbench as their workmates watch from a safe distance and the driver waits to put the circular saw blade into motion. On contract work the square van in the centre was the driver's living quarters if his job was too far from home to walk or cycle. The heap of off-cuts was useful fuel for the winter months. On some estates and farms workers received firewood as an important 'perk' if they carted it home in their own time.

20 to 30-year old coppiced ash cleaves (splits) well into straight spars suitable for the bars and uprights of hurdles and rustic fencing. This old craftsman at Wellington has a pile of freshly made fence panels stacked beside him. Surrounded by chips he splits a 7-foot spar ready for use. Woven split ash hurdles were used for folding sheep on turnips for winter feed or for making temporary lambing pens, and with care would last for years.

A useful byproduct of the timber industry was oak bark, an important source of tannin, used in the preparation of leather. Quite small branches, as well as the trunks, were stripped of bark for this purpose. Large quantities were sent from Bucknell station yard to the Midlands for processing. It was surprisingly valuable. Two 1881/2 insurance policies on two ricks (stacks) of bark standing in William Head's timber yard near the Wye Bridge, Hereford valued them at £400 and £500 each. A local user was the Wrekin Chemical Works near Pontrilas station which 'produced naptha, tar, limesalt, sulphur and charcoal

by the destructive distillation of wood' from timber unsuitable for other uses. Another user of bark was the tannery in Tanyard Lane, Ross.

Before large iron pipes became commonly available, elm trunks were used to make water pumps in wells. Elm wood resists water and was used in piers and lock gates on canals, where it remained permanently wet. For pumps, freshly felled timber was used, as it lasted longer and did not split when worked with the sap still in the wood. The first phase of the pump maker's job was to square off the trunk on a saw pit so that he could mark out his intended work accurately with chalk. Mr Barber of Kingsthorne was photographed in about 1900 drilling out a freshly cut baulk of elm with a 15-foot long auger. Securely fixing his auger so that it could not move, Mr Barber aligned it through a wooden horse (post) onto carefully drawn chalk lines on the sides of the baulk. The nose auger he used cut a straight bore irrespective of the line of the wood's grain, with accuracy in the initial alignment essential. It was usually a two man job to turn the 5-foot long auger handle, but he seems to have managed alone despite his age, judging by the pile of wood shavings beneath the hole. Another elm baulk with a hole ready bored out lies beyond his work. Wells over 20 feet deep had pumps made in two or three sections, shaped to fit snugly together. Lower sections had a two inch bore, while the upper was augered five inches wide to accommodate the bucket, also made of elm with a leather valve in the bottom. The pump handle and ironwork were the work of a local blacksmith. Made of rural materials by local craftsmen, these wooden pumps could last for years, especially as they were unaffected by frost damage, unlike the iron ones that replaced them.

The Women's Forestry Corps banner reads 'Many more women required to work in the country converting timber to make aeroplanes. Healthy Open Air Work near home is possible.' The Women's Land Army banner announces 'We all feed you in the Land Army'. They were taking part in a War Weapons Week parade through Hereford to encourage more recruits. Nationwide, about 16,000, mainly middle class, ladies joined the WLA. In Herefordshire in 1917 there were 33 members of the WLA at work on farms beside an unknown number of country women who simply replaced their absent menfolk. As usual, advertising masked the truth. Very little of the timber these ladies cut ended up in aeroplanes. The vast bulk of their output was converted to other military uses, like duckboards to cross the mud to the front line trenches, posts and planks to strengthen the dugouts and the many other uses for which timber was required to keep the Army at war functioning. Home production of pit props and fence posts was needed also to reduce the amount of timber imported. The Women's Forestry Corps contributed a valuable workforce to maintain timber production while the men were away.

The less glamorous side of their work is shown in this photograph taken in the winter of 1915 as WFC volunteers sawed cordwood with heavy cross-cut saws.

A WFC member demonstrates she could fell a tree as well as a man.

Basketweaving

In an age of mass production woven wickerwork baskets remain items defying mechanised production and they must be made by hand. They are woven from osiers (or withies), the annual growth of willow stumps cut every year. Depending on their intended use they are either stripped of their bark immediately, or stored for later use. After storage for five or six months they are selected for size and placed in a stream to start regrowth. When signs of regrowth show, they are stripped of their bark, dried and tied in bolts until needed. The basket maker selects enough for a day's work and soaks them until pliable for weaving. A buff coloured rod was obtained by boiling. Peeled rods were reckoned to be stronger than those with the bark still on. Most English supplies now come from Somerset. Basket

After a period of storage, osiers were stripped of their bark before weaving. This meant pulling each one separately, butt end first, through a stripping brake. Two of these implements can be seen in front of the woman and the lad in this 1897 photograph. In the days before plastic bags and boxes there was sufficient demand in most towns for several basket makers. In 1867 there were four in Ross, dwindling to one – Henry Dowell, landlord of the Hope and Anchor in 1909. He continued making and repairing basketwork there for at least another 30 years, obtaining some of his osiers from the nearby withy beds at Wilton. His workers wove a variety of different sized and shaped baskets for farmers, tradesmen and housewives
– virtually any shape his customers required.

weavers work from left to right, preferring to rand (weave) one rod at a time as the finished article is stronger than those woven with three rods simultaneously. This method is called slewing and is a quick way to produce a weaker basket. A surprising number of different baskets are still in use, including wickerwork baskets slung under the hot air balloons in our summer skies, preferred for their light weight, resilience and strength.

An elderly basket maker at Brampton Abbotts demonstrates with practised ease how to weave handles into a wicker skip to make it easier to carry. Handles were often a weak point, especially on skips used for heavy work like carrying fodder to cattle, and needed to be well woven into the skip's fabric.

Coopers

Coopering (the difficult art of making wooden barrels) has a long history. To learn its intricate skills a young man had to serve a 7-year apprenticeship before qualifying. Herefordshire's coopers were kept busy making and maintaining the thousands of oak barrels and casks used in breweries and the cider industry. Oak was used as it did not taint the drink with unwanted flavours. Old barrels found a final use as rain water butts. Coopers' specialised skills demanded high wages, often double the average. In 1918 the Herefordshire Fruit Company was offering 50 to 60 shillings per week for skilled coopers, at a time when the average wage was about 35 shillings. Some men, however, preferred to be self-employed.

Above: An unknown cooper shows how to use a flagging iron to fit a new head into an old barrel. The iron hoops by his knee will be replaced to hold it tight in place. On the shelf behind is a croze (a curved plane), used to cut the circular groove in the top of the staves where the flat top of the barrel fits.

Left: Surrounded by the tools of his trade, a cooper replaces a broken stave in a 36 gallon barrel. On the left is a 6-feet long jointer, an upsidedown type of plane, made of beech, on which he shaped his oak staves. For stability, one end was set in the ground and the other angled up to a convenient height of about three feet, so that he could see his work as he planed the angles on each stave. In front of him is a block of ash or elm let into the ground, his equivalent of the blacksmith's anvil. Set in the stone block stands an iron bick, like a narrow anvil, on which he can rivet the ends of the iron hoops which hold the cask together. These will be fitted when he has finished using a downright plane to smooth the edges of the new stave flush with the side of the cask.

Chairmaking

This photograph of Philip Clisset in his workshop at Staplow near Bosbury was taken in 1909, when the 92-year-old craftsman was still making a few of his by then famous chairs. He is surrounded by a lifetime's store of well-used woodworking tools. Born at Birtsmorton in Worcestershire in 1817, he started making his distinctive wooden chairs in 1838 after settling at Staplow, where he died in 1913. There was plenty of local timber available, so he used ash for the framework and elm for the seats. The legs and spars he turned as green timber on the pole lathe in the centre of the workshop. These he then dried slowly by the fire. His early work was all in wood, but in later years he started making chairs with rush seats. On average he could produce one chair a day. A 1909 invoice in the Butcher's Row Museum in Ledbury shows that he sold a set of four high backed rush seated chairs for £1 10s and on the same day two ordinary rush seated chairs for 5s 6d each. To put this into context, farm labourers' wages were then about 12 shillings per week. Never moving from Staplow, he had some of his chairs exhibited in London in 1888, which considerably enhanced his reputation in the district. He received occasional commissions to make sets of chairs for wedding presents, and some of these are still loved and used by the couples' descendants. The quality of the workmanship of his chairs means that any that appear in local auctions now realise good prices. Despite the competition he faced in his later years from cheap factory-made chairs from the High Wycombe area, his local clientele appreciated his craftsmanship to such an extent that he had work if he wanted it throughout his long life.

Philip Clisset, chair maker (1817-1913)

Blacksmiths

In the days of four legged horse power, blacksmiths or more properly farriers, were in constant demand to ensure that the thousands of horses in use on farms, for riding and for transporting goods were properly shod. The 1907 Agricultural Returns for Herefordshire record 15,381 horses employed in farming and 9,300 unbroken colts. Many more were employed in road haulage in all its forms, and the gentry owned many carriage horses and hunters. Consequently, there were blacksmiths' forges in every town and village to cope with their demands. A young blacksmith had to serve five years' apprenticeship even if he was the owner's son and likely to take over his father's business eventually. After passing the test at the end of his five years, he went to work for another blacksmith as an improver to gain more experience before becoming fully qualified. For the independent, it cost about £100 to set up business as a self-employed village blacksmith in 1900. It was hot, heavy and tiring job, but essential, and varied too. Waggoners holding their horses and idling passers-by regarded the forge as a social centre, where they could pass the time of day, gossip about market prices or politics or exchange the latest joke. On wet days when land work was impossible, horsemen would bring their horses for new shoes and enjoy the warmth of the forge as sparks flew and the iron shoes were heated and shaped before being fitted to the hooves of the patient horses. This was the scene until the 1940s when blacksmiths' forges disappeared as horses were finally replaced by tractors, cars and lorries.

Village boys gather round the blacksmith's shop to listen to their elders chat as Ebenezer Randall, Preston on Wye's blacksmith, prepares to shoe a shire horse from a local farm.

Joseph Seymour's smithy at 8 Gloucester Road, Ross, with an ornate scroll design over its narrow entrance. On the left Joe Seymour holds a paring knife to trim the hooves of the hunters held by a groom. The assistant third from the left holds a rasp ready to smooth any rough edges after Mr Weaver (in the tattered leather apron) has finished shoeing the horses. Hammers, tongs, pliers and other tools of their trade lie ready to use in the traditional wooden boxes at their feet as they pose for a photograph taken about 1902 by Richard Edwin Phipps Davies, who ran the 'Wye studio' in Cantilupe Road.

About to shoe a horse, this handsome young blacksmith, Frederick Hanks, is seen in about 1919 outside his wooden forge at Tretire on the Abergavenny road, near St. Owen's Cross. Other forges in the area were said to be built of stone. At the outbreak of war in 1914 he was 18 and like many of his Herefordshire friends was an early recruit to the King's Shropshire Light Infantry. As a skilled man he found himself still working as a farrier, suddenly responsible for shoeing the 500 horses and 1,000 mules used for transporting supplies to his battalion. After demobilisation in 1919 he married a local girl, Edith Galliers, who worked in the nearby post office. Between the wars, as horses disappeared, repairing farm tools and machinery became an increasing part of his job, though he preferred shoeing horses and bought a portable forge to take to where he could still do the work he loved. After 1945 the farrier's trade more or less ended, and he finished his working life as a plumber.

As mechanisation took over, blacksmiths were forced to turn their skills to repairing tractors and machinery. Naturally this varied from village to village. In Shobdon, for example, at the outbreak of the Second World War there was only one tractor, and the blacksmith was still quite busy. In 1938 in Lyonshall Evan Evans is seen adjusting lawnmower blades outside his quiet smithy. The postcard was sent from Hereford to Evans's mother in Birmingham in 1941, at a time of severe food rationing and reads, 'the foods plenty of it and as much as you like. Do you good hear [sic] for a week.'

Index

Page numbers in italics refer to illustrations

IMPERIAL DEATH STAR

DS-1 Orbital Battle Station

Owner's Workshop Manual

Ryder Windham

Chris Reiff and **Chris Trevas**

CONTENTS

↑ Imperial Schematic Design System data, obtained by a rebel agent from a military communications complex on Galvoni III after the Battle of Yavin, yielded schematics for a concept "Death Star" with a superlaser cannon located on the sphere's equator.

TO: His Imperial Majesty, Emperor Palpatine

FROM: Governor Tarkin, Seswenna Sector, Eriadu

REGARDING: Increasing the security of the Empire

▶ Your Majesty, it has long been my contention that your New Order needs one undeniable and overwhelming symbol to impress and, yes, frighten the masses. The average citizen has no grasp of numbers nor a head for calculation. I maintain that the effectiveness of the Star Destroyer stems from not only its massive firepower but also from its size. When citizens look at a Star Destroyer and then compare it to the craft which might be mustered to attack it, they have a tendency to dismiss such a notion as suicidal rather than approach the problem tactically.

This natural state can be exploited to a far greater degree, as the average citizen deals in symbols, not rational analysis. If we present the galaxy with a weapon so powerful, so immense as to defy all conceivable opposition against it, a weapon invulnerable and invincible in battle, then that weapon shall become the symbol of the Empire. We need only a handful, perhaps as few as one, of these weapons to subjugate a thousand worlds. It must have force enough to dispatch an entire system, power enough to shatter planets. The fear such a weapon will inspire will be great enough for you to rule the galaxy unchallenged. What do you need with the Senate when you can give direct control of territories to your hand-picked regional governors? Sweep away the last remnants of the Old Republic and let fear keep the local systems in line—fear of our ultimate weapon.

I am ready to begin work to implement these steps at your word.

TO: Grand Moff Tarkin

FROM: Imperial Advisor Ars Dangor, for the Emperor

REGARDING: The Tarkin Doctrine

▶ You have read correctly, valued servant. Everything you have suggested will be implemented in a policy to be officially known as the Tarkin Doctrine. Rule through fear instead of through idealistic government agencies has a satisfying appeal to the Emperor. As such, the following title is bestowed upon you immediately, along with all relevant powers pertaining to such.

▶ You are now Grand Moff Tarkin, the first of a new order of Imperial officials.
▶ You have complete authority and control of Oversector Outer, which includes most of the sectors considered the Outer Rim Territories.
▶ You are to implement under extreme secrecy the design and construction of your ultimate tool of fear, code-named the Death Star Project.
▶ You have command of four Sector Groups to use to maintain the peace and to provide security for the Death Star Project.

The Emperor is pleased, Grand Moff Tarkin. Do not disappoint him.

THE HISTORY OF THE DEATH STAR

Nearly three decades before the Battle of Yavin, starship engineer Raith Sienar conceived the Expeditionary Battle Planetoid, a one-hundred-kilometer sphere with a smaller sphere at each pole, a large turbolaser at its core, and the capability to destroy an entire planet. Realizing that such a weapon would require a huge implosion core for power as well as great advances in hypermatter technology, Sienar dismissed his own concept as impractical.

Despite his misgivings, Sienar presented his concept for the Expeditionary Battle Planetoid to his friend, Republic Outland Regions Security Force Commander Wilhuff Tarkin, a native or Eriadu. Tarkin believed the concept had potential, and after he entered a career in politics and became the lieutenant governor of Eriadu, he conveyed his strong interest in the weapon to the Republic's leader, Supreme Chancellor Palaptine.

Palpatine assigned engineer and architect Bevel Lemelisk to pursue the necessary advances in hypermatter science. As the battle station project shifted from conceptual stage to architectural planning, work moved to the planet Geonosis, where Lemelisk teamed with the hive-minded Geonosians to hammer out structural and power supply issues. The weapon's schematics were in a laboratory on Geonosis when the Geonosians joined the Separatist movement, which represented numerous worlds that wanted to secede from the Galactic Republic. The Separatist leader Count Dooku, a former Jedi, absconded with the schematics during the battle that launched the Clone Wars.

Although Palpatine and Dooku led the opposing factions in the Clone Wars, both men were actually Sith Lords and allies. It remains unknown whether Wilhuff Tarkin—who served as a Republic Navy officer in the Clone Wars—was aware that either man was a Sith Lord. Following the Clone Wars, Palpatine and Tarkin continued working on the code-named Death Star project in secret, their goal to create a weapon that would permanently silence all who dared to resist Imperial rule.

Tarkin oversaw construction of the 120km-diameter Death Star in the Horuz system, in orbit of the prison world of Despayre. Supply and labor issues, unexpected technical difficulties, and acts of sabotage delayed the project for years. When construction was finished, the Death Star's laser targeted Despayre, and reduced it to asteroidal dust. Members of the Rebel Alliance stole the superweapon's schematics, and delivered them to technicians at the rebel base on Yavin 4, but not before the Death Star also destroyed the planet Alderaan.

With little doubt that the Empire's next target would be Yavin 4, the rebels raced to find any strategic vulnerability in the weapon's design. They found a flaw, an unshielded thermal exhaust vent, and the rebel pilot Luke Skywalker was able to destroy the Death Star by firing proton torpedoes into the vent.

Four years later, the rebels discovered the existence of a second Death Star that was still under construction in the Endor system. More than a weapon of terror, this Death Star was part of an elaborate trap, as the Empire knew the rebels would be unable to resist mounting an assault. Despite incredible odds, the rebels managed to first destroy the shield generator that protected the Death Star, and then the battle station itself. Within a month after the Battle of Endor, Rebel Alliance leader Mon Mothma declared the end of the rebellion and the birth of the New Republic.

Today, the Death Star remains a symbol of the Empire's oppression but also represents the Empire's greatest weakness: the belief that technology was supreme, and all foes insignificant.

← Imperial TIE fighters patrol the orbit of the under-construction Death Star.

TRADE FEDERATION BATTLESHIP

During the early stages of transforming Raith Sienar's concepts for the Expeditionary Battle Planetoid into an actual superweapon, Bevel Lemelisk's team of engineers drew inspiration from the *Lucrehulk*-class cargo freighters that the Trade Federation had converted into battleships.

Originally manufactured by Hoersch-Kessel Drive, the *Lucrehulk* is over three kilometers in diameter, and resembles a flattened disc that forms a split ring around a central sphere. The ring is split at the front of the craft, revealing two mammoth docking bays lined with forward docking claws. The ring also houses cavernous hangar bays, which were cargo holds in the ship's previous freighter configuration. The sphere contains the ship's massive computer and multiple power systems, and a compact hypermatter-annihilation reactor. A tower on the sphere houses a spacious command bridge; on *Lucrehulk*-class LH-3210 Cargo Haulers converted to serve as control ships for the Trade Federation's droid armies, a military control tower was also installed.

Although the *Lucrehulk* is an extremely powerful vessel, the conversion from freighter to warship was not entirely effective. The reactor-support assemblies retained independent fusion-powered triggers and confinement-field generators for the hypermatter main reactors, and were extremely volatile. The addition of retractable turbolasers along the equator of the ship left large blind spots that enemy starfighters could exploit by flying close to the hull.

← The Trade Federation used their battleships to blockade worlds they sought to conquer, but the warships were vulnerable to attack by small starfighters.

SPECIFICATIONS

CRAFT: *Lucrehulk*-class Battleship (converted freighter)
MANUFACTURER: Hoersch-Kessel Drive Inc. (primary contractor)
DIAMETER: 3,170m (10,400ft)
SUBLIGHT ENGINES: Rendili stardrive proton 2 (primary); proton 12 (secondary)
HYPERDRIVE: Class 2
HYPERDRIVE BACKUP: Class 10
SHIELDING: Equipped

NAVIGATION SYSTEM: Navicomputer
ARMAMENT: 42 quad laser emplacements
CREW: 25 (command staff)
PASSENGERS: 139,000 battle droids
CARGO: 500 million tons
CONSUMABLES: 500 days
COST: Not for sale (black market value 40,000,000)

TRADE FEDERATION CORE SHIP

After the Battle of Naboo, the Republic Senate ordered the Trade Federation to dissolve its army and disassemble its battleships. The Trade Federation pretended to comply but instead converted the central spheres into detachable core ships, which were engineered for planetary landings and equipped with land and air defenses. Used at the Battle of Geonosis and throughout the Clone Wars, the core ships were serviced in special landing pits on planets affiliated to the Trade Federation. The pits were lined with gravitational reflectors, which assisted the core ship's repulsors, and enabled the ships to retreat into space and reattach to the hyperdrive-equipped outer rings. Following the Clone Wars, most of the few remaining Trade Federation battleships and core ships wound up in the Corporate Sector.

1. Forward control tower
2. Droid-feedback rectenna
3. Command bridge tower
4. Scanner array
5. Docking ring
6. Equatorial bay
7. Hull section covers
8. Repulsorlift suspensors
9. Landing gear retractors
10. Foot pads

SPECIFICATIONS

CRAFT: Trade Federation Core Ship
MANUFACTURER: Hoersch-Kessel Drive Inc. (basic Core Ship);
   Baktoid Combat Automata (droid-army control core)
DIAMETER: 696m (2285ft)
HYPERDRIVE: None
HYPERDRIVE BACKUP: None
SHIELDING: Equipped
NAVIGATION SYSTEM: Navicomputer

ARMAMENT: 280 point-defense light laser cannons
CREW: 60 Trade Federation supervisors; 3,000 Droid Crew;
   200,000 maintenance droids
PASSENGERS: stateroom capacity for 60,000 trade
   representatives
CARGO: approx. 66 million tons
CONSUMABLES: 300 days
COST: Not for sale (black market value 25,000,000)

Although the Jedi Order was decimated in the purge that concluded the Clone Wars, dozens of Jedi younglings managed to take refuge at a Jedi enclave that had been established decades earlier on the planet Belsavis. The enclave lay in the Plawal rift, a series of geothermal-heated valleys that rested between wind-scoured glaciers, and was protected from above by an immense transparisteel dome. Soon after the Jedi purge, Emperor Palpatine secretly ordered the construction of an automated "battlemoon", its singular goal to wipe out the surviving Jedi on Belsavis. The battlemoon was named the *Eye of Palpatine*.

According to reconstructed Imperial documents, Palpatine specifically indicated that the battlemoon should resemble an asteroid, complete with impact craters, and he maintained such camouflage was necessary to deceive or baffle sensor scans from enemy worlds and vessels. However, given that the Death Star project was already in the works when Palpatine issued the order to build his battlemoon, historians have theorized that the Emperor was less interested in creating a natural-looking superweapon than he was intent on keeping secrecy, and hesitant to reveal the grandness of his evil ambitions so early in his rule. Had he blatantly promoted his intent to wipe out

every inhabitant in the Plawal rift, most of whom were children, his actions would have caused untold outrage in the Senate.

Imperial engineer Ohran Keldor designed the battlemoon, which was constructed at the shipyards of Rothana and also Patriim. Keldor utilized an asteroid from the Patriim system as a source of raw materials as well as a foundation upon which he installed huge engines and turbolaser cannons. The result was a 19,000-meter-long weapon, paid for by government funds that had been diverted by Palpatine himself. To further maintain secrecy, Palpatine also arranged for the *Eye* to pick up contingents of stormtroopers on various worlds throughout the Outer Rim.

Despite the Emperor's schemes, two Jedi sabotaged the *Eye of Palpatine*, and brought it to a stop before it ever picked up the waiting stormtroopers. The inhabitants of Belsavis escaped, and the furious Emperor imprisoned many of those responsible for losing the *Eye*. For nearly three decades, the *Eye* remained dormant amidst the asteroids in the Moonflower Nebula in the Wild Space region of the galaxy. Eight years after the Battle of Endor, Luke Skywalker and two of his Jedi students discovered the battlemoon, and worked together to destroy it.

⬇ With its rocky, cratered surface, the *Eye of Palpatine* remained unnoticed for decades in an asteroid belt in the Moonflower Nebula.

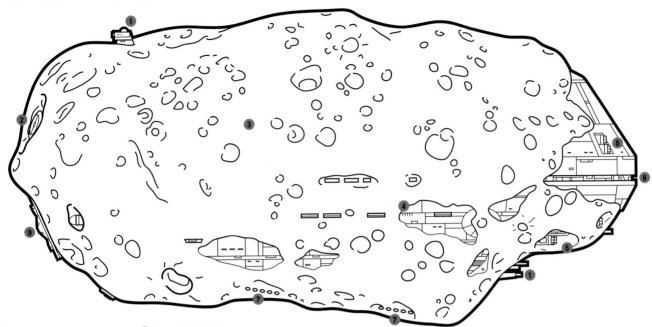

1 Deflector shield generator
2 Sensor arrays
3 Hollowed asteroid shell
4 Hangar bays
5 Sublight engines
6 Hyperdrive
7 Ventral turbolaser batteries
8 Main bridge
9 Laser targeting beam emitter
10 Forward focused turbolaser batteries

⬇ Palpatine, Emperor of the Galactic Empire.

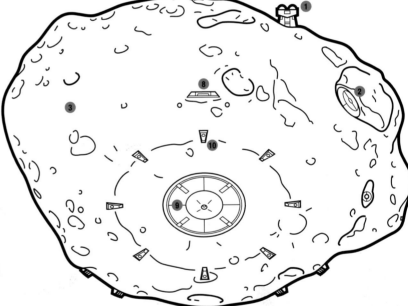

SPECIFICATIONS

CRAFT: **Eye of Palpatine**
TYPE: **Automated battlemoon**
MANUFACTURER: **Rothana Heavy Engineering**
LENGTH: **19,000m**
HYPERDRIVE: **Class 5**
HYPERDRIVE BACKUP: **Class 20**
SHIELDING: **Merr-Sonn *Guardian*-class shield generators**

NAVIGATION SYSTEM: **Advanced AI Navicomputer**
ARMAMENT: **Turbolaser cannons**
CREW: **Unmanned**
PASSENGERS: **Imperial stormtroopers**
CARGO CAPACITY: **Unknown**
CONSUMABLES: **90 days (estimated)**
COST: **Unknown**

TORPEDO SPHERE

A dedicated siege platform produced for the Empire by Loronar Defense Industries, the Torpedo Sphere is designed for the singular purpose of disabling planetary defense shields. The primary armament of a Torpedo Sphere is an assembly of 500 proton torpedo tubes. The tubes are arranged in an inverted conical formation, a design that enables all torpedo-launchers to fire simultaneously at one target. The tubes are circled by ten heavy turbolaser batteries.

The Torpedo Sphere is covered in thousands of dedicated energy receptors (DERs) designed to analyze energy shield emissions. Planetary shields are never uniformly even and experience power anomalies and fluctuations. To make an assault, the Torpedo Sphere arrives in a planet's orbit, and then trains its DERs to search for weak points in the planet's shielding. These weak points rarely show a power drop of more than 20 percent, and rarely larger than a six-meter square, but are nevertheless sufficiently vulnerable areas. The Torpedo Sphere's sensors cannot penetrate full planetary shields, so the only way the Sphere's crew can determine the location of a planet's shield generators is to study the power waves and seek their initial source.

Because a station the size of a Torpedo Sphere cannot fire-link weapons, the torpedo tubes must be carefully coordinated by more than 100 heavy-weapons technicians. The process for determining the location of a planetary shield's weak point and calculating an attack on that specific point can take hours. This time-consuming process precludes the possibility to fire the tubes together at anything more mobile than a planet. Although it is possible to take some fire-links off the normal weapon control system and fire normally at starship-sized targets, only fifty tubes can be managed at a time in this manner.

Once the weak points in a shield have been found, the technicians fire the proton torpedos in unison at one weak point. This action is followed with a barrage of turbolaser blasts directed at the planetary defense generators. Planetary defense shields are rarely disabled for more than a few microseconds, so if the first barrage does not shatter the shield, the process must start all over again.

The siege platform's ovoid-shape and considerable firepower have encouraged some Imperial officers to liken the Torpedo Sphere to a "miniature Death Star." While the Torpedo Sphere is hardly capable of destroying a planet, it is a formidable weapon. Six Torpedo Spheres are currently in service.

⬇ Although the Empire maintained control of all Torpedo Spheres, Emperor Palpatine blanketed the planet Coruscant with powerful shield generators that were engineered to withstand an orbital bombardment of proton torpedoes.

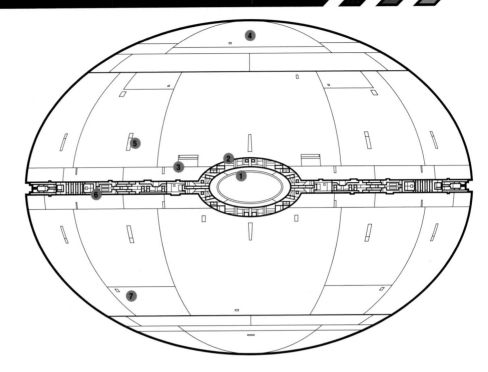

1. **Torpedo tube array**
2. **Turbolaser batteries**
3. **Deflector shield generator**
4. **Main bridge**
5. **Dedicated energy receptors**
6. **Hangar bays**
7. **Sensor arrays**
8. **Sublight engines**
9. **Hyperdrive**

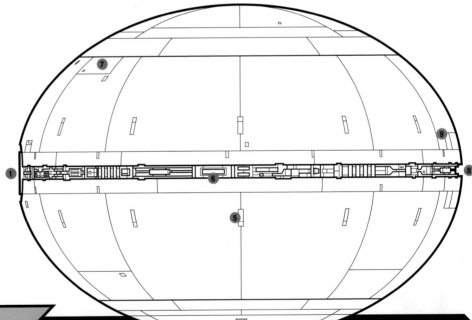

SPECIFICATIONS

CRAFT: Loronar's Torpedo Sphere
TYPE: Dedicated siege platform
MANUFACTURER: Loronar Defense Industries
LENGTH: 1,900m
HYPERDRIVE: Class 3
HYPERDRIVE BACKUP: Class 18
SHIELDING: Loronar DS-13 projectors
NAVIGATION SYSTEM: Sienar Fleet Systems navicomputer

ARMAMENT: 10 turbolaser batteries; 500 proton torpedo tubes
CREW: 61,245 gunners; 2,030 skeleton
PASSENGERS: 8,540 (troops)
CARGO CAPACITY: Unknown
CONSUMABLES: 4 years
COST: Not for sale (construction cost unknown)

lthough the Rebel Alliance claimed victory at the Battle at Yavin, the era of the Death Stars was far from over. Emperor Palpatine had already ordered the construction of a second Death Star, and was also manufacturing a pair of mammoth warships—*Eclipse*-class Super Star Destroyers—at Kuat and Byss. To test the technology of the *Eclipse*-class's ship-mounted superlasers, and also to divert the Alliance's attention from the second Death Star, the Emperor assigned Bevel Lemelisk to develop a prototype of the *Eclipse*-class into an operational weapon that would also serve as a test bed for new

⬇ **Grand Moff Tarkin aboard the Death Star. Both the Death Star and the Tarkin were paid for by funds diverted from the Departments of System Exploration and Public Works.**

technology. The result was the *Tarkin*, named in honor of the martyred Grand Moff Tarkin.

Most of the members of Lemelisk's design team were unaware of the fact that their assignment was to build a prototype, and were led to believe that the *Tarkin* was intended as an official Imperial battle station. They replicated the Death Star's main offensive battery, the ionic cannon superlaser, and essentially bracketed the weapon with a set of giant engines and defensive shield generators. Not surprisingly, the design team did not leave any thermal exhaust ports exposed, effectively removing the flaw that had allowed the Rebel Alliance to destroy the first Death Star.

The *Tarkin* was built in secret at a dry dock in orbit of the garrison planet Hockaleg in the Patriim system, and construction was overseen by Imperial Admiral Nod Warfield. The prototype's superlaser came to the attention of Imperial Grand Admiral Martio Batch, who had been assigned by the Emperor to develop cloaking technologies. Although cloaking devices for starships had once been common, the technology had become virtually obsolete since the mines of Aeten II, an Outer Rim world in the Dreighton Nebula, had been depleted of the rare stygium crystals required for the devices. Batch diverted the *Tarkin* to Aeten II and used the prototype's superlaser to shatter the entire world, which released thousands of stygium crystals that were subsequently collected by Batch's forces.

After the *Tarkin* returned to Hockaleg's orbit for additional modifications and further testing, a Rebel Alliance officer, Captain Maraba Tev, was on a high-risk spy mission in the Patriim system when he discovered the Empire's secret weapon. Tev managed to obtain the *Tarkin*'s schematics, which enabled a rebel assault squad to infiltrate the enormous vessel. The assault squad included Princess Leia Organa, who sabotaged the ionic cannon's activation mechanism by switching two wires to reverse the polarity modes of the cannon's fire controls. After the squad escaped the *Tarkin*, the Imperials attempted to fire their superlaser at the squad's ship, but Leia's sabotage made the cannon fire on itself, causing the *Tarkin* to self-destruct.

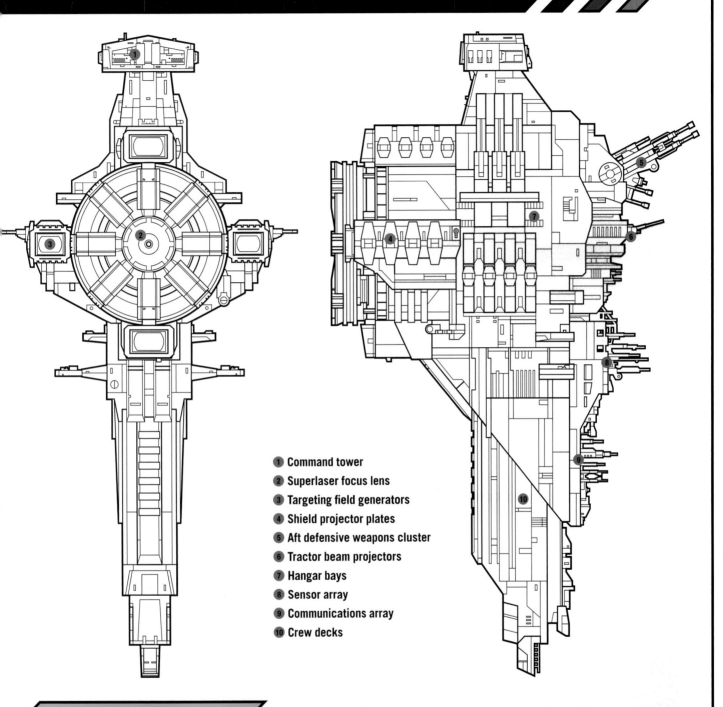

1. Command tower
2. Superlaser focus lens
3. Targeting field generators
4. Shield projector plates
5. Aft defensive weapons cluster
6. Tractor beam projectors
7. Hangar bays
8. Sensor array
9. Communications array
10. Crew decks

SPECIFICATIONS

CRAFT: **The Tarkin**
TYPE: **Battlestation**
MANUFACTURER: **Imperial Department of Military Research**
LENGTH: **42km**
HEIGHT: **70km**
HYPERDRIVE: **Class 4**
HYPERDRIVE BACKUP: **Class 20**

SHIELDING: **Borstel Galactic Defense field generators**
NAVIGATION SYSTEM: **Sienar Fleet Systems navicomputer**
ARMAMENT: **Superlaser**
CREW: **43,863 (35,705 operational staff, 8,158 gunners)**
PASSENGERS: **105,417**
CONSUMABLES: **2 years (estimated)**
COST: **Unknown**

GRAND MOFF TARKIN

A native of Eriadu, Wilhuff Tarkin graduated from the Academy, joined the Republic Outland Regions Security Force, and quickly gained a reputation for quelling piracy around Eriadu and other Rim worlds. He reached the rank of commander before retiring, then entered politics and became lieutenant governor of Eriadu. When Senator Palpatine was elected to the office of Supreme Chancellor, Tarkin realized a major political shift had occurred, and he insinuated himself to become recognized as one of Palpatine's most ardent supporters.

Tarkin befriended the engineer Raith Sienar, who described his idea for an "expeditionary battle planetoid". Tarkin eventually relayed the idea to Palpatine, who was intrigued. During the Clone Wars, Tarkin served as the Seswenna sector's governor. After Palpatine became Emperor, he appointed Tarkin as the Galactic Empire's first sector governor, which carried the designation Moff.

Tarkin formulated what became known as the Tarkin Doctrine. Officially known as Imperial Communiqué #001044.92v, the Doctrine consisted of Tarkin's plans for increasing security and maintaining order within the Empire. His plans included the proposal for *"a weapon so powerful, so immense as to defy all conceivable opposition against it"*, which would be used to *"rule through the fear of force rather than through force itself"*.

Palpatine subsequently appointed Tarkin as the first Grand Moff, and gave him oversight of the construction of Sienar's conceived superweapon, which was dubbed the Death Star.

RAITH SIENAR

Born into a family of wealthy industrialists, Raith Sienar trained at the Rigovian Technical University, and became an engineer and hyperspace explorer. He mapped dozens of new hyperspace lanes, discovered exploitable systems in the Unknown Regions, and amassed his own fortune by the age of 20.

He founded Sienar Design Systems as well as its clandestine division, Advanced Projects Laboratory, and specialized in one-of-a-kind contracts, designing starships for wealthy clients. Eventually, he became CEO of his family's most profitable company, Sienar Technologies. An innovative and by all accounts brilliant engineer, Sienar frequently drew inspiration from mistakes made by others. He invested heavily in the scrapped projects of his competitors and searched the designs for new ideas that had failed for simple reasons, and which could be corrected to serve his own purposes, such as transforming stock vessels into fast, unique starships. He pushed ion-drive technology to its limits, and produced the first Twin Ion Drive (T.I.E.) starfighter.

Sienar's longtime friend Wilhuff Tarkin ensured Sienar Technologies secured numerous contracts with the Republic for Sienar's companies. After Palpatine became Emperor, Sienar nationalized Sienar Technologies, and gave the company a new name: Sienar Fleet Systems. His T.I.E. design was utilized for the Imperial TIE fighter, TIE bomber, infiltrator, Advanced, and other TIE variants.

← **Grand Moff Tarkin in uniform, shortly after the end of the Clone Wars.**

BEVEL LEMELISK

An engineer and architect, Bevel Lemelisk studied under Nasdra Magrody, founder of the Magrody Institute of Programmable Intelligence. During the Clone Wars, he worked with the esteemed engineer Walex Blissex, and assisted Blissex in designing the *Victory*-class Star Destroyer for the Grand Army of the Republic. After Palpatine declared himself Emperor, Grand Moff Tarkin assigned Lemelisk to the Maw Installation, where he became chief engineer of the Death Star project.

As chief engineer, Lemelisk essentially outranked everyone affiliated with the Death Star's construction except for Tarkin. Along with Imperial scientist Frap Radicon and weapons engineer Umak Leth, he spent years working on the secret weapon. Lemelisk also discreetly enlisted the help of the Twi'lek scientist Tol Sivron, who conducted his research in a laboratory on his homeworld Ryloth. However, to maintain secrecy, Lemelisk deliberately gave limited data to Sivron, preventing him from knowing that he was working on a superweapon. At some point, Lemelisk was appointed Master of Imperial Projects. After completing the Death Star, he was assigned to work on Torpedo Spheres.

Despite Lemelisk's many contributions to the Empire, Emperor Palpatine held him personally responsible for the design flaw that enabled the Rebel Alliance to destroy the Death Star. According to various reports, Lemelisk attempted to flee Imperial authorities but was eventually captured and executed. However, other reports suggest that Palpatine—after the Battle of Yavin—assigned Lemelisk to oversee construction of the *Tarkin*. Rumors persist that Palpatine considered Lemelisk too valuable to kill, and opted to torture the engineer instead. Whether dead or alive, Lemelisk's current whereabouts remain unknown.

DEATH STAR PROTOTYPE

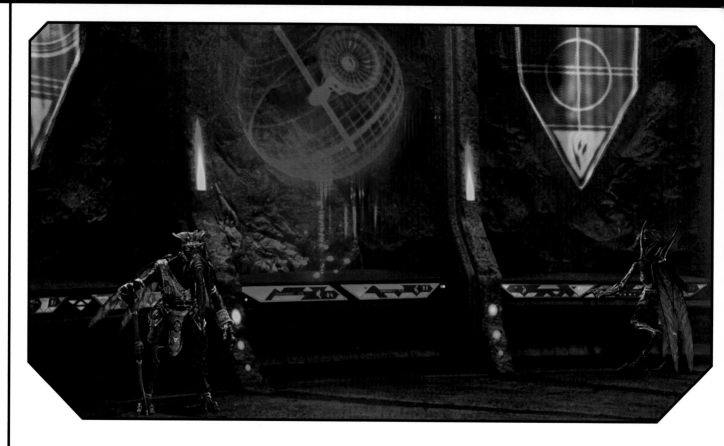

By the time Moff Tarkin had been promoted to Grand Moff Tarkin, numerous flaws in the original Geonosian plans for the Death Star battle station, as well as intelligence leaks and scattered efforts at sabotage, had led to ongoing construction delays. As the Imperial engineers continued to have great difficulty in adapting the Geonosian plans into a working model, Tarkin ordered a think tank of engineers to review the schematics for feasibility from top to bottom and create a working prototype Death Star.

For the prototype's construction, Tarkin also founded and selected the location of a top-secret research facility, built within and amidst linked asteroids inside a hidden island of gravitational stability in the exact center of the Maw black-hole cluster near Kessel. Eventually, the Twi-lek administrator Tol Sivron came to run Tarkin's Maw Installation, which was guarded by four Star Destroyers under the command of Admiral Natasi Daala.

Many proof-of-concept components, theoretical models, and performance tests were undertaken to hone the Death Star design. Work crews of Wookiee slaves assembled a scaled-down version of the core

SPECIFICATIONS

CRAFT: Death Star Prototype
TYPE: Battlestation
MANUFACTURER: Imperial Department of Military Research
LENGTH/WIDTH/HEIGHT: 120 kilometers
HYPERDRIVE: None
HYPERDRIVE BACKUP: None
ENGINE UNITS: Ion engines (for sublight travel only)
SHIELDING: Borstel Galactic Defense field generators

NAVIGATION SYSTEM: Interplanetary navicomputer
CREW: 258
PASSENGERS: Stormtroopers and gunners
CARGO CAPACITY: Unknown
CONSUMABLES: 2 months
COST: Unknown

superlaser, which was mounted inside a stripped-down superstructure, an armillary sphere with a diameter of 120 kilometers. Because the prototype was never intended to be a practical weapon of war, the designers had no need to install maintenance and repair machinery, an immense computer core, or the enormous hyperdrive engines that were necessary for the full-scale Death Star. The only visible components inside the prototype's sphere were the giant reactor core, engines for sublight travel, and the prototype superlaser itself. A small command cabin with slave-rigged computer systems controlled the superlaser and drive units, and also minimized personnel requirements.

Compared with the working model of the first Death Star, the prototype superlaser had several disadvantages. The targeting system was never perfected, and the superlaser was incredibly wasteful of power, its storage batteries requiring several hours to recharge fully. Although the superlaser could be fired at reduced power, its destructive ability was reduced significantly. Firepower was only sufficient to destroy a planet's core and render the planet uninhabitable, but could not completely vaporize the targeted world.

The prototype proved effective, and construction resumed on the full-scale Death Star, which had been relocated to the Horuz system. Eleven years after the Death Star's destruction at Yavin, the prototype was still in orbit of the asteroid laboratories of the Maw Installation, and still guarded by Admiral Daala's forces, when New Republic agents, including Kyp Duron, discovered the superweapon at the secret facility. Kyp Duron subsequently managed to destroy the prototype by luring it into the Maw's black hole.

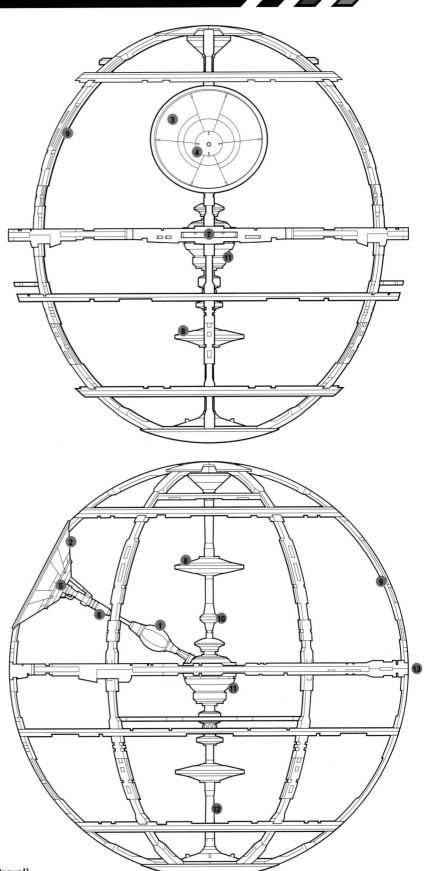

1. **Power amplification system**
2. **Focus lens frame**
3. **Superlaser focus lens**
4. **Amplification crystal prototype**
5. **Laser crystal**
6. **Superlaser power distribution shaft**
7. **Command cabin**
8. **Reactor core**
9. **Frame**
10. **Power cell coupling**
11. **Main reactor**
12. **Power distribution shaft**
13. **Ion engines (for sublight travel)**

DEATH STAR

To: Major Arhul Hextrophon, Executive Secretary and Master Historian, Alliance High Command
From: Lieutenant Voren Na'al, Assistant Historian
Regarding: Revised summary for the Death Star battle station

Although the conception and development of the Death Star occurred years before the Republic fell to Palpatine's Empire, there is little doubt that Palpatine knew such a superweapon would be vital to his goal to rule thousands of worlds. Because he was determined to gain respect as well as inspire fear throughout the galaxy, the Emperor demanded that the Death Star would defy all planetary defenses, and have the ability to destroy an entire world with one devastating stroke.

An equatorial trench divided the Death Star into two hemispheres, each of which was subdivided into 12 bridge-controlled zones for a total of 24 zones. Each zone was similar to a sub-batttle station, and had its own food replicators, hangar bays, detention blocks, medical centers, armories, and command centers. The upper hemisphere housed the superlaser, and all Imperial estimates indicated that a single blast would equal the combined firepower of the entire Imperial fleet.

The station's surface was covered with thousands of 'city sprawls', manned stations dedicated primarily to defense. These sprawls housed the majority of the Death Star's shield projectors and communications arrays. Most of the station's 'habitable' areas were on the surface or within the two to four kilometer thick crust. All of the 'below surface' facilities within the crust were considered part of the city sprawl. All data gathered by the clusters' sensors and manned stations were relayed to each zone's respective bridge, which was in turn relayed to the overbridge, a vast command center that constantly monitored all the work stations and datafiles on the battle station.

At the Death Star's core was an immense, cavernous housing for the battle station's power matrix. A fusion reactor, fed by stellar fuel bottles that lined its periphery, produced the raw energy demanded by the Death Star's superlaser. The reactor core, sublight and hyperdrive systems, and the superlaser housing filled approximately half of the battle station's interior. Sublight propulsion systems and defense field generators lined the outer equatorial regions.

When the first Death Star's construction was finished, it was the single largest object ever built.

↑Although the Death Star was equipped with mooring platforms for Imperial Star Destroyers, ship-to-ship transfers were typically made via shuttles.

↓ Arriving upon the Death Star in the Alderaan system, the crew of the YT-1300 freighter *Millennium Falcon* initially mistook the battle station for a small moon.

↑ 35 kilometers in diameter, the superlaser focus dish was the Death Star's most prominent surface feature.

SPECIFICATIONS

CRAFT: Mk. 1 deep-space mobile battle station
MANUFACTURER: Imperial Department of Military Research/Sienar Fleet Systems
DIAMETER: 120km (74.6 miles)
HYPERDRIVE: Class 4
HYPERDRIVE BACKUP: Class 20
SHIELDING: Equipped
NAVIGATION SYSTEM: Navicomputer

ARMAMENT: 1 superlaser, 15,000 Taim & Bak D6 turbolaser batteries, 2,500 Borstel Galactic Defense SB-920 laser cannons, 2,500 Borstel MS-1 ion cannons, 768 Phylon tractor-beam emplacements, 11,000 combat vehicles
CREW: 342,953 (285,675 operational staff, 57,278 gunners)
PASSENGERS: 843,342
CARGO CAPACITY: Over one million kilotons
CONSUMABLES: 3 years
COST: Unknown

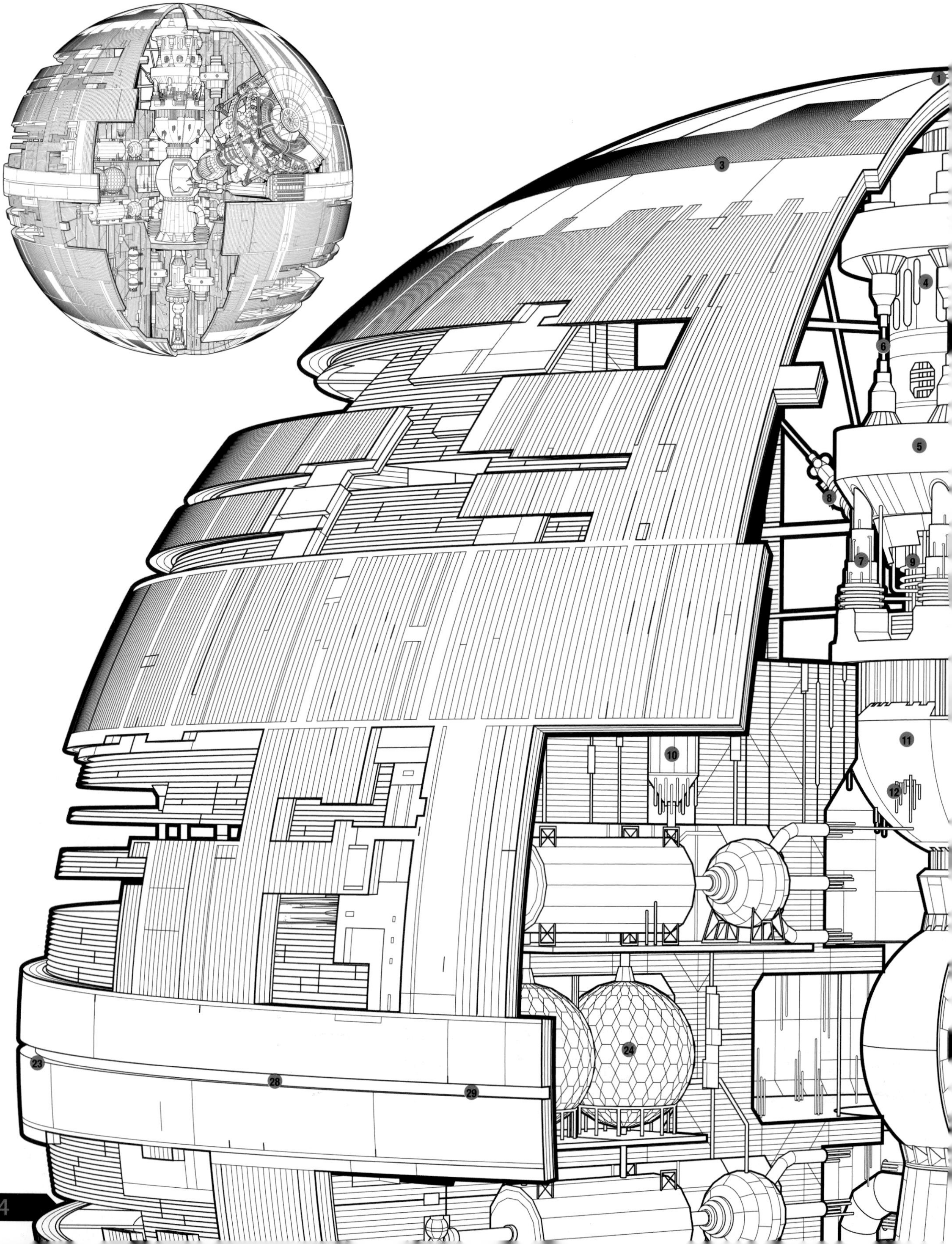
1
3
4
6
5
8
7
9
10
11
12
24
23
28
29

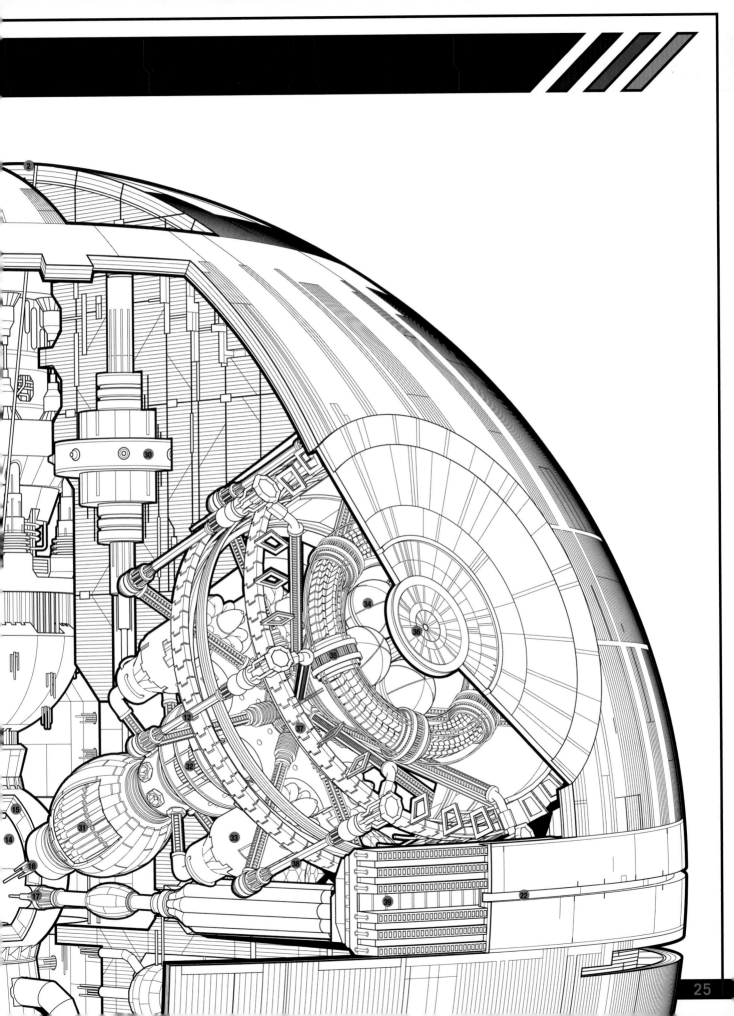

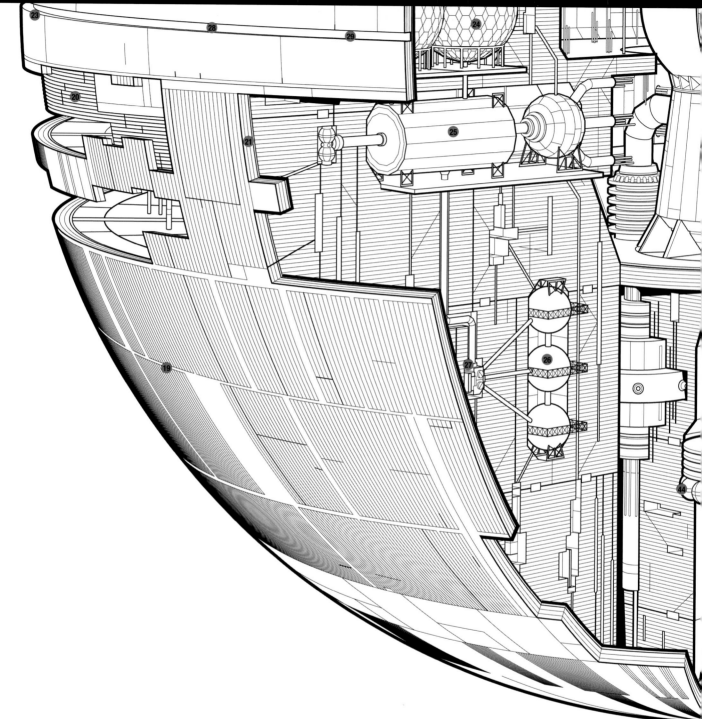

1. Main exhaust port
2. Thermal exhaust port
3. Polar trench
4. Secondary power converters
5. Central power column
6. Tractor-beam reactor coupling
7. Tractor-beam generator tower
8. Emergency radiation discharge
9. Power processing networks
10. Sector computer cluster
11. Main power generator
12. Static discharge tower
13. Energy exchanger
14. Hypermatter reactor
15. Insulator plating
16. Superlaser power diverter
17. Hyperdrive power diverter
18. Raw power diversion selonoid
19. Mid-hemisphere trench
20. Stacked interior decks
21. Concentric surface decks
22. Equatorial trench
23. Ion sublight engines
24. Ion-drive reactor

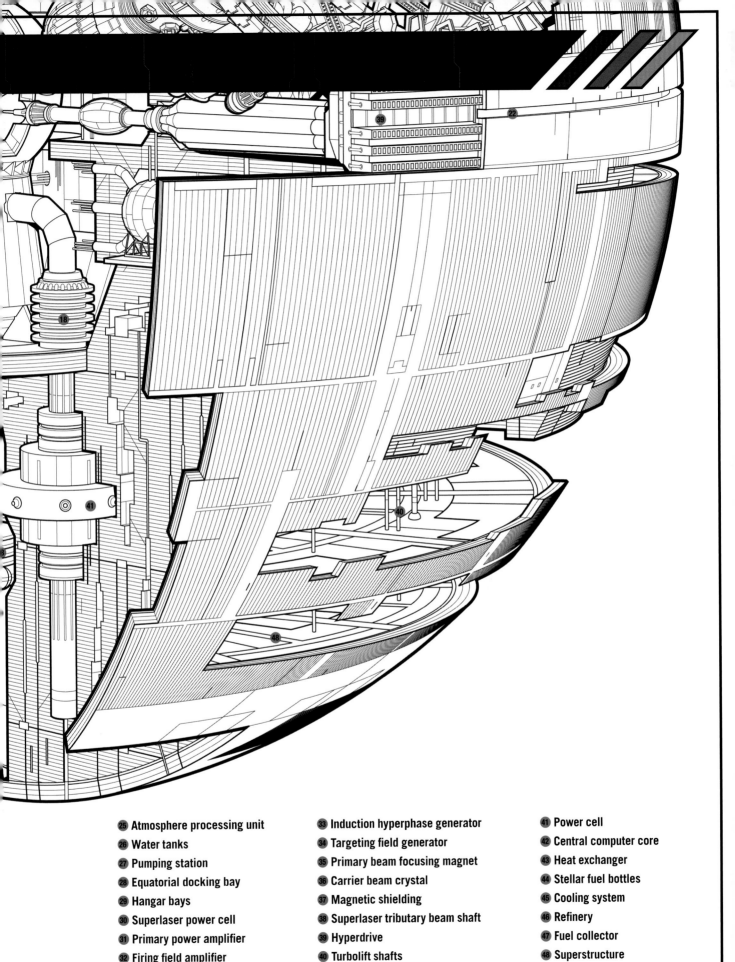

25 Atmosphere processing unit

26 Water tanks

27 Pumping station

28 Equatorial docking bay

29 Hangar bays

30 Superlaser power cell

31 Primary power amplifier

32 Firing field amplifier

33 Induction hyperphase generator

34 Targeting field generator

35 Primary beam focusing magnet

36 Carrier beam crystal

37 Magnetic shielding

38 Superlaser tributary beam shaft

39 Hyperdrive

40 Turbolift shafts

41 Power cell

42 Central computer core

43 Heat exchanger

44 Stellar fuel bottles

45 Cooling system

46 Refinery

47 Fuel collector

48 Superstructure

1. Main exhaust port
2. Thermal exhaust port
3. Secondary power converters
4. Central power column
5. Tractor-beam reactor coupling
6. Tractor-beam generator tower
7. Emergency radiation discharge
8. Main power generator
9. Hypermatter reactor
10. Concentric surface decks
11. Ion sublight engines

12. Ion-drive reactor
13. Atmosphere processing unit
14. Water tanks
15. Overbridge
16. Superlaser power cell
17. Primary power amplifier
18. Firing field amplifier
19. Induction hyperphase generator
20. Targeting field generator
21. Primary beam focusing magnet
22. Carrier beam crystal

23. Magnetic shielding
24. Superlaser tributary beam shaft
25. Hyperdrive
26. Power cell
27. Central computer core
28. Sector computer cluster
29. Heat exchanger
30. Stellar fuel bottles
31. Cooling system
32. Refinery
33. Fuel collector

EXTERIOR

31. Quadanium steel outer hull
32. Polar trench
33. Superlaser focus lens
34. Equatorial trench
35. Mid-hemisphere trench

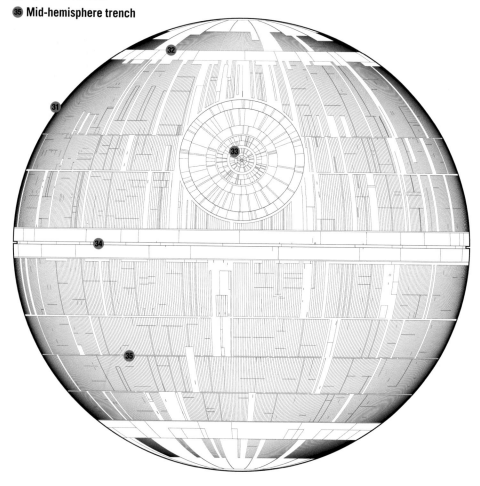

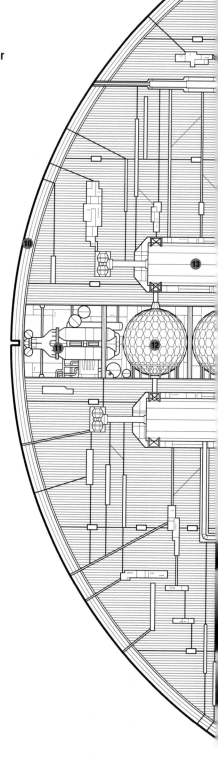

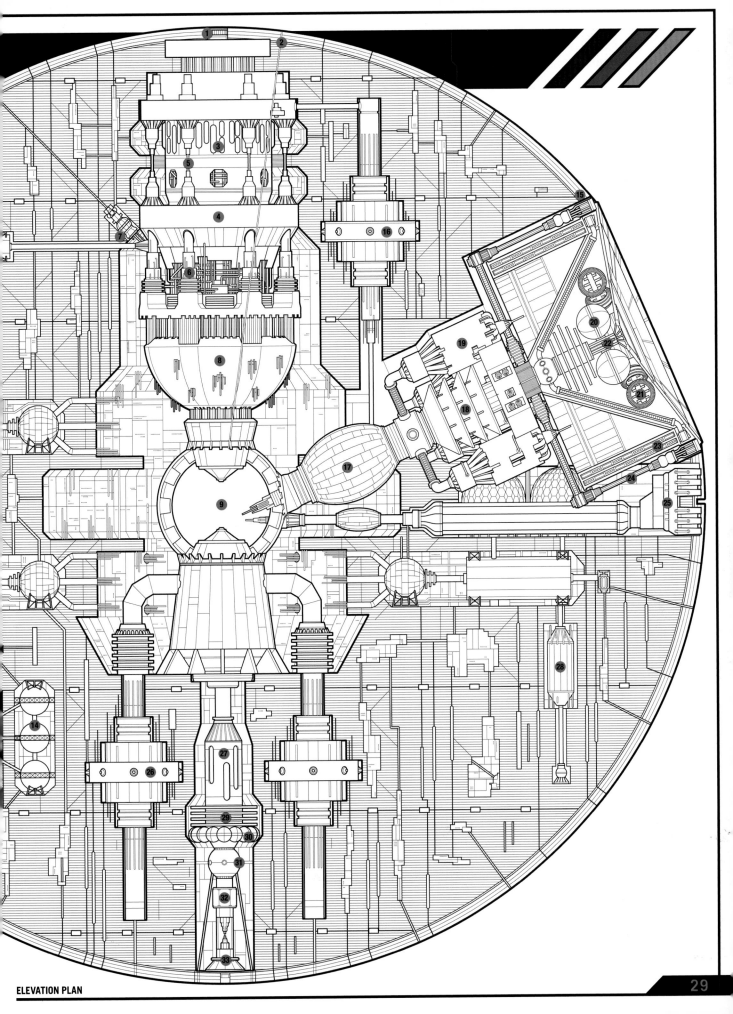

SUPERSTRUCTURE

esigned and engineered to accommodate an enormous reactor core and superlaser, the Death Star's superstructure resembled a vast network of crisscrossing girders, braces, compression-resistant struts, and interconnected tubes used for ventilation, repulsorlift travel, and the routing of energy systems. The superstructure's structural integrity was so great that the Death Star could easily withstand bombardment to its exterior or collisions with large spacecraft, and was also more resilient to external gravitational forces than smaller, non-spherical battle stations.

The voids between the superstructure's crisscrossing components were spacious enough to allow construction droids and service vehicles to travel from one area of the Death Star to another during construction. After construction was completed, repulsorlift-equipped maintenance droids moved between the components,

⬇ From the bridge of an Imperial Star Destroyer, Emperor Palpatine and his Sith Lord lieutenant Darth Vader surveyed the construction of the Death Star.

scanning for any sign of pressure leaks, weak welds, or other hazards that posed even a slight threat to the structure's integrity.

Despite the superstructure's strength, the first Death Star's designers did not anticipate several acts of sabotage during construction. In one instance, a bomb detonated in a cargo hold, causing significant damage to the hold and the area around it, which prompted an investigation by Darth Vader. Despite this and other acts of sabotage, and also an assault of rebel starfighters at the Battle of Yavin, the Death Star's superstructure remained sound until that battle's explosive conclusion. At the Battle of Endor, the Rebel Alliance was able to take advantage of the fact that large regions of the second Death Star's superstructure remained exposed, enabling pilots to travel straight to the station's reactor core.

→ The Death Star's bowels was a multilayered maze of tubes, girders, and machinery.

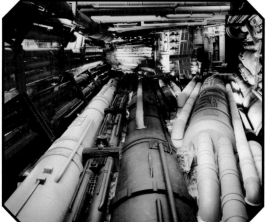

← Excess energy from the reactor core was diverted to lighting systems inside the superstructure, enabling construction crews to clearly see their work areas.

↓ Although substantial voids were included for the passage of large service vehicles, such voids did not compromise structural integrity.

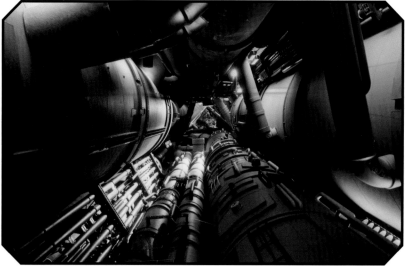

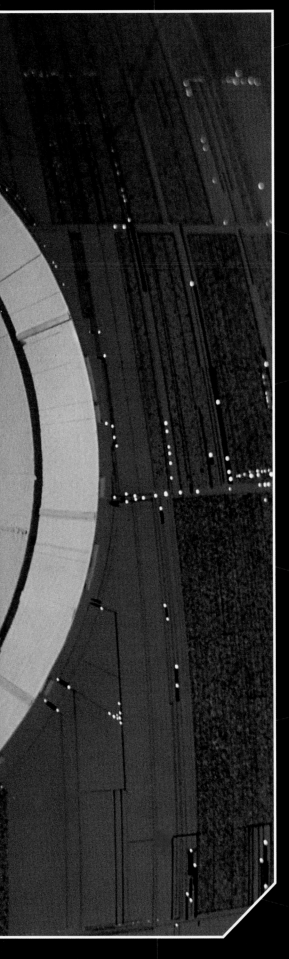

WEAPONS & DEFENSIVE SYSTEMS

Excerpts from Personal Data Journal Entries #476 and #481, Tarkin recording

The Death Star must feature a single weapon of mass destruction. This weapon must emit energy of such a degree as to rock a target planet to its very core.

In addition, the Death Star must include surface defenses rivaling that of the Imperial core worlds. Planetary shielding, surface-to-air turbolasers, 360-degree sensor capability, powerful multi-directional tractor beams, and heavy cannons for use against capital-class ships are not only necessary but vital to the design and mission of the battle station.

Chief Bevel Lemelisk assures me that he can include a weapon he calls a "superlaser" into the final design. In fact, the entire sphere will be dedicated to the support and maintenance of this single weapon. Not only will it be able to rock a planet, Bevel claims that the superlaser will shatter worlds. Only asteroid ruins will remain afer the weapon is trained upon a target.

However, to achieve such immense destructive power, I must lose all but the most rudimentary shielding capabtilities. Bevel assures me that the surface-to-air defenses will more than make up for the loss.

← Full view of the Death Star's superlaser focus lens, which was frequently referred to by Death Star gunners as "The Eye".

TRACTOR BEAM REACTOR COUPLING

Tractor beams are invisible, maneuverable force fields that can capture, shift, or redirect objects with great precision. The force field is produced by a tractor-beam generator, then released by a tractor-beam projector—also called an emitter tower—which is usually mounted on a rotating turret. Standard equipment in all spaceports and space stations, tractor beams are typically used for traffic control to guide starships into and out of hangars and docking bays.

Each zone of the Death Star featured 24 tractor-beam emplacements that housed modified Phylon Q7 tractor beam projectors—the same models used on Imperial Star Destroyers—as offensive weapons. Every zone could concentrate from one to all 24 emplacements on a single target, and at great distances, enabling the Death Star to snare distant enemy ships in a virtually unbreakable bubble of

energy. The long-range projectors were so powerful that a ship could be captured before its sensors could identify the "small moon" in its vicinity as a battle station. Each Phylon Q7 tractor beam projector required a crew of ten to operate properly.

The Death Star's tractor beams were coupled to the station's main reactor to provide a steady stream of energy, which prevented accidents caused by generator malfunctions. The Death Star had seven power coupling terminals; each standing atop a generator tower 35km tall, and providing energy for more than 700 tractor beams. If the tractor beam's connection to the reactor was severed at any one of the coupling sites, the beam became inoperative. Maintenance and technician droids accessed the reactor coupling controls via a bridge that wrapped around the terminal.

➜ **As revealed by visual data obtained from a military communications complex on Galvoni III, Imperial stormtroopers did not detect the Jedi Knight Obi-Wan Kenobi as he shut down Tractor Beam 12 in Section N6 of the Death Star.**

WEAPONS & DEFENSIVE SYSTEMS

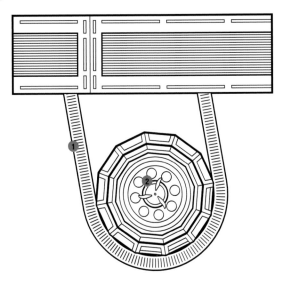

1. Maintenance bridge
2. Energy emitter
3. Control levers
4. Power level indicator
5. Status display
6. Manual override
7. Generator tower

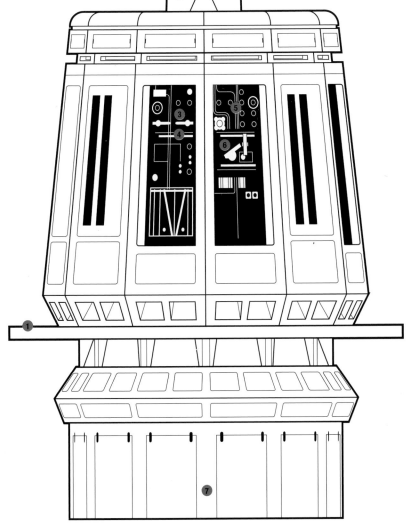

↑ The tractor beam power level indicator also displays data related to the reactor coupling's location with the Death Star.

↓ Located in the Death Star's central core, the Tractor Beam Reactor Coupling tower was approximately 35km tall.

ENERGY SHIELDS

Shield-projection towers emitted energy fields that covered the Death Star's city sprawls. These energy shields protected the sprawls from space debris, and offered limited defense against energy weapons, as most of the Death Star's energy was harnessed for operations related to the superlaser. A typical city sprawl was protected by at least three shield projection towers. Power cells, machinery, and shield-operator stations were located in the enclosed complex located at the base of each tower. The most heavily shielded area of the Death Star was the tower that accommodated the Emperor's throne room.

Shield operation fell under the jurisdiction of Battle Station Operations. Officers, operators, and technicians manned the shield-projection tower's stations to ensure the shields were always in full working order. In the event of an attack, towers from neighboring sprawls could overlap their shields to create a continuous blanket of energy over the Death Star's surface.

1 **Shield-projection tower**   **3** **Energizer**
2 **Shield generator**   **4** **Power tap to main reactor**

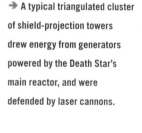

➜ A typical triangulated cluster of shield-projection towers drew energy from generators powered by the Death Star's main reactor, and were defended by laser cannons.

ARMORED PLATING/HULL

Much of the metal for the Death Star's hull plating was drawn from asteroidal material, and processed into military-grade Quadanium steel. As if the sourcing and manufacturing of the plating were not enough of a challenge, Bevel Lemelisk's design team was also tasked with the enormous undertaking of the plating's installation.

The incredible magnitude of the project prohibited the possibility of building the space station's entire hull and pressurizing its interior before beginning interior construction, as the amount of air necessary for pressurization would have been tremendous. However, pressurized areas would be required for the estimated hundreds of thousands of laborers who would be conscripted to work on the Death Star, and those laborers would require somewhere convenient to live during the construction, as it would have been neither time nor cost effective for the Empire to shuttle laborers back and forth for any distance between shifts.

Lemelisk's team determined that the most efficient solution was to build, seal, and pressurize individual sectors while the hull was being laid. This allowed storage space for supplies during construction, and also for temporary habitats for laborers.

↑ From a distance, the Death Star's hull appeared relatively smooth to the naked eye.

⬇ Heavily armored towers were constructed for turbolaser emplacements and also mooring platforms for Imperial Star Destroyers. These also served as directional markers for TIE fighter pilots.

TURBOLASER TOWER

The most common capital ship weapons in the galaxy, turbolasers are two-stage supercharged laser cannons. The small primary laser produces an energy beam that enters the turbolaser's main actuator, where it interacts with a stream of energized blaster gas to produce an intense blast. The barrel's galven coils focus the beam, providing a range that is double or triple that of conventional laser cannons. The destructive power of the fired energy bolt can punch through an enemy warship's shields and thick armor plating.

The Death Star had 5,000 Taim & Bak xx-9 heavy turbolaser towers. A typical tower featured four distinct sections housed within an armored hull. The top section housed the gun turret, which rotated in a full circle to provide a continuous arc of fire. Twin laser barrels jutted from the turret, and swivel mounts allowed the barrels to cover the vertical field of fire.

The second section of the tower contained rows of capacitator banks, which stored energy that the laser actuator converted into charged beams of intense light. This energy-storage capability was crucial to enable the turbolasers to maintain rapid fire.

The third section housed the support crew and maintenance stations, and also the substantial turbine generators required to power the tower.

The lowermost section of the tower contained the gunnery stations and the tracking and targeting computers. Although gunners wore specialized helmets that helped them provide limited targeting for their guns, only the targeting computers could keep track of multiple targets and devise fire patterns to pick out fast-moving enemy starfighters.

Safety features built into the targeting computers didn't allow the lasers to fire when any portion of the Death Star was within their sights. The Alliance exploited this vulnerability by flying their starfighters so close to the Death Star that the Imperial weapons automatically held their fire.

➜ ⬃ Turbolasers deliver a big punch but require a delay of at least two seconds between shots to allow the capacitators to build up an adequate charge.

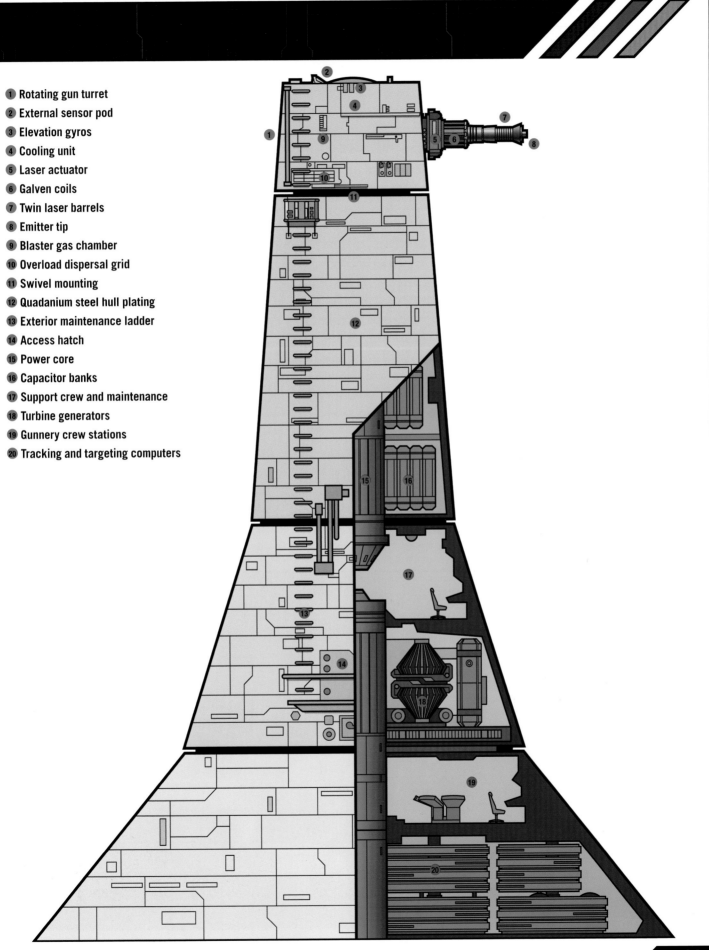

1. Rotating gun turret
2. External sensor pod
3. Elevation gyros
4. Cooling unit
5. Laser actuator
6. Galven coils
7. Twin laser barrels
8. Emitter tip
9. Blaster gas chamber
10. Overload dispersal grid
11. Swivel mounting
12. Quadanium steel hull plating
13. Exterior maintenance ladder
14. Access hatch
15. Power core
16. Capacitor banks
17. Support crew and maintenance
18. Turbine generators
19. Gunnery crew stations
20. Tracking and targeting computers

TURBOLASER TOWER

MANNED LASER CANNON SB-920

Defenses along the Death Star's trenches included Borstel Galactic Defense Super Blaster 920 laser cannons, exotic energy weapons manufactured exclusively for Imperial starships. The SB-920 is capable of destroying shields and armor on capital ships, and can destroy a starfighter with a single shot.

Like most laser cannons, the SB-920 funnels volatile blaster gas from a supercooled and armored chamber, combines the gas with a power charge, and directs the resulting energy through a long barrel. Circuitry in the barrel increases the beam's power. Where the SB-920 differs substantially from other laser cannons is that instead of relying on a built-in computerized targeting system to help a single gunner track targets, the cannon is linked to tactical computer systems throughout the Death Star, and requires a crew of three: a standing gunner, a seated targeting technician, and a seated energy technician. The SB-920 also has a faster recharge rate than most laser cannons.

Each member of the SB-920 crew wears protective, specialized computer helmets equipped with arrays to assist with their respective duties. The targeting technician monitors and analyzes the targeting computer systems to help the gunner select the best target, be it a fast-moving fighter craft or a specific

shield generator on a capital ship. The energy technician ensures the cannon doesn't overheat or run out of power. The gunner selects targets, maneuvers the cannon, and operates the trigger.

The SB-920 utilizes an advanced Target Acquisition and Tracking (TAT) system similar to certain Imperial surface-to-air defensive systems. The TAT acquires a signature lock on targets in a designated vector while the computer selects a primary target, and simultaneously updates and calculates trajectories of alternate targets. The TAT extrapolates the position of receding targets at long range, and the SB-920 crew is quite capable of bringing those targets down.

At the Battle of Yavin, Death Star gunners prevented most of the rebel starfighters from reaching the battle station's exhaust port canyon. However, data recovered from an Imperial communications complex on Galvoni III revealed that shortly before the Battle of Yavin, an overzealous officer under General Tagge, in a misguided attempt to encourage Death Star gunner crews to become effective in any combination, redistributed the gunners in alphabetical order throughout the battle station. By that one order, the close-knit unity of the gun crews and their targeting coordinators may have been swept away, and aided the rebel victory at Yavin.

→ Death Star gunners are stationed in pressurized enclosures to fire the cannons directly through magnetic force-field ports. Gunners wear specialized computer helmets equipped with arrays to assist with targeting fast-moving fighter craft.

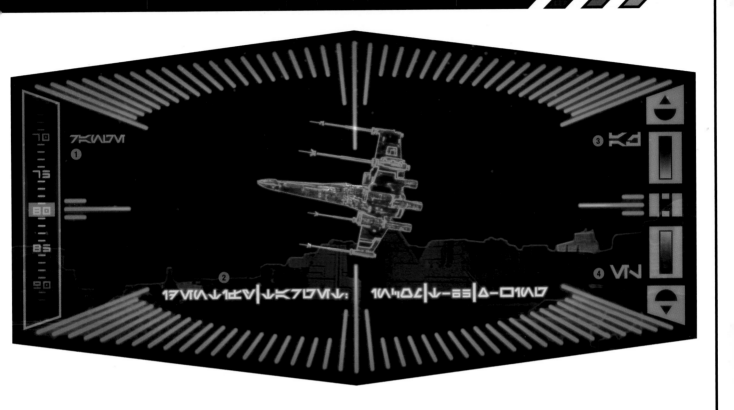

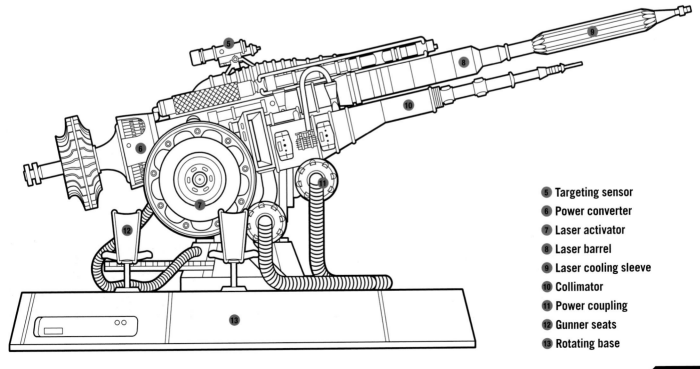

⬆ An example of a Target Acquisition and Tracking (TAT) system technical readout, displayed within an SB-920 gunner's computer helmet, presents an attack simulation of an enemy X-wing starfighter above a Death Star trench.

1 Range indicator
2 Target identifier
3 Azimuth (degree of rotation)
4 Elevation (vertical angle)

5 Targeting sensor
6 Power converter
7 Laser activator
8 Laser barrel
9 Laser cooling sleeve
10 Collimator
11 Power coupling
12 Gunner seats
13 Rotating base

MANNED LASER CANNON SB-920

SUPERLASER

The majority of the Death Star's interior volume was dedicated to housing and supporting its primary weapon: the superlaser keystone to Emperor Palpatine's "Doctrine of Fear". The weapon's energy originated deep within the battle station, and was channeled into an array of eight initiator laser cannons. The tributary beams from the eight cannons converged at a central amplification nexus over the superlaser cannon well—the vast concavity in the Death Star's upper hemisphere—to form a powerful single beam. The power of this beam could be controlled and scaled to suit the destruction of various targets. A beam of one power level could be used against enemy capital ships. The most powerful beam had more firepower than half the Imperial Starfleet, and could instantly reduce a world to asteroid fragments and space dust.

At an early stage of the Death Star's development, the challenges of building an operational superlaser led to a proposal for an alternative weapon: a composite beam superlaser. This weapon would have fired proton beams capable of destroying a planet's core, and leaving the targeted planet uninhabitable. The composite beam superlaser would have required an immense mechanical arm to move the superlaser's concave dish out of a locked position—flush with the battle station's spherical surface—before firing. However, engineers were able to resolve the technical difficulties of the planet-shattering superlaser, and plans for the composite beam superlaser were scrapped.

The superlaser's power required recharging between firings, and the intensity of each firing determined the per-day firing frequency, from once per minute against spaceborne vessels to once every 24 hours against planetary targets. Recovered Imperial reports indicate the superlaser, prior to destroying Alderaan, also destroyed the *Fortressa*, a *Lucrehulk*-class battleship under rebel control, and the prison planet Despayre.

⬇ **Front view of the Superlaser. The cannon well's diameter was approximately 35km.**

1. **Primary power amplifer**
2. **Inulator plating**
3. **Induction hyperphase generator**
4. **Firing field amplifer**
5. **Superlaser tributary beam shaft**
6. **Magnetic shielding**
7. **Primary beam focusing magnet**
8. **Targeting field generator**
9. **Carrier beam crystal**

DEATH STAR GUNNERS

A special sub-unit of the Imperial pilot corp, Death Star gunners were culled from the best fighting units in the galaxy. Many were originally Imperial Navy pilots-in-training or pilots who failed to qualify for flight assignment, who nonetheless possessed keen eyes, superior reflexes, and a rapport with specialized equipment. Gunners were expected to be able to handle everything from a single light laser cannon to turbolaser battery emplacements.

Death Star gunners were trained to work as a group, to operate gun towers and defend against large-scale assault, and specialized in unified fire and probability-generated spread patterns. In the event of attack from enemy starfighters, gunners would operate cannons from multiple emplacements to blanket the Death Star in a defensive net of blaster fire. The Death Star's highest-ranking and best-trained gunners were assigned to the superlaser.

The gunners wore specialized computer helmets that not only offered protection but were equipped with macrobinocular viewplates, sensor arrays to assist with targeting fast-moving fighter craft, and sophisticated tracking systems for better fire control assistance. Each helmet was also equipped with a tongue-operated comlink.

Prior to the Battle of Yavin, Death Star gunners spent months calibrating their weapons, running through countless scenario engagements. Utilizing battle plans devised by Tarkin's staff, a thousand simulated rebel fleets engaged the Death Star, and a thousand rebel fleets were repelled and destroyed. Evidently, it never occurred to the Imperials that they should test themselves against a simulated attack by small squadrons of starfighters instead of just a large armada.

⬇ **Computer-linked helmets and thousands of hours of drilling enabled Death Star gunners to aim, power-up, and fire the superlaser with synchronized precision.**

SUPERLASER FIRING STATION

1. System status boards
2. Energy transfer relays
3. Radiation levels
4. Emitter crystal harmonics
5. Laser station sychronization
6. Targeting sensor refinement
7. Targeting displays
8. Tributary beam alignment
9. Focus-field polarity
10. Charge status-indicator
11. System ignition keypad
12. System ignition keypad

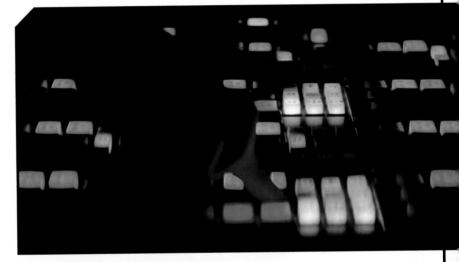

Eight individually manned laser stations produced the beams of super-charged energy for the Death Star's superlaser. In case one of the main laser stations malfunctioned, four back-up laser stations were always on active standby.

The eight beams of energy converged at a central amplification nexus in front of the huge, concave focus lens. For optimum performance, the superlaser was manned by 168 Imperial gunners, with a minimum of 14 soldiers manning each of the initiator laser cannons.

SUPERLASER TRIBUTARY BEAM SHAFT

Of all the Death Star's technological challenges, the greatest was engineering the superlaser, and all its numerous safeguards, to prevent the battle station from being destroyed by its own incredible power. Some of these challenges had already been addressed and resolved by Project Hammertong, a top-secret weapon project that originated during the Clone Wars.

Authorized by then-Supreme Chancellor Palpatine, Hammertong was developed to explore the use of laser-stream technology for a new weapon. Hammertong incorporated crystal technology that Republic forces seized from an experimental power source on the planet Mygeeto, where the native Muun had long drawn power from synthesized crystals, and built their cities around enormous capacitor towers that stored and distributed energy. Hammertong's laser-stream weapon required tributary beam shafts, which—after the foundation of the Empire—were constructed at

Desolation Station, an Imperial facility in the Atrivis sector. Evidently, the Death Star project superseded Hammertong, for the beam shafts were subsequently transported to the Death Star's construction site.

Eight tributary beam shafts, each with its own amplification crystal, were positioned around the circumference of the superlaser's immense concave cannon well. The shafts were lined with focusing coils to maintain each beam's integrity. The tributary beams had to be perfectly calibrated and aligned, or the central beam would misfocus and dissipate, and generate a flurry of backscatter that could severely damage or destroy the superlaser housing. The firing process also generated magnetic fields and gravitational flux, which had to be dissipated to prevent the amplification crystals from becoming misaligned, and to prevent the battle station from being torn apart.

➡ Although the visors on Death Star gunner helmets were designed to protect the gunners' eyes, visual data obtained from an Imperial communications complex reveal some gunners in the tributary beam shaft routinely left their lower faces partially exposed, presumably to maintain direct audio communication with fellow gunners when the shaft was filled by static charges from the tributary beam.

1. Principle energy inducer
2. Primary focusing coils
3. Gravitational flux dampeners
4. Amplification crystal chamber
5. Galven coils
6. Collimator
7. Pulse capacitor
8. Magnetic dissipators
9. Fine targeting coils

↑ The locations of the Death Star's tributary beam shafts are illustrated on page 43.

← Despite the gunners' protective visors, control stations in the tributary shaft were positioned so the gunners would stand with their backs to the beam, preventing them from glancing at the brilliant stream of energy directly. Gunners closed their eyes before the beam blazed at full intensity.

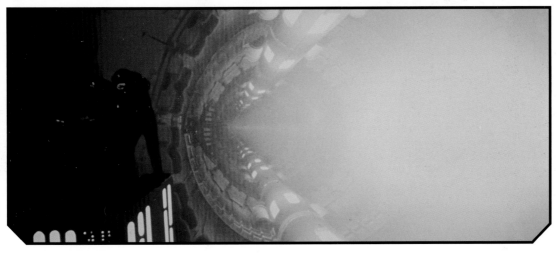

ENERGY & PROPULSION

Excerpts from Personal Data Journal Entries #461 and 481, Grand Moff Tarkin recording

Because the Death Star's energy requirements are as staggering as the challenges of building a weapon that can actually contain and release such energy without destroying itself, it's easy to understand why Raith Sienar essentially abandoned his concepts for the Expeditionary Battle Planetoid. To generate and control such energy, the battle station must be enormous. Much of its interior will consist of housing for the giant power cells, engines, weapons systems, and other machinery necessary to support living beings and actually move the sphere through space.

The Death Star not only needs to move through normal space but it must also have the capacity to travel through hyperspace or it is useless to us. While hyperspace speeds need not be great, since a planet would not be able to evade this station, it would be pleasing to achieve a moderate hyperdrive multiplier.

Moving the sphere will be accomplished through the use of massive ion sublight drives while in realspace, and through redundant hyperdrive engines for travel from system to system. Make no mistake, though. The Death Star will be slow. It will seem to crawl through the void between planets, and even in hyperspace it will be no faster than the most ancient tramp freighter. [Engineer] Bevel [Lemelisk] believes that he can get the hyperdrive multiplier down to three, but he warns me that it could be as high as five or six. No matter. It is fitting that targets of this station have an exceptionally long period of time to fear their ultimate fate.

HYPERMATTER REACTOR

→ Holographic schematics revealed the second Death Star held a more sophisticated hypermatter reactor than its predecessor.

The Death Star's primary power generator was a cavernous SFS-CR27200 hypermatter reactor, a chamber lined by stellar fuel bottles that fed a fusion reaction of prodigious proportions. This reactor powered all systems on the battle station, including the superlaser and turbolaser emplacements, 123 Isu-Sim SSP06 hyperdrive generators and two Sepma 30-5 sublight engines, energy shields, and life-support.

The hypermatter reactor was located at the center of the Death Star's cylindrical polar column, which served to distribute power and stabilize the station's rotational capabilities. Capacitor panels were layered around the reactor core, and reactor shafts extended outward to the station's circumference.

The Death Star was engineered with innumerable redundant engine and electrical subsystems to ensure power could be directed to any area of the battle station when necessary. Not only were all of the Death Star's subsystems interconnected but they were also connected to the main reactor system in order to provide maximum power to all subsystems at all times.

↓→ Although visual recordings of the first Death Star's hypermatter reactor may be lost to time, the Rebel Alliance obtained close-up views of the second Death Star's power transference assembly, and images of the considerably larger reactor.

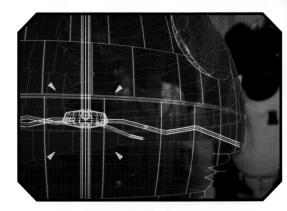

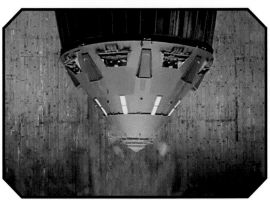

FIRST DEATH STAR'S HYPERMATTER REACTOR

1. Lines out to power distribution nodes
2. Main power generator
3. Static discharge vanes
4. Clean/filtered power manifolds
5. Energy exchanger
6. Raw power manifolds
7. Radiation insulator plating
8. Containment field coils
9. Reaction chamber
10. Superlaser power diverters
11. Raw power to superlaser
12. Hyperdrive power diverter
13. Raw power to hyperdrive
14. Fuel injectors
15. Power diverter manifold control
16. Primary fuel exciters
17. Fuel control valves
18. Raw fuel supply lines (from stellar fuel bottles)
19. Power regulators
20. Emergency raw power diversion solonoid
21. Line out to power cell

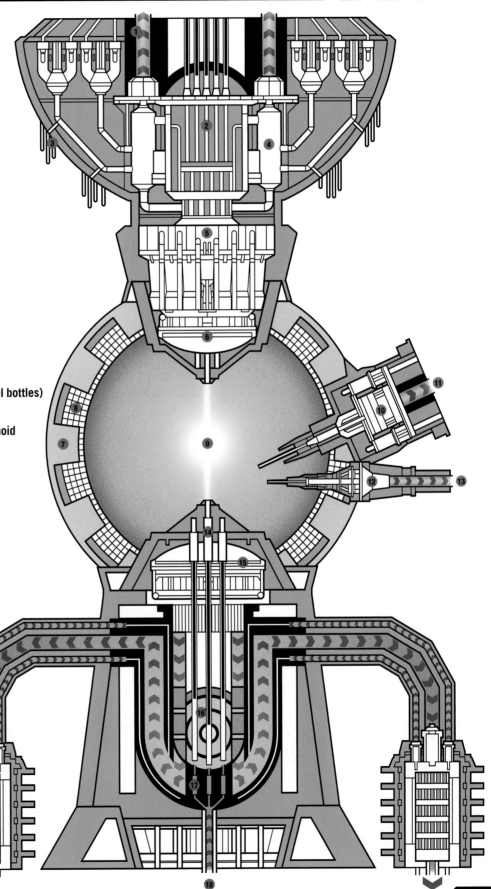

THERMAL EXHAUST PORT

Excess energy produced by the Death Star's hypermatter reactor was expelled into space by way of thermal exhaust ports, which were scattered over the battle station's surface. Although the exhaust ports effectively prevented excess heat and radiation from damaging the station or injuring crew members, they were especially vulnerable to attack, as they opened upon shafts that lead directly to the reactor. The Death Star's designers, knowing that an explosion within an exhaust port could trigger a chain reaction that might damage or destroy the main reactor, utilized ray-shield generators to protect the exhaust ports from laser bombardment.

⬇ **Technical readouts revealed that an innocuous, two-meter-wide thermal exhaust port was the Death Star's most vulnerable area.**

After obtaining the Death Star's technical readouts, the Rebel Alliance determined protective ray shields could be breached by projectiles such as proton torpedoes. The Alliance concluded that a precise hit on one exhaust port's shaft would ignite an explosion that would start a series of energy backlashes that would travel from subsystem to subsystem, and explode in proximity to the main reactor. Alliance tacticians surmised that if the Death Star's designers had not engineered the station with so many interconnected systems, a single proton torpedo might have partially crippled the battle station but would not have destroyed it.

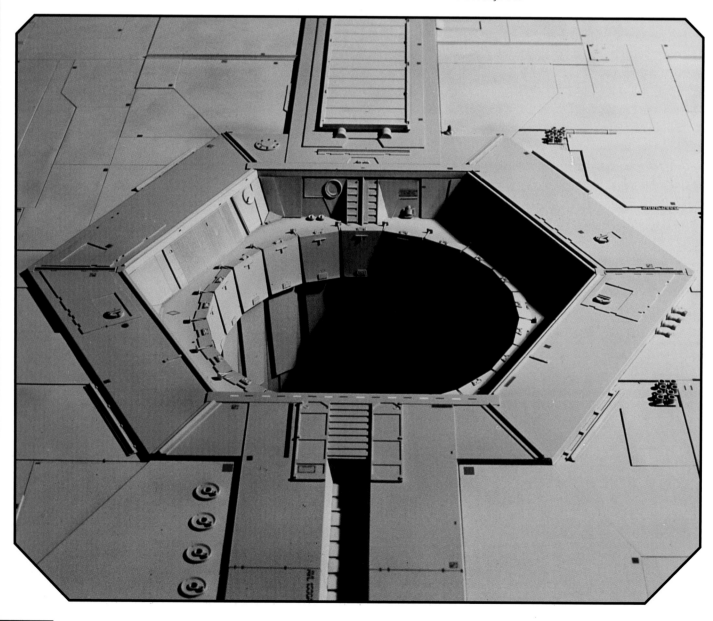

← Inside the rebel base on Yavin 4, a viewscreen displayed the Death Star's technical readouts while General Jan Dodonna briefed pilots and astromech droids on his strategy to attack the battle station. Dodonna instructed the pilots to fire proton torpedoes into a specific thermal exhaust port.

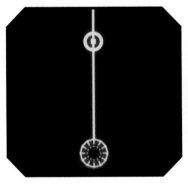

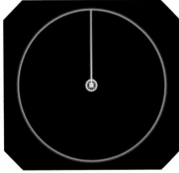

↑ Strategic animatic of a proton torpedo traveling into the shaft beneath the exhaust port.

↑ The ray-shielded exhaust port's shaft led directly to the Death Star's reactor system.

↑ A precise hit would trigger a chain reaction that would destroy the entire battle station.

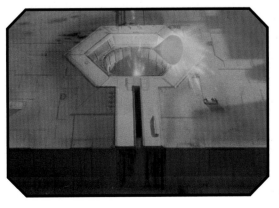

← Rebel starfighters swarmed the Death Star in a coordinated effort to reach their target.

Although hyperdrives are considered much 'cleaner' than their highly-radioactive sublight drive counterparts, they require more power to hurl their host beyond lightspeed. The Death Star's hyperspace motivator units comprised linked banks of field generators—the same systems used by Imperial Star Destroyers. One hundred twenty-three individual hyperspace generators, tied into a single navigational matrix, were necessary to carry the Death Star beyond the speed of light. The intense power generated within the battle station, combined with its great mass, gave it both magnetic and artificial gravitational fields equal to those of a natural body many times its size.

Every hypedrive station on the Death Star had dedicated astrogation/hyperdrive computers. Collectively, these computers housed coordinates for every system in Imperial Space, and also thousands of other systems that the Empire intended to conquer. As with any hyperdrive-equipped vessel, all hyperspace jump calculations had to be incredibly precise to guarantee that the Death Star would arrive completely intact at any given destination. Engineers and technicians manned the hyperdrive stations' control stations, checking and cross-checking their linked computer monitors to make certain that all of the Death Star's hyperdrives worked in unison.

Retractable footbridges extended between the hyperdrive stations' control stations and the central power core, allowing engineers and technicians to inspect the power core's energy readouts, check for stresses or leaks, and make any necessary repairs. Because of high radiation levels, Imperial personnel relied on droids to inspect the power core while the Death Star was traveling through hyperspace.

⬇ From the Overbridge, Darth Vader and Grand Moff Tarkin monitored the battle station's hyperspace jump to Alderaan. Moving such a large mass through hyperspace required the coordinated effort of all hyperdrive stations.

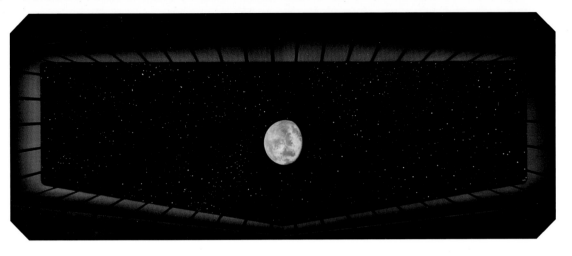

← A view of the planet Alderaan from the Death Star, shortly before Alderaan's destruction. The Death Star's hyperdrive system was linked with the navicomputer to deliver the battle station to strategic areas beyond the hazardous range of planetary or stellar gravitational forces.

1 **Charge coils**
2 **Effect channels**
3 **Energy junction**
4 **Field stabilizer plating**

5 **Horizontal boosters**
6 **Power regulator**
7 **Regulator access platform**
8 **Control station**

9 **Retractable footbridge**
10 **Turbolift**
11 **Open vertical shaft**
12 **Astrogation/hyperdrive computers**

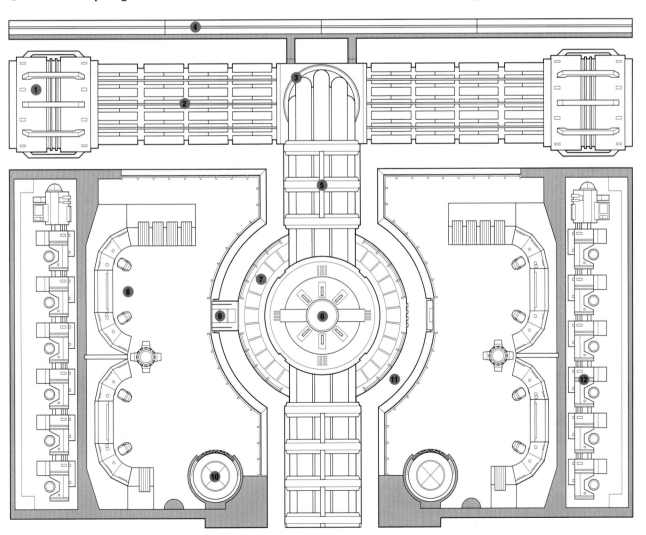

ION SUBLIGHT ENGINES

➔ After exiting hyperspace in the Yavin system, the Death Star used sublight engines to enter orbit around the giant gas planet Yavin.

The Death Star's realspace propulsion was handled by an external array of powerful ion engines, which converted the raw fusion energy of the station's core into fusion reaction particles. The converted energy was used to achieve thrust, and pressed the station's great mass into any motion dictated by the *Death Star*'s huge navicomputer banks. Engine blocks were located along the battle station's equator and also at its poles,

providing the thrust to move the massive vessel through space. While ion engines of such magnitude are highly radioactive, no other system could provide the directional control necessary for a station of such great size. Powerful vents were utilized to force the radiation out of the drive stations and into space. Engineering personnel assigned to monitor ion vent operations routinely wore protective gear to ward off radiation spillage.

1 **Thrust beam**
2 **Focusing field stabilizer**
3 **Exhaust pre-stabilizer screen**
4 **Thrust pressure manifold**
5 **Ion accelator**
6 **Sychronizing interconnectors**
7 **Magnetic chamber**
8 **Magnetic field stabilizer**
9 **Initiating coils**
10 **Support framework**
11 **Electron injectors**
12 **Power line from reactor**
13 **Drive station**

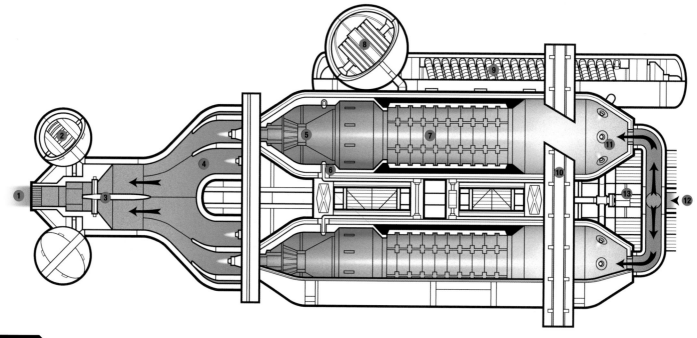

SUBLIGHT DRIVE STATION D-639

Engineering had the sole assignment of keeping the Death Star's sublight and hyperdrive engines in working order. Sublight Drive Station D-639 was a typical layout, designed for engineers and technicians to operate and monitor the sublight drives. Two main consoles overlooked a crew pit, where personnel were tasked with ensuring the sublight drives remained fully operational at all times. Although the numerous controls

and equipment in the sublight drive station were constructed with durable materials, Imperial designers anticipated that the constant use of various controls would inevitably lead to some becoming damaged. The station's small parts shop enabled the engineering team to make minor repairs quickly and without leaving the station. Droid technicians were also on standby to repair or upgrade delicate circuitry.

1. **Radiation vents**
2. **Sublight drive units**
3. **Power cells**
4. **Power level monitoring**
5. **Crew pit**
6. **Main consoles**
7. **Briefing room**
8. **Computer room**
9. **Turbolift cluster**
10. **Small parts shop**
11. **Engineer office**
12. **Auxiliary helm**

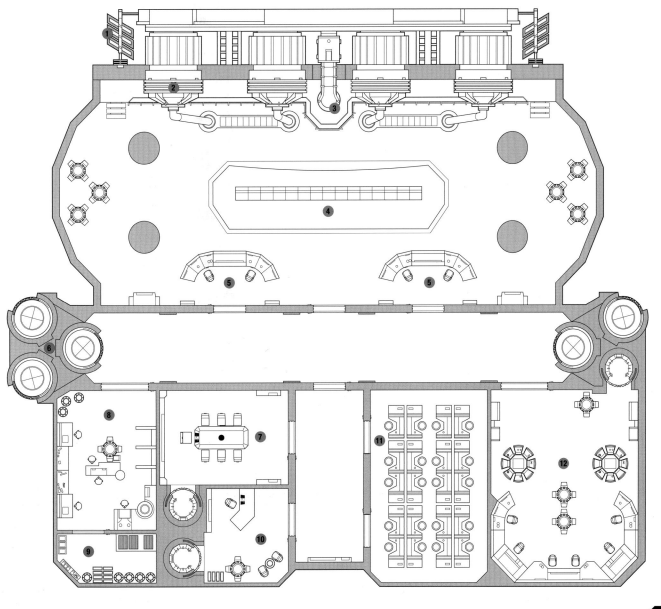

HANGAR BAYS

Excerpts from Personal Data Journal Entry #463, Grand Moff Tarkin recording

In his initial concept designs for the Expeditionary Battle Planetoid, Raith Sienar was so preoccupied by the energy and space requirements for the massive weapon systems that he neglected to consider accommodations for the spacecraft necessary for the battle station's defense, maintenance, and other purposes. To his credit, his concepts did incorporate docking systems for large warships, and also a sophisticated network of multidirectional lift tubes, but as the design process progressed toward the construction of a much larger battle station, it became apparent that small shuttles would be more often the most efficient means of travel from one surface sector to another. Obviously, such travel would only be workable if the station had an abundance of hangars and docking bays. Furthermore, the Emperor agreed that the superweapon should be as autonomous as possible, that it would more effectively induce fear as a singular weapon of destruction than if it moved across the galaxy with a conspicuous armada.

Not surprisingly, Bevel Lemelisk's designs for the hangars have exceeded my expectations. The Death Star will easily accommodate thousands of TIE fighters, and will boast more hangar bays than the average commercial spaceport. He has strategically positioned numerous tractor beam projectors and docking bays for the express purpose of capturing enemy spacecraft.

A subtle yet most impressive accomplishment in Lemelisk's design addresses how the Death Star's many hangars and bays will be oriented with the station's expansive gravity systems. Although the majority of the Death Star's inhabited areas will be engineered for a gravity orientation that is toward the core, most of the hangar bays and the corridors that immediately surround the hangars will be built perpendicular to the core. In other words, nearly every hangar above and below the equator, as well as those along the equator itself, is engineered so gravity seems to generate from the same direction, so from almost any given hangar, the station's south pole is perceived as "down" and the north pole as "up". This orientation will not only allow ships to arrive and depart from the station in remarkably uniform trajectories, but will simplify many junctures of the lift tube systems and encourage an innate awareness to hierarchy throughout the station.

I admit, I had assumed Lemelisk would follow Sienar's original plan to place hangars at various angles along the station's surface area, but Lemelisk's solution is more than brilliant. It embraces the greatness of Imperial technology and defies the natural laws of gravity. Simply put, the Death Star is perfection.

EQUATORIAL DOCKING BAYS (BAY 327)

Numerous and various-sized hangar bays ringed the Death Star like latitude lines. The larger bays were surrounded by support decks which contained vehicle maintenance shops, emergency medical stations, pilot ready rooms, and repulsorlift shafts connecting to deep storage bays. Smaller shuttle hangars could handle one or two craft and were found all over the battle station. They were normally used for station personnel movement. Ships first arriving at the Death Star or leaving for deep space normally worked with a latitude bay control tower.

Like most Death Star hangars, Docking Bay 327 had tractor beam projectors and interior emergency repulsor fields to deal with damaged vessels. Tractor beams guided craft that had lost engines or directional thrusters, and emergency generators could flood a bay with a repulsorfield cushion landings. The walls and decks were lined with power cell chargers sockets where parked craft could obtain fuel for their next mission. Directional markings etched into the deck were

illuminated by the tower to guide ships to a safe resting place. The deck was also equipped with a large lift that transported troops, vehicles, cargo, and maintenance equipment to and from the barracks, workshops, and supply rooms located below the hangar.

DEEP STORAGE DOCKING BAYS

The Death Star's innermost hangar bays held the complement of land vehicles, backup shuttles and starfighters, and special-service vessels that were not expected to be used routinely. These vehicles were contained within stasis fields that protected them from dust and vermin, keeping each craft in perfect condition. When a ship was requisitioned from a deep storage bay, repulsor-generated antigrav fields were projected into the bay, and moved the ship out of stasis and into a repulsor shaft. From the repulsor shaft, the ship could be transported to a latitude surface hangar anywhere within the battle station.

The stasis fields were checked regularly to maintain

↓ Images obtained from an Imperial communications complex reveal a YT-1300 freighter, the *Millennium Falcon*, as it was guided by Death Star tractor beams into an equatorial docking bay. Standing beside turbolaser emplacements, stormtroopers monitor the captured craft's progress.

their integrity. Security guarded the deep storage docking bays with the same dedication as personnel who oversaw the Death Star's armories.

↑ View of Hangar Bay 327 from the docking bay control room window.

↓ A large lift delivers additional stormtroopers to the docking bay.

DOCKING BAY CONTROL ROOM

Every hangar and docking bay on the Death Star had a control room, sometimes called control towers, that overlooked the hangar. Each control room was staffed by a team that monitored the approach and departure of all craft into and out of the hangars. Control teams reported to and received orders from their zone's main control tower, which was commanded by a complete staff of maintenance

→ Imperial records confirmed the identity of Lieutenant Pol Treidum, gantry officer in charge of Docking Bay 327. Treidum surveyed the docking bay from his control room window.

personnel, emergency medical teams, and flight support personnel and droids. Each zone's main control tower contained sensor relays, flight-tracking screens, ship-to-ship communication capabilities, tractor beam and repulsorlift controls, and consoles for regulating the magnetic fields in each of the hangars and docking bays within the respective zone.

A typical docking bay control room housed computer consoles that could be used to access data and monitor other areas of the Death Star. A rack of blaster rifles was positioned close to the room's doorway so the crew would have quick access to weapons in the event that an enemy infiltrated the hangar. The room also held various security supplies, including binders to secure prisoners during their escort to the detention levels.

Each zone of the Death Star had a main control tower, which contained sensor relays, flight tracking

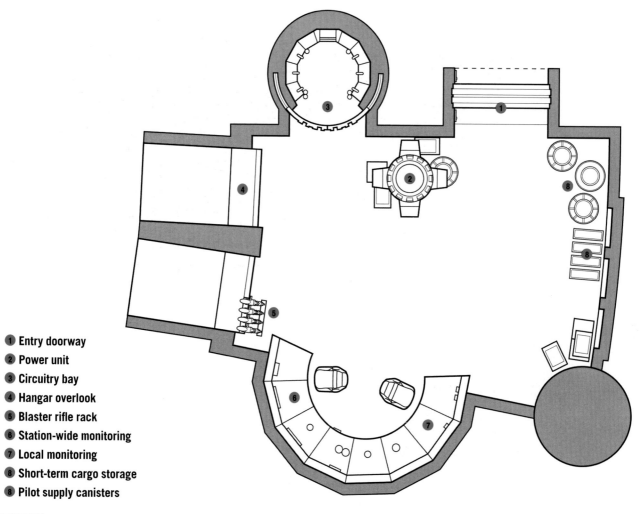

1. **Entry doorway**
2. **Power unit**
3. **Circuitry bay**
4. **Hangar overlook**
5. **Blaster rifle rack**
6. **Station-wide monitoring**
7. **Local monitoring**
8. **Short-term cargo storage**
8. **Pilot supply canisters**

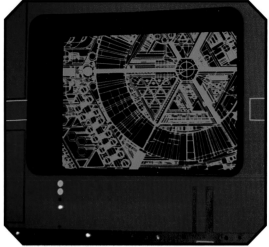

screens, ship-to-ship communication capabilities, tractor beam and repulsorlift controls, and consoles for regulating the magnetic fields in each of the hangars and docking bays within the respective zone. The tower was commanded by a complete staff of maintenance personnel, emergency medical teams, and flight support personnel and droids.

⬆ Docking bay control room officers monitored consoles with built-in comlinks, allowing them to communicate with Imperial stormtroopers and other personnel stationed aboard the Death Star.

⬆ On the control room's consoles, monitors typically displayed data regarding vehicles, personnel, and general status inside the adjoining hangar, but could also display schematics for almost every area of the Death Star.

⬅ After arriving on the Death Star with the crew of the *Millennium Falcon*, the droids C-3PO and R2-D2 accessed data from the docking bay control room's computer to help their allies liberate the captive Princess Leia Organa and escape the battle station.

EXECUTIVE DOCKING BAY

➜ **Darth Vader arrived in an executive docking bay on the second Death Star, and was met by Moff Jerjerrod, the Imperial officer who had been assigned to overseeing the battle station's construction.**

Reserved for high-ranking Imperial officers and visiting dignitaries, the Death Star's executive docking bays were located within the battle station's equatorial trench, and were extremely expansive. These bays were more heavily reinforced than those used by typical Imperial transports and starships, with additional energy-shield generators, tractor-beam projectors, and laser cannons emplaced in and around the trench walls to ensure trouble-free arrivals and departures. Small droids equipped with micro-cleaning systems were tasked with keeping all surface areas within the bays spotless and free of dust.

The largest executive docking bay was constructed specifically for Emperor Palpatine, and could accommodate hundreds of troops for arrival ceremonies. A smaller executive docking bay, reserved for Darth Vader, was located near the Emperor's bay. Both bays were designed to receive and deploy *Lambda*-class shuttles.

Like other Death Star docking bays, the executive bays had openings that appeared to be exposed to the vacuum of space. The openings were protected by powerful magnetic fields that maintained the atmosphere within the bays, but the fields could be manipulated in intensity to allow starships to enter and exit the bays. If bay control crews anticipated the arrival of a vessel with shield or engine damage, they could empty the bay of all personnel except for those in protective gear, and close the bay's blast doors to form vacuum-worthy seals to retain station atmosphere integrity.

⬇ **During the Death Star's construction, scores of Imperial stormtroopers stood in formation as the Emperor arrived to inspect the battle station.**

➔ One of the Death Star's docking bay's was reserved for Darth Vader's *Lambda*-class T-4a shuttle, manufactured by Cygnus Spaceworks.

➔ From the moment that an executive vessel's ramp was lowered, all personnel within the docking bay were required by Imperial regulations to stand at attention.

➔ Flanked by a receiving party, a senior officer was prepared to immediately debrief Darth Vader about the Death Star's status.

TIE HANGAR

While many of the Death Star's hangar bays were equipped to accommodate shuttles and other transports, most were engineered specifically to house, deploy, and service Imperial TIE fighters, which are not equipped with landing gear. The Death Star carried more than 7,000 TIE fighters. Smaller hangars contained as few as two TIE fighters, while larger hangars contained six squadrons, or 72 TIE fighters.

Each TIE hangar bay had ceiling-mounted racks that held the TIEs several meters above the deck. Pilots climbed across a gantry above the racks to reach their starfighters, and entered the TIEs through ceiling hatches. After the pilot was seated behind the controls and the hatch was sealed, the rack disengaged and dropped the TIE into the waiting repulsorlift field below. The field maneuvered the TIE to the bay opening where tractor beams automatically took control, catapulting the TIE through the hangar's magnetic forcefield and into space. When the TIE returned to the hangar, tractor beams would guide the TIE back onto the rack.

Surrounding decks were designed to offer total support to the starfighters and their pilots. The Death Star's largest TIE bays accommodated two full wings of TIEs, dwarfing similar TIE-exclusive bays in most Star Destroyers, which only held half of a wing.

1 **Ship gantry**
2 **Pilot catwalk**
3 **Boarding platform**
4 **Ladder**
5 **Ingress/egress hatch**
6 **Cockpit viewport**
7 **Retaining claw**
8 **Launch release guide**
9 **Solar array wing**
10 **Wing brace**
11 **Laser cannon**

⬇ **An elite corps within the Imperial Navy, Imperial pilots undergo a strenuous screening and testing process for admission into the TIE training program. The Death Star had 167,216 pilots.**

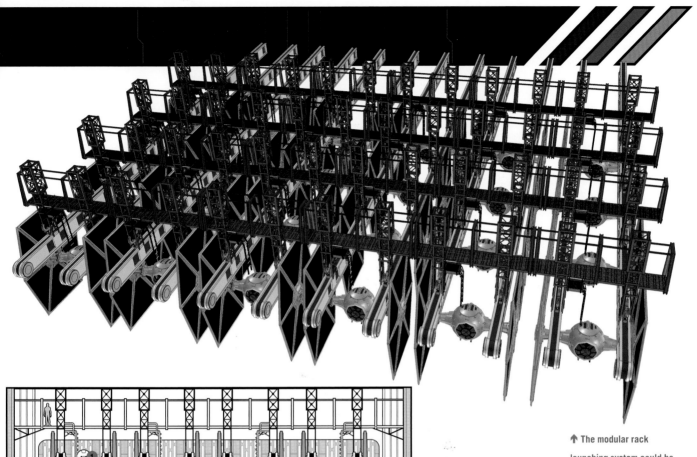

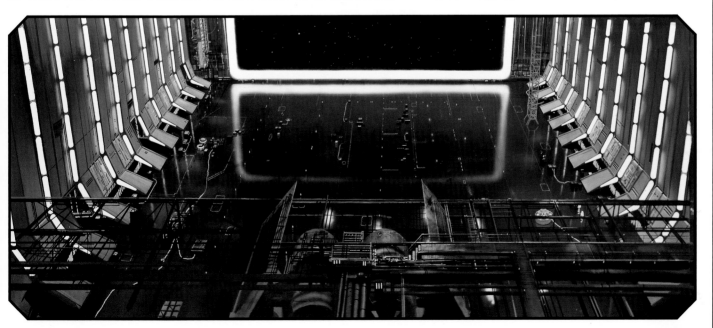

1 Open hatch
2 Transfer tunnel
3 Access doors
4 Refueling pod
5 Open blast doors
6 Service gantry

⬆ The modular rack launching system could be adjusted to accommodate the maximum capacity of TIEs in different sized hangars.

⬇ A TIE bomber, secured above a hangar bay floor, carried a payload that included orbital mines and proton bombs.

CITY SPRAWLS & TRENCHES

Excerpt from the Personal Diary of Imperial Admiral Conan Antonio Motti, commander of the Naval operations aboard the Death Star.

From a distance, the Death Star resembles an airless, runaway moon with a large, single impact crater. But upon closer inspection, it becomes apparent that this 'moon' is hardly a natural body. The crater has an obvious symmetry that could never be the result of some random impact. Below the crater, a dark line wraps around the sphere's equator, bisecting its upper and lower hemispheres. Canyons, ridges, and valleys come into view, but unlike natural formations these surface details run in parallel lines and at right angles, and form true geometric patterns.

The 'crater', of course, is what Death Star gunners call the 'Eye', the collector lens that focuses the superlaser. The dark line at the equator is a trench that holds docking bays and weapons emplacements, and this trench is linked to many others. And all the formations on the surface are actually expanses of modular Imperial constructions that form city sprawls. Although the superlaser is certainly the battle station's most prominent feature, the trenches and sprawls are no less amazing. All those interconnected clusters and masses of thermal exhaust ports, heat sinks, sublight thrusters, hyperdrive thrusters, transparisteel viewports, cosmic-ray sinks, energy flush vents, and navigation lights add up to the most awe-inspiring invention, the most incredible weapon.

I wish I could see the faces of the Empire's enemies when they first behold the Death Star, and they immediately realize that they are powerless to defend themselves. I want very much to personally witness the fear in their eyes.

← This image, recorded by a damaged astromech droid from the aft of a rebel-piloted X-wing starfighter, shows a TIE fighter and a TIE Advanced x1 prototype fighter in the Death Star's latitudinal polar trench during the Battle of Yavin.

Because prefabricated Imperial building materials were used for most of the Death Star's habitable sections, structures and layouts of the city sprawls strongly resembled planetary Imperial outposts and research stations. City Sprawl North 7: A68, located in the Death Star's northern hemisphere, zone N7, was typical of the hundreds of regional constructs that dotted the battle station's surface. Turbolasers were housed on multi-storied towers that were grouped into skyline batteries, all strategically positioned to work together in combined offensive attacks. Huge workstations supported and operated shield projectors alongside space-traffic control towers. Giant communications islands, bordered by myriad sensor arrays, handled outgoing and incoming holo and voice transmissions.

Although City Sprawl North 7: A68 operated as an independent 'village', its sensors and communications nets constantly fed data to Zone N7's command sector computers, which in turn fed to the overbridge interior central computers for analysis and compilation. The computers collectively created a complete view of all activity and the overall status of the Death Star's exterior for the command sector's perusal. When more coordinated activity was necessary to examine, repair, or defend city sprawls, the overbridge could take control of the computers in every zone.

City Sprawl North 7: A68 had representatives from all the major sectors operating aboard the Death Star. Command, military, security, service/technical, hangar, and general sectors maintained operation centers within the confines of the sprawl. Each operation center had a commanding officer who reported to interior command. The chain of command worked up to Operations Command and the command triumvirate of Grand Moff Tarkin, Admiral Motti, and General Tagge.

⬇ **Zone N7 of the Death Star's northern hemisphere.**

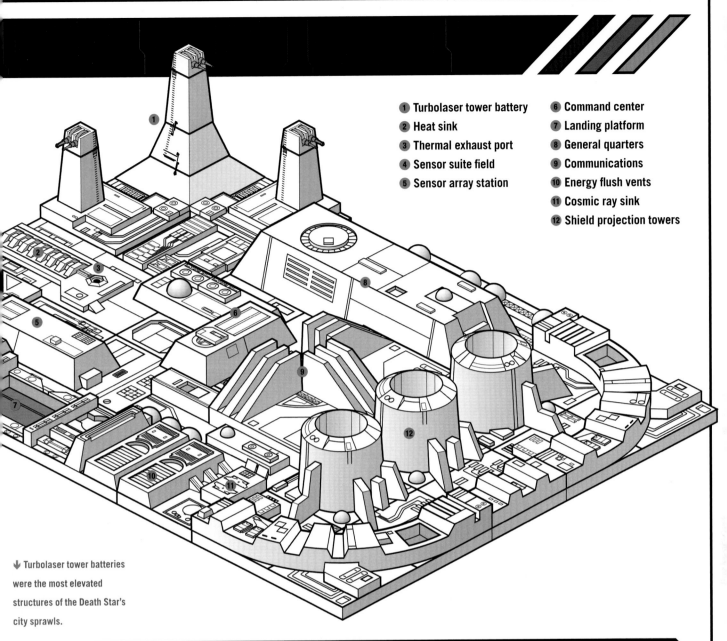

1 Turbolaser tower battery
2 Heat sink
3 Thermal exhaust port
4 Sensor suite field
5 Sensor array station
6 Command center
7 Landing platform
8 General quarters
9 Communications
10 Energy flush vents
11 Cosmic ray sink
12 Shield projection towers

⬇ Turbolaser tower batteries were the most elevated structures of the Death Star's city sprawls.

TRENCH VIEWS

The long trenches that cut across the Death Star's surface at right angles contained service ports, docking bays and hangars, and also vents and ports for expelling built-up heat. Typical trenches stretched for many kilometers in a straight line, and some circumnavigated the entire sphere. The most prominent trench wrapped around the battle station's equator.

Major and minor trenches were used by pilots of shuttles and starfighters as directional markers. Because traveling via shuttle between distant zones on the Death Star was often more efficient than traveling via turbolifts, shuttle pilots also used the major trenches as flight paths.

While low-energy shield projectors covered the many access and disposal ports in the trenches, the main source of protection came from the XX-9 heavy turbolaser towers that were positioned along the top of the trenches as well as along the trench floors. The trenches' defensive systems were programmed to prevent the turbolaser batteries from accidentally blasting each other or damaging the station's hull and surface structures.

Major trenches divided numerous city sprawls, but

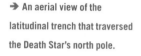

➜ An aerial view of the latitudinal trench that traversed the Death Star's north pole.

⬇ The battle station's latitudinal trench was wide enough to accommodate three single-pilot starfighters in attack formation.

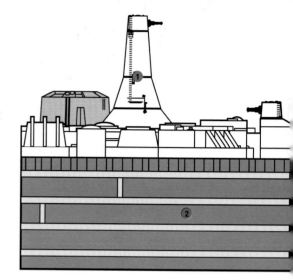

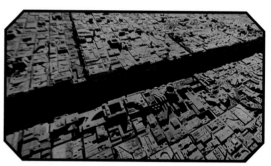

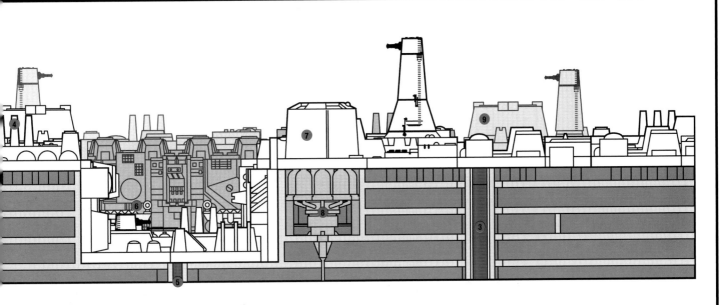

some minor trenches traversed sprawls. Maintenance crews used tractor beams to ensure that jettisoned trash would not fall back or drift into any trenches.

Although the Death Star's designers were aware of the fact that the trenches were accessible to enemy starfighters, they were confident that such an attack could be readily defeated by Imperial firepower, and would not cause significant damage.

1. **Turbolaser tower**
2. **Sub-surface levels**
3. **Turbolift shaft**
4. **Communications array**
5. **Thermal exhaust shaft**
6. **Ray shield projectors**
7. **Shield projection tower**
8. **Shield generator**
9. **Defense-field generator**
10. **Power distribution nodes**
11. **Service access port**
12. **Shuttle landing pad**
13. **Cosmic ray sink**
14. **Sensor suite field**
15. **Energy flush vent**
16. **Heat sink**

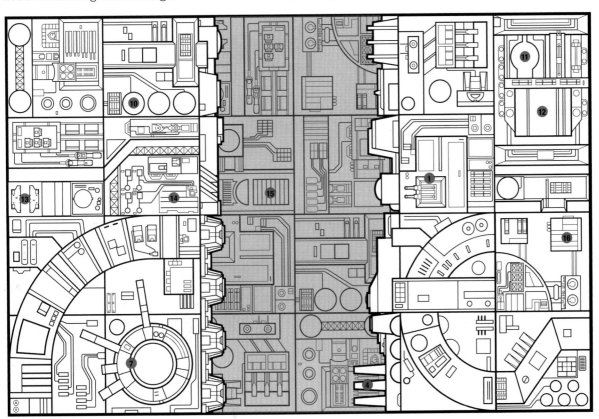

GENERAL QUARTERS

All of the operating forces stationed in North 7: A68 resided in a large general quarters building. Living quarters ranged from austere barracks for the crew to multi-room luxury apartments for the senior officers. Lower officers shared their quarters with as many as three other officers of the same rank, while higher officers received private quarters. The crew quarters bunked as many as 50 individuals per room, but combat pilots and highly-skilled technical crew members received better accommodations than the average service tech.

In addition to living quarters, the general quarters building had recreational areas, mess halls, and sport courts. Maintenance and management of general quarters fell to Battle Station Operations, but the building was divided into areas where army and navy operations had jurisdiction, and their own respective support personnel monitored the activities of the crew and officers.

The crew ate in a large, open room full of tables and benches. Meal trays were delivered by droids, and the fare was cultivated from the Death Star's food and water synthesization plants. The officer mess halls featured more secluded dining facilities, and the food came from the huge stores of refrigerated and dried goods imported by Imperial cargo ships.

→ Imperial officers were quartered close to their stormtrooper barracks in their sectors, allowing the officers to summon and mobilize the troops quickly.

→ Except for when they were asleep or assigned to individual sentry posts, stormtroopers were rarely alone in any area of the Death Star.

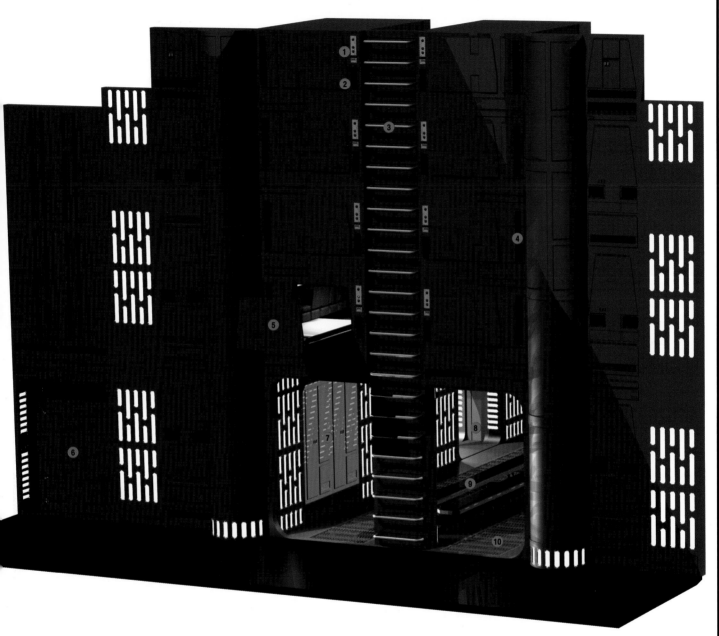

STORMTROOPER BARRACKS

Taking inspiration from barracks used by Republic Army clone troopers during the Clone Wars, the Death Star's designers created ladder-accessible enclosed chambers for stormtroopers. Each chamber held a single, extendible bunk, and was equipped with a viewscreen, comlink, controls for lighting and air conditioning, and built-in sensors that allowed stormtrooper squad leaders, droid medical teams, and Imperial Intelligence agents to monitor the stormtroopers. If Imperial Intelligence had reason to suspect a stormtrooper was a Rebel Alliance agent,

1. Bunk control panel
2. Trooper ID plate
3. Bunk access ladder
4. Independent air handler
5. Open trooper bunk
6. Refresher
7. Gear lockers
8. To sonic showers
9. Benches
10. Ventilated flooring

they were authorized to use remote controls to lock the stormtrooper within his chamber. Stormtroopers placed their armor and weapons in lockers before ascending to their respective bunks.

→ A Stormtrooper takes aim with a BlasTech SE-14r light repeating blaster.

The Death Star's recreation areas typically consisted of a main chamber filled with running tracks, weight-training machines, calisthenic and aerobic training space, martial-arts sparring areas, and other personal exercise stations. Side chambers featured lockers and sonic showers, holo obstacle and combat training simulation facilities, equipment and exercise droid storage, refreshment bars, multipurpose sport courts, puttie course, and recreation staff offices.

Every member of the Death Star's crew was encouraged to use the exercise equipment. To maintain their fighting skills and learn new techniques, all crew members were periodically assigned to the combat training and obstacle course facilities. Combat training included refresher courses in handling blasters, grenades, and heavy weapons, and lessons or assigned instructions in melee and biological weapons. The obstacle course's computer held programs that generated an endlessly expandable variety of holographic representations of terrain and situations, all engineered to test the crew's limits of ability and ingenuity.

↓ A selection of blasters issued aboard the Death Star and used regularly in combat training.

The recreation facilities' refreshment bars served healthy drinks that replenished vitamins and vital fluids lost after a strenuous workout or examination. The sport courts could be configured for playing various popular games, including wallball, kel tag, and repulsor puck.

BlasTech DLT-19 heavy blaster rifle

Merr-Sonn Power 5 heavy blaster pistol

BlasTech E-11 blaster rifle

1. **Lift to track**
2. **To refreshment bar**
3. **Sparring courts**
4. **Melee training lane**
5. **Benches**
6. **Exercise stations**
7. **To showers/lockers**
8. **Calisthenics area**
9. **Weight machines**
10. **Elevated track**
11. **Chief trainer's office**
12. **Refresher**
13. **Maintenance office**
14. **Holo obstacle &**
    combat simulation
15. **Multipurpose courts**
16. **Equipment room**
17. **Practice range**
18. **Range office**
19. **Turbolift cluster**
20. **Shaft**

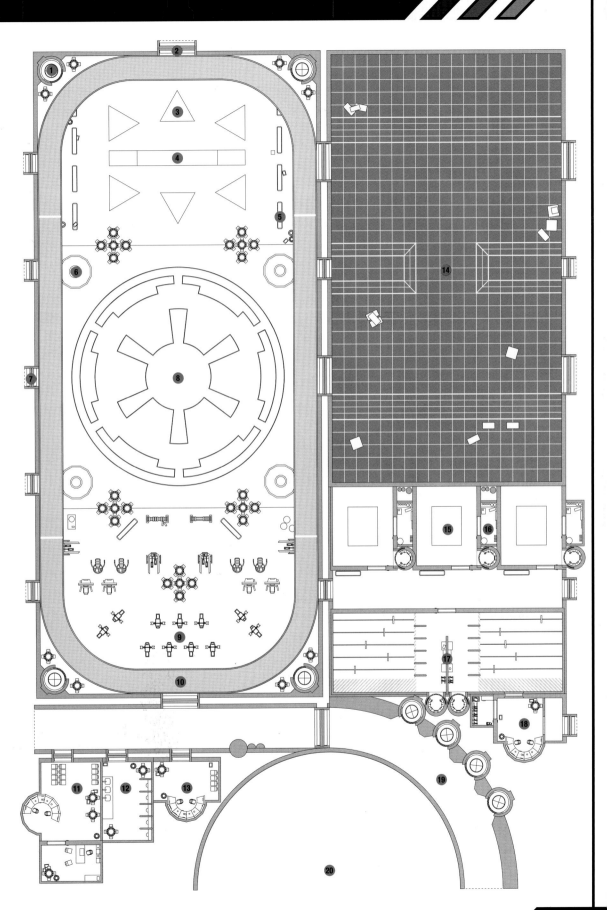

TURBOLIFTS

Turbolift conveyances utilize repulsorlift field generators—the most common form of technology in the galaxy—to transport passengers through architectural shafts or hollow tubes. By filling long stretches of crisscrossing cylindrical shafts with repulsor fields, Bevel Lemelisk's design team created an efficient travel system that connected all sectors of the battle station.

On any given level of the Death Star, turbolift conveyances were positioned every few hundred meters and typically in clusters to guarantee at least one turbolift car would always be waiting for Imperial personnel. Turbolift cars raced at incredible speeds, and could cover many kilometers per minute. Despite the speed and availability of the cars, it was often faster and more convenient to take a shuttle from one hangar bay to another that was close to the final destination, especially when traveling between different zones on the surface of the Death Star.

The turbolift cars were engineered to rotate, which was necessary because most of the battle station's inner gravity orientation transitions were accomplished by turbolifts. During transit, the car rotated to match the orientation of the destination deck, while compensators

→ A cross-sectional turbolift map illustrates the major routes within zones 3 and 9. Knowing that shuttles would be a more efficient mode of transport between widely separated sections of the Death Star, the designers incorporated lift tubes that led directly to shuttle systems.

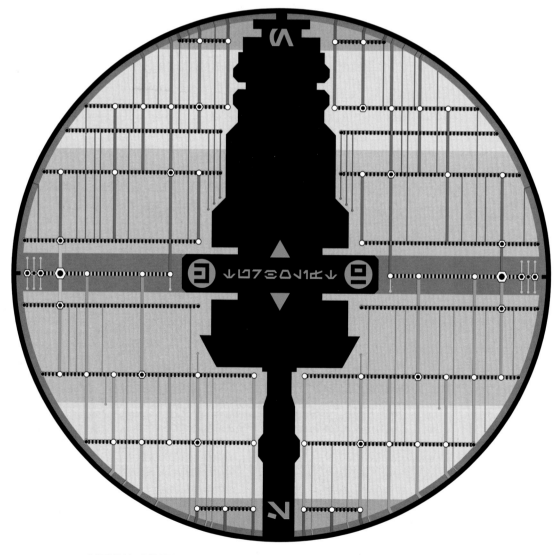

LATERAL SHUTTLE SYSTEM
EQUATORIAL LIFTS
NORTHERN HEMISPHERE LIFTS
SOUTHERN HEMISPHERE LIFTS
POLAR REGION LIFTS

◉ CONNECTION POINT TO CONCENTRIC SHUTTLE SYSTEM

○ CONNECTION POINT TO LATERAL SHUTTLE SYSTEM

kept passengers comfortable and unaware of any change in gravity orientation.

Turbolift cars were activated by voice command, but access to certain areas of the Death Star required a rank cylinder key, as such areas were limited to specific crew designations and ranks. If a crewman requested a turbolift car to take him to an area that was closed to his classification, and he failed to provide a rank cylinder key, the turbolift's computer would prevent the car from moving. If the requested destination was an especially sensitive area, the computer would inform security of the crewman's possible intent to trespass.

1 **Upper repulsor**
2 **Orientation sensors**
3 **Power charge coils**
4 **Magnetic guide rails**

5 **Outer doors (open)**
6 **Artificial gravity plate**
7 **Repulsor lift**
8 **Emergency mag-brake**

⬇ **Executive lift tubes were reserved for Darth Vader and high-ranking officers. Concealed scanners and security devices prevented unauthorized use.**

⬋ **Rebel authorities have confirmed the stormtroopers in this image were actually Luke Skywalker and Han Solo, accompanied by their 'captive', Chewbacca.**

CORRIDORS

The Death Star's gray-and-black corridors appeared strictly utilitarian, but were actually part of the battle station's complex network of linked systems. Energy from the station's reactor was channeled through and around the corridors to provide power for lighting, ventilation, and air-conditioning, and was also utilized for the station's artificial gravity systems.

Gravity within the station was maintained by omni-directional gravity boosters built into decks, walls, and ceilings. Easily adjustable gravity boosters were designed to allow gravity orientation to be altered from sector to sector, or even corridor to corridor. While hangar bays imposed gravity perpendicular to the battle station's core, adjoining corridors shifted the gravity orientation toward the core. To prevent accidents, numerous warning signs were activated when the gravity orientation changed from one section to the next.

The corridors were designed not only for pedestrian access throughout the battle station but also for military drilling exercises. At any given time, patrols of stormtroopers could be found marching on various levels of every zone while security personnel used restricted corridors to test their weapons and scanners in mock hunts for rebel interlopers.

① **Luminous conduits**   ④ **Air vents**
② **Light diffuser**   ⑤ **Air return**
③ **Perforated front panel**   ⑥ **Power lines**

➜ Always on the lookout for saboteurs and rebel insurgents, Imperial stormtroopers were an intimidating presence as they marched through the Death Star's corridors.

BLAST DOORS

The Death Star was equipped with two types of doors: regular doors, which were generally found between rooms and corridors in general quarters areas, and blast doors, which separated corridors from command centers, docking bays, and adjoining corridors. Both types retracted into walls, ceilings, and floors. Blast doors utilized magnetic seals, making them virtually impossible to unlock without proper authorization codes, and were impervious to standard blaster fire.

The Death Star's security personnel issued rank cylinders to Imperial officers and crew members. Rank cylinders allowed users to access secured areas and doors, as well as to navigate and access information from the Imperial computer network. Stormtroopers used their comlinks to contact security officers when they required blast doors to be opened or closed at specific locations.

Blast doors that separated docking bays from corridors were well guarded, and could be opened and closed remotely by the docking-bay control room, and also by way of consoles on the walls beside the doors. The docking bay blast doors were reinforced to protect the rest the station from potentially dangerous cargoes.

← Wide blast doors retracted into doorways and separated corridors at practical and strategic intersections. To trap or eliminate trespassers, corridors could be rapidly sealed, locked, and depressurized.

← Recovered from a military communications complex on Galvoni III, recordings from a Death Star security camera yielded images of two interlopers making a narrow escape through a closing blast door.

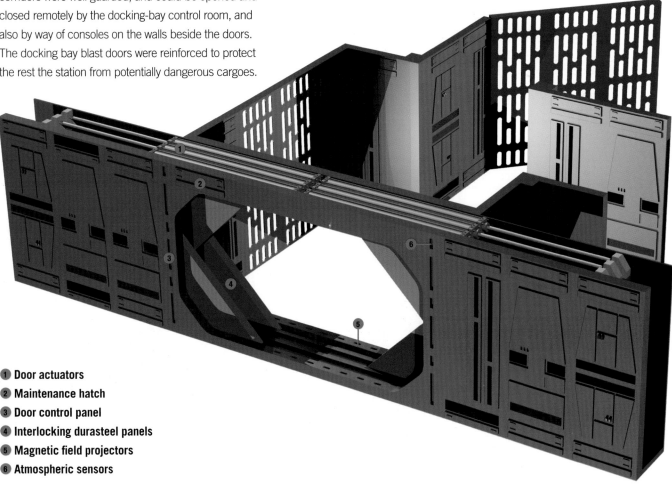

1. **Door actuators**
2. **Maintenance hatch**
3. **Door control panel**
4. **Interlocking durasteel panels**
5. **Magnetic field projectors**
6. **Atmospheric sensors**

AIR SHAFTS & EXTENDIBLE BRIDGES

Numerous areas throughout the Death Star consisted of vast air shafts. These shafts helped circulate air, pressurize the battle station's habitable sections, and also channeled heat that expended from generators located within the shafts. All shafts incorporated Imperial-designed superannuated System Four ventilation systems, and were built in compliance with Imperial standards.

Death Star personnel could traverse the air shafts via extendible bridges, which retracted into the shaft walls. Controls for the bridges were built into the frames of doorways for bridge-access areas. Although most bridges were wide enough to allow at least two personnel to walk abreast, few bridges had protective railings, as they were conceived specifically for use by Imperial stormtroopers and ambulatory service and maintenance droids, who by their respective training and programming did not experience vertigo. Imperial officers and other crew members typically avoided the bridges, and claimed the lift tubes were a much more efficient mode of transportation within the station.

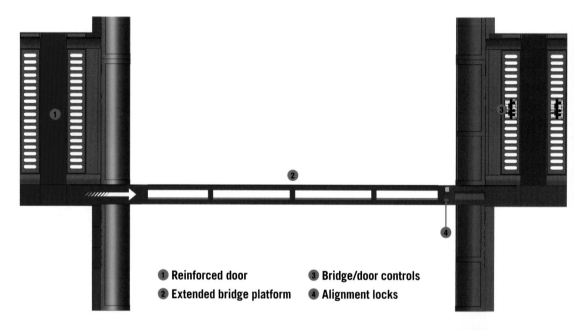

1 Reinforced door   **3** Bridge/door controls

2 Extended bridge platform   **4** Alignment locks

➜ Recovered from an Imperial communications complex on Galvoni III, this image shows Princess Leia Organa and Luke Skywalker on the edge of a retracted bridge in the Death Star's central core shaft.

↑ After a group of rebels infiltrated the Death Star's central core shaft, stormtroopers took advantage of upper-level hatches as strategic firing points.

↓ Kuat PJC 223 power generators were mounted to the walls of the Death Star's central core shaft. Imperial designers were only concerned by the functionality and structural integrity of the generators, and never imagined that the units' lower pipes might provide trespassers with an opportunity for escape.

1. **Maintenance hatch**
2. **Controls to extend bridge**
3. **Reinforced door**
4. **Magnetic alignment pins**
5. **Non-slip plating**
6. **Edge safety sensors**
7. **Retracted bridge**
8. **Bridge alignment locks**

SECURITY SECTOR

Recovered Imperial Datafile #003729.61v:
Grand Moff Tarkin's introductory address
to Death Star Security Officers

As you all have access to Imperial personnel records, I must assume that you are familiar with certain details of my own military career, that long before my appointment to this battle station, I was the Republic Outland Regions Security Force Commander. I mention this to assure you that I am more than well aware of your duties and responsibilities as members of the Death Star's security sector.

I have always maintained that the primary purpose of security is to maintain the peace. But as security officers, I expect you to not only honor the rules and regulations of the Imperial military establishment but also adhere to proper decorum at all times, especially when maintaining the security of high-ranking officers and visiting officials.

I must stress that the Death Star is not just a battle station, but a community comprised of hundreds of neighborhoods. The survival of the community depends upon its members getting along and working together smoothly.

Unfortunately, all communities suffer some level of tension and personal violence. Should any crewmember stray from their duties, or any officer abuse the power entrusted to him, I expect the surveillance branch to report such transgressions to the wardens immediately. Should an argument or discussion between crewmembers get, shall we say, out of hand, I fully expect the enforcement wardens to put down the disturbance and restore order.

← Darth Vader leads a contingent of Imperial officers through a security sector on the Death Star.

Charged with patrolling and guarding vital or off-limits areas aboard the Death Star, Imperial security officers—known throughout the Empire as wardens—also maintained the detention cell blocks, policed corridors, and protected visiting officials. Wardens were among the only Imperial officers on the battle station to carry personal weapons at all times. They were assigned to several different security divisions, including enforcement, protection, surveillance, and detention.

The surveillance division worked with enforcement and protection to create a complete umbrella of security aboard the battle station. Relying on a myriad of hidden cameras, sensors, mobile remotes and droids, surveillance stations remained on alert throughout all duty shifts.

The wardens themselves were under constant surveillance and observation, as each standard security sector was required to provide office space and reasonable assistance to the Imperial Security Bureau (ISB). The ISB served as a fact-finding and special-

assignments division of the Imperial bureaucracy, and was represented by agents who specialized in surveillance, investigations, internal affairs, interrogation, re-education, and enforcement. Because the ISB's policing and surveillance techniques were even more harsh than typical Imperial security standards, and because they were known to place undercover agents among military and technical-support personnel, security forces throughout the Empire maintained a tense relationship with the ISB.

Each security sector maintained its own armory store. Amories contained a wealth of weapons, ammunition, and protective gear. Blaster pistols and rifles, grenades, mounted laser cannons, melee weapons, and body armor were typically stored behind locked blast doors. Turbolifts delivered security personnel to larger armories that were connected to nearby hangar bays, and which held the Army's land combat vehicles, including AT-AT walkers and repulsortanks.

⬇ Although white-armored stormtroopers assisted Imperial security officers on the Death Star, they were hardly subservient, as they also served to ensure that all officers complied with the policies of the Emperor's New Order.

← Imperial scanning crews used portable equipment that included an Idellian Arrays ILF-4500-2 life-form scanner. More sophisticated than the Death Star's military-grade long-range sensors, the ILF-4500-2 can more readily detect concealed life forms.

→ The floor plan of Security Sector N7: A68-1 was typical of similar facilities on the Death Star.

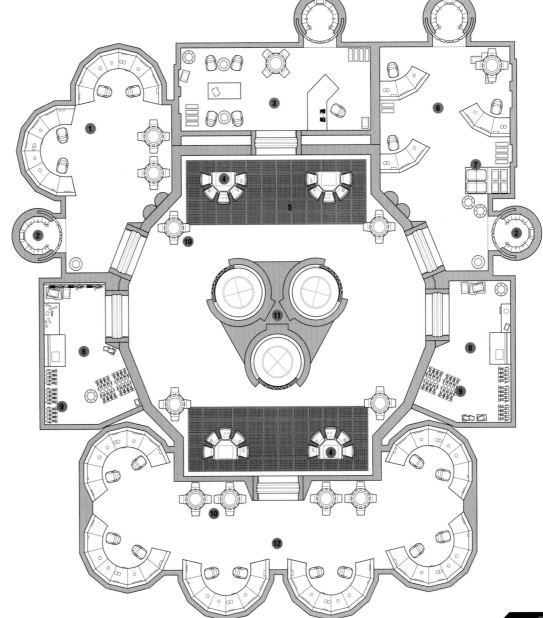

1. **Watch stations**
2. **Circuitry bay**
3. **Imperial Security Bureau office**
4. **Guard posts**
5. **Grated flooring**
6. **Security office**
7. **Equipment rack**
8. **Armory**
9. **Blaster rifle racks**
10. **Power units**
11. **Turbolift cluster**
12. **Surveillance stations**

Detention was the branch of security that maintained the Death Star's detention blocks which held individuals who had been charged for infractions. Typical 'guests' in the detention block cells included political prisoners, criminals, saboteurs, and Imperial personnel who disobeyed orders.

Detention blocks were located away from the main command and personnel areas in the Death Star, and were accessible by turbolifts. Like most chambers in the battle station, the walls were dark gray metal, but the floors were grilled and illuminated by red lights. Detention wardens and guards were stationed in the block's control room, and were trained to handle prisoners and maintain their cells. Cells had magnetic-locked doors and extremely utilitarian interiors, consisting of little more than bare-metal walls and a built-in metal bench.

The guard stations in the control room held monitors linked to wall and ceiling-mounted holocam units, which kept a constant watch over everyone and every movement in the block's workstations. The security cameras were in turn linked to wall-mounted BlasTech Class VI automated laser projectors, and fed targeting data to the laser's combat computer. Beyond the control room, a flight of steps ascended to the cell bay, a long corridor lined with cell doors.

The grilled floors were engineered so that the entire cell bay, including the cells themselves, could be sluiced out automatically, removing all traces of blood and other unpleasant by-products of torture and terror. Grills were also located along the side of the corridor to allow the waste to exit.

⬇ Imperial records confirmed the identity of Lieutenant Shann Childsen (foreground), who was in charge of the Imperial wardens in the control room of Detention Block AA-23. Armed with blaster pistols, wardens monitored prisoners, maintained authority, and prevented escapes.

① **Multi-dimensional cameras**
② **Thermographic sensor**
③ **Status indicator lights**
④ **Audio sensor**
⑤ **Lens plate**
⑥ **Mounting plate**

➔ Ceiling-mounted automated holocam units recorded all proceedings within the battle station's detention block and transmitted visual and audio data to each zone's command sector authority.

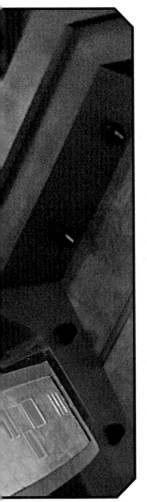

⬅ This image of rebel infiltrators attacking a Death Star detention block was recovered from a transmission to the Imperial communications complex on Galvoni III.

⬅ The Death Star's detention block walls were lined with embedded BlasTech Class VI automated laser projectors. Nicknamed laser traps, these automated blasters were typically found in Imperial prisons and labor camps, where they were used to suppress inmate uprisings.

MSE DROID

The most common droid aboard the Death Star was the MSE-6 general-purpose droid. Each MSE-6 is a Class-3 droid equipped with a single modular circuit matrix that can hold only one skill at a time, but the matrices are inexpensive and so easy to install that one MSE-6 can reprogram another without difficulty. Standard MSE-6 skill matrices include elementary repair, security checks, message delivery, janitorial cleanup, and basic computer programming.

The MSE-6 was introduced years ago by the now-defunct Chadra-Fan company Rebaxan Columni. Chadra-Fan engineers patterned the MSE-6 after the pleeky, a diminutive pet animal from their homeworld, Chad III, and were so confident that the droid would appeal to countless consumers that they manufactured hundreds of billions of units. Unfortunately, consumers from dozens of worlds quickly realized that the small, scurrying droids and their audiocast patterns resembled various species of disease-carrying vermin, and Rebaxan Columni was inundated with billions of returns and requests for refunds. The company managed to stave off bankruptcy by offering a cut-rate deal on the entire production run to the Republic Army and Navy, who needed the droids for their warships. Subsequently, MSE-6s were adopted by the Imperial Army and Navy, and can be found on nearly every Imperial vessel and station.

The MSE-6's outer casing can conceal two retractable manipulator arms, one for heavy-duty work and the other for delicate operations. A sensitive auditory sensor is located on either side of the casing, and an electro-photoreceptor and miniature holocam are located on the front. When the MSE-6 is used a courier, it utilizes a small compartment to hold sealed orders and classified documents. Once locked, the compartment cannot be opened without an authorized voice-code.

The MSE-6 travels on a maneuverable set of treaded wheels and can move forward and backward quite rapidly. Despite their inflexible programming and propensity to flee from almost any unfamiliar noise, the Empire relied upon the droids to guide troops through the Death Star's labyrinthine corridors. These droids were also routinely sent into the battle station's ventilation ducts to inspect damage from mynock infestations and to drive off the energy-eating creatures.

→ Staying close to walls in Death Star corridors, MSE droids formed trains to conserve energy, maintain orderly lines of travel, and avoid collisions with other droids and Imperial personnel.

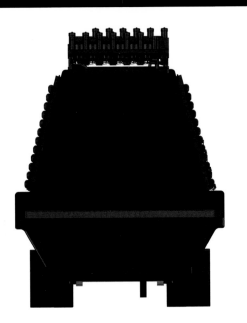

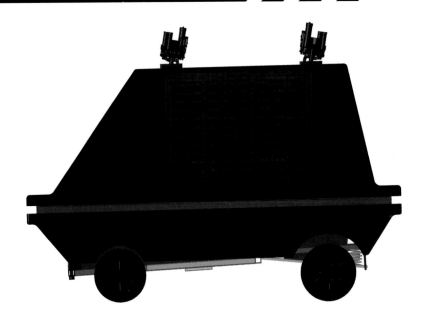

1. Encoded order/command cylinders
2. Mission sub-processor module
3. Logic processor module
4. Command processor module
5. Acoustic navigation sensors
6. Electrophoto sensor band
7. General diagnostic port
8. Holo-encoder cartridge
9. Protective casing
10. Environmental imager

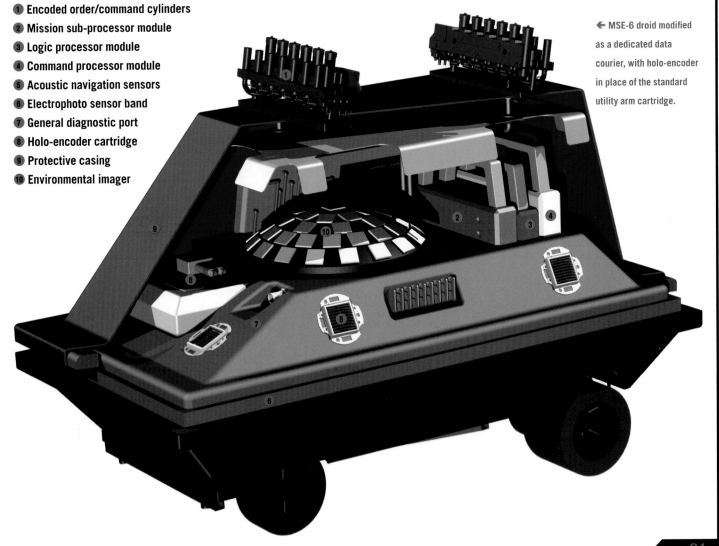

← MSE-6 droid modified as a dedicated data courier, with holo-encoder in place of the standard utility arm cartridge.

IT-O INTERROGATOR DROID

Developed by the Imperial Security Bureau, the IT-O interrogator droid uses numerous tools of torture to obtain information from enemies of the Empire.

The spherical droid, less than a meter in diameter, is encased in a glossy black shell, and hovers above the ground on low-power repulsors. Its surface is studded with an array of needles, probes, optic sensors, and audio receptors. Although the droid is equipped with a vocabulator capable of producing speech, the droid typically serves as a silent partner to an Imperial Security Bureau agent or other personnel authorized to question prisoners.

In designing the IT-O, Imperial engineers incorporated technology from top-of-the-line medical droids as well as ultra-secret assassin droids. Like medical droids, the IT-O has sophisticated medical diagnostic matrices and expert programming in medicine, psychology, surgery, and humanoid biology. However, instead of analyzing what is wrong with a body system, the IT-O attempts to discover how to make a healthy system go wrong. Its vital-sign monitors make it capable of predicting and preventing the onset of catalepsy or unconsciousness, enabling the droid to bring prisoners back from the brink of death so they can endure further questioning.

A hypodermic injector syringe, deliberately oversized to inspire anxiety and fear, is one of the droid's most prominent devices. The needle dispenses a variety of liquid chemicals that are stored in internal reservoirs. These drugs can lower pain thresholds, stimulate cooperation, and trigger hallucinations. The most frequently used drug is the remarkably effective truth serum Bavo Six.

The IT-O also features a laser scalpel, a grasping claw, and power shears. Not surprisingly, the very sight of an IT-O is sufficient to frighten most prisoners into divulging secrets and submitting admissions of guilt. The droid's sensors can easily analyze a prisoner's heart rate, muscle tension, and voice patterns to evaluate whether the prisoner has told the truth. Despite the Imperial Security Bureau's boasts about the effectiveness of their interrogation droids, it is possible for strong-willed subjects to withstand the torments of an IT-O.

⬇ **Darth Vader used an IT-O droid to interrogate Princess Leia Organa on the Death Star. Image obtained from the Imperial communications complex on Galvoni III.**

1. Voice stress analysis
2. Visual recording
3. Status indicators
4. Drug dosage level
5. Subject vital signs

6. Sonic torture device
7. Function indicators
8. Electroshock assembly
9. Grasping claw
10. Confession & medical diagnostic recorder
11. Shell release handle
12. Repulsorlift
13. Interrogation drug syringe
14. Auditory sensor
15. Visual input eye
16. Repulsorlift engine housing

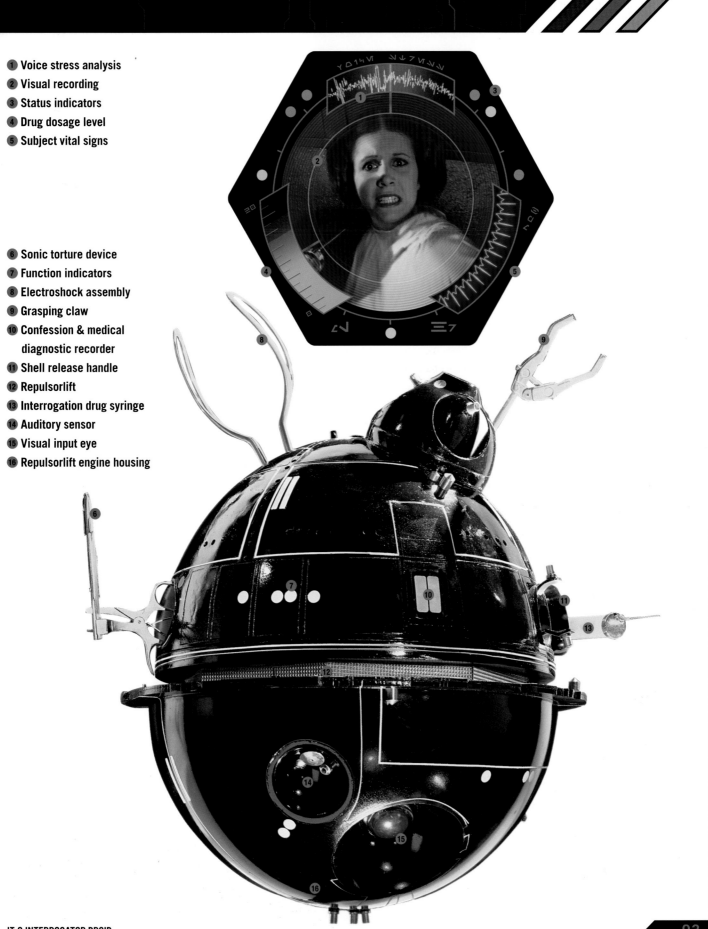

SERVICE & TECHNICAL SECTORS

Personal Data Journal Entry #478,
Grand Moff Tarkin recording

Recent exchanges with Chief Lemelisk have made it abundantly clear to me that the Death Star's ongoing service and technical requirements will require even more personnel than originally projected. Constructing a superweapon for the Empire may be our primary goal, but of tantamount importance is the need to maintain the battle station's thousands of kilometers of maintenance tunnels, accessways, trash compactors, and ventilation ducts. These areas will be the domain of the service sector, and the more I think of it, the more convinced I am that service shall be the true backbone of the station's operation.

Service technicians will spend the bulk of their duty time inspecting, maintaining, repairing, and replacing machinery. From highly-skilled technicians trained to build components from scratch, to almost-mindless droids programmed to clean corridors, service will likely be taken for granted by other sectors. Though it seems unlikely that any number of rebel attacks could ever cause a significant hull breach, the service sector's most important duty may be the upkeep of the station's protective and emergency gear.

As for the technicians who won't be part of the service sector, they shall be assigned to the technical sector, and work in the science stations, medical bays, research laboratories, programming facilities, and engineering sections. While it's hard to imagine a weapon more destructive than the superlaser, I imagine the technical sector may eventually be tasked with developing an even more powerful weapon.

However, the service and technical sector must never be allowed to become deluded into thinking they are somehow *more* important than the military sector. Their strength is not in their numbers or capabilities, but in their service to the Empire. And more specifically, in their services to the Death Star.

← Imperial astromech droids were stationed in
all hangars and docking bays on the Death Star.

MAINTENANCE SECTION 19-52

Every general sector on the Death Star had at least several maintenance areas. A typical maintenance section within a sprawl featured a series of connected repair stations, a storage warehouse full of spare parts, monitoring stations which received continual diagnostic reports and could hook into a droid's visual sensors, and machinery for repairing worn components or even constructing new components from raw materials.

All corridors and duty stations contained concealed but easily accessible emergency equipment that had to be charged with power or replaced on a regular basis. A standard emergency gear locker contained breath masks, environmental suits, food, water rations, glow rods, location beacons, laser cutters, and comlinks. Anticipating the possibility that a hull rupture could leave some personnel unable to reach escape pods, the Death Star's service

sector made sure each emergency gear locker also contained temporary environment pouches. Using these pouches personnel would be able to survive the breach of space for up to 12 hours.

When service techs were not busy performing repairs or routine maintenance on the Death Star's machinery, they were stationed at monitoring posts, where they checked temperature and performance readings or waited for system-failure alarms to sound. All machinery was installed with built-in diagnostic systems that fed performance information to the monitors in maintenance. These readings measured coolant levels, air quality, noise output, heat generations, and a score of other indications that were constantly compared to factory norms and Imperial standards. Any significant dips or rises in the data resulted in warning sensors alerting on-duty techs to make more detailed investigations.

⬇ An image obtained from an Imperial communications complex revealed Imperial MSE droids with a motley assortment of droids in Maintenance Section 19-52. Rebel allies identified the non-Imperial droids as property stolen from Jawas on Tatooine.

Vehicle maintenance shops were located on the decks below and around the latitude hangar bays. Every bay had a lift that lowered spacecraft either directly into a waiting shop or to a repulsor shaft that connected to a shop. Maintenance crews and droids cleaned carbon buildup, changed components, and overhauled engines. The shops provided routine tune-ups and overhauls for Imperial starfighters, strike cruisers, and shuttles, and were equipped with parts and materials to repair damaged spacecraft.

DEATH STAR DROIDS

Manufactured by Arakyd Industries, the RA-7 protocol droid was conceived to serve Imperial officers. The Imperial Security Bureau ordered thousands of RA-7s, and installed sophisticated programming to enable the droids to be used as spies. Although RA-7s were outnumbered by MSE droids on the Death Star, they became known as Death Star Droids because of their ubiquitous presence in all areas of the battle station, including maintenance sections.

↓ **Death Star service technicians were expected to maintain everything from Imperial probe droids to TIE fighter pilot gear.**

1 **Magnetic sensor**
2 **Broadband photoreceptors**
3 **Resonating vocabulator**
4 **Interface connection port**
5 **Advanced auditory sensors**
6 **Magnetic-grip foot plates**

The Death Star was in every way a warship, but the designers did not overlook the need for medical facilities to ensure the Imperial crew and soldiers remained healthy and fit for duty, and also to administer treatment to those who were injured during their service. A typical facility was Medical Station 381-N3, which was staffed by medical technicians of varying rank and ability, and by droids that specialized in medical techniques, including surgery, anesthesia, and prosthetics.

Arranged around a convenient turbolift cluster, Medical Station 381-N3 featured large open chambers that served as either examination rooms or operating theaters. The chambers contained diagnostic examination platforms and operating tables, and each could be partitioned to form three separate rooms.

The Death Star reportedly carried large supplies of bacta, an exotic chemical compound that can heal almost any wound. While minor wounds could be treated with disposable patches coated with bacta gel, patients with more serious injuries were completely submersed in cylindrical bacta tanks. Medical Station 381-N3 had two bacta tank wards with a total of 16 bacta tanks, which were manufactured by Zaltin Baca Corporation.

Although the restorative properties of bacta remains the fastest and most effective method for healing, bacta baths were reserved for only the most seriously injured patients. Life-threatening injuries were handled by a special intensive care ward that combined bacta-tank treatments with life-support machinery. Non-life-threatening injuries were treated and the patients were sent to recuperation wards.

1. **Dividable exam room**
2. **To recuperation wards**
3. **Medical Officer station**
4. **Medical lab**
5. **Bacta tank wards**
6. **To command offices**
7. **Turbolift cluster**
8. **To intensive care ward**
9. **Medical duty station**
10. **Secure medical storage**
11. **Sterilization field**
12. **Dividable operating room**
13. **To general sector**

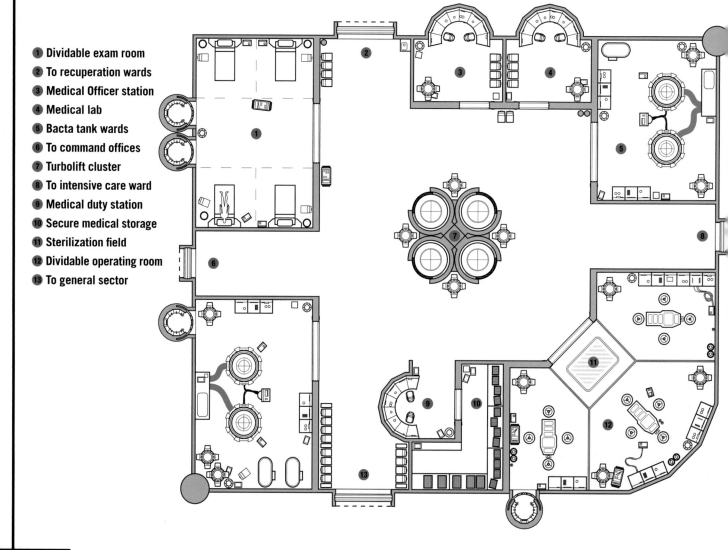

← Medical droids on the Death Star included the Emdee series of diagnostic, laboratory technician, and microsurgery mechanicals.

↑ During the Galactic Civil War, the Emperor forged alliances with two bacta corporations, Zaltin and Xucphra, making it nearly impossible for all but Imperial forces to acquire bacta.

↓ Manufactured by Medtech Industries, multi-armed FX-10 medical assistant droids were stationed in all Death Star medical stations.

1 Multiwave visual sensors
2 Hydraulic lines
3 Medical diagnostic computer
4 Computer interface socket
5 Servogrip pincers
6 Torso sheath
7 Hypodermic injector

WASTE REMOVAL

The Death Star's service sector was responsible for trash removal and processing. All personal quarters had their own refuse disposal points that fed into the larger chutes like tributaries into a river. Every corridor and room on the battle station had a trash disposal chute that led to a large waste-collection bin. Each city sprawl shared a single bin.

The entire process of waste management and disposal was controlled by central computer. Droids broke trash down, separating recyclable materials such as plastics, metal, food, and water from unrecyclable waste. Recyclable materials were sent for processing to the manufacturing centers within the zone or to the bulk storage and replication sections in the Death Star's deeper levels. Waste was directed through an elaborate system of garbage chutes and distributed into each zone's numerous trash compactors.

To maximize the amount of refuse that could be stored inside the compactors, the compactors' metal walls were designed to close together and crush trash into the smallest possible size. The compactors' maintenance hatches were magnetically sealed to prevent possibly toxic and combustible combinations of refuse from causing damage, and to prevent waste materials from leaking into outer chambers and nearby compartments. Despite the efforts at recycling, Imperials gave little thought to disposing of large, damaged girders and other construction materials, and tended to use the compactors like common dumpsters.

After being compacted, the trash would be moved to a jettison compartment along one of the trenches. As with other Imperial Navy vessels, the Death Star jettisoned unrecyclable trash immediately prior to hyperspace jumps.

⬇ Images obtained from an Imperial communications complex revealed Princess Leia Organa, Chewbacca the Wookiee, Han Solo, and Luke Skywalker landed within the confines of Death Star trash compactor 3263827 after their escape from Detention Block AA-23.

DIANOGA

Sometimes called 'garbage squid', dianoga evolved as marine scavengers on the swamp world Vordan. Ages ago, dianoga slithered into the hold of a space freighter, and the creatures quickly spread their populations to many planets. Thriving in sewers and river canals of large urban areas throughout the galaxy, dianoga feed on all types of refuse, and can consume almost anything except pure metals. A dianoga possesses seven tentacles used for locomotion and to catch food, and has a single, flexible eyestalk, which can extend around corners, or up like a periscope from underwater. Because dianogas can consume vast quantities of garbage, the Death Star's service sector not only tolerates their presence, but actually breeds them for use in the trash compactors.

↖ After a dianoga snared Luke Skywalker, Han Solo attempted to tug him free. The tentacled creature did not release Luke until the compactor walls began to move.

↑ In a desperate effort to stop the compactor's walls from converging, Princess Leia and her allies attempted to shift large pieces of scrap metal to jam the walls.

↓ Imperial technicians ignored scans of dianoga in the Death Star trash compactors because the creatures helped break down garbage and posed no threat.

COMMAND SECTOR

Excerpt from Personal Data Journal Entry #49, General Tagge of the Imperial Army recording

The Imperial command structure aboard the Death Star will be as strict as any organization found in the Empire. Command sectors will be found throughout the battle station, and will include many controls rooms. Imperial officers of no less than lieutenant rank shall supervise the command sectors.

The battle station will be under the command of a triumvirate headed by Grand Moff Tarkin, myself, and Admiral Motti of the Imperial Navy. The Chiefs of Navy, Army, and Battle Station Operations will be held by officers with the rank of colonel. Below each Operations Chief, eight majors will serve as chiefs of specific departments under heir branch of operations. In addition, four majors will be responsible for the general, service, technical, security, and military sectors. The military sectors will include Army troopers, the Navy's Death Star troopers, gunners, and pilots.

Two significant portions of the Death Star complement will not fall under the normal command structure, but are worth noting. The first is the Emperor's emissary, Lord Darth Vader, who will answer to Grand Moff Tarkin, and will not be subject to any other authority aboard the Death Star. Second, the Imperial stormtroopers. Both the Army and Navy may call upon the services of the stormtroopers, but with the firm understanding that these soldiers fall under the jurisdiction of neither, and that their primary loyalty is to the Emperor alone.

Although the Emperor rarely ventures from Coruscant, it is his decree that the Death Star must include a throne room. We must prepare this chamber with the full expectation that the Emperor will visit the battle station. The maintenance and management of the throne room shall also fall to the command sector.

← When Emperor Palpatine was aboard the Death Star, his throne room was in every way the pinnacle of the command sector.

A vast command center that monitored all workstations and datafiles on the Death Star, the overbridge was the primary headquarters for the battle station's command triumvirate: Grand Moff Tarkin, General Tagge, and Admiral Motti. All information collected by the Death Star's bridges, sensor arrays, communication centers, and space traffic control was routed through the station's central computers and displayed on banks of monitors and holoprojectors situated throughout the overbridge. A secure holo communications booth allowed for private transmissions between the Grand Moff or Darth Vader and the Emperor.

Each member of the triumvirate had his own command station, and also stations for the operation chiefs at their respective services. They were assisted by lesser officers, droids, and enlisted crew who worked throughout each duty shift. In emergencies, the overbridge could cut off all lesser command centers and control the entire Death Star.

Although the overbridge was quite capable of controlling the battle station during non-emergency situations as well, the triumvirate acknowledged it was more efficient to assign each zone's active bridge to be responsible for their own operations. Although the Death Star's designers believed it was highly unlikely that the overbridge could ever be damaged beyond repair, Emperor Palpatine insisted on a contingency plan for one of the

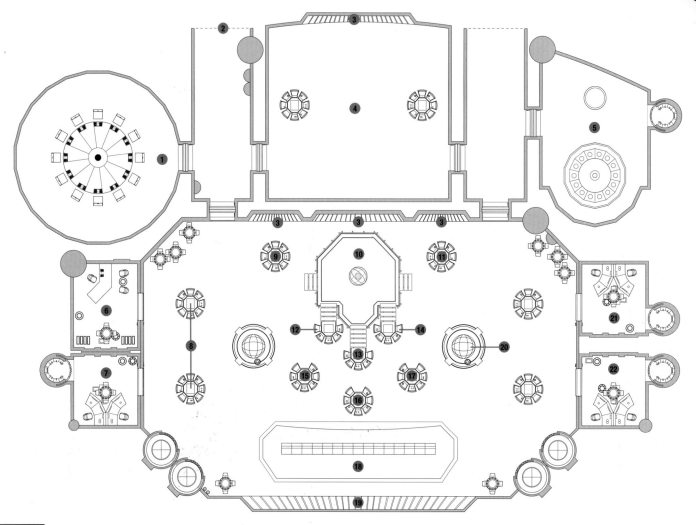

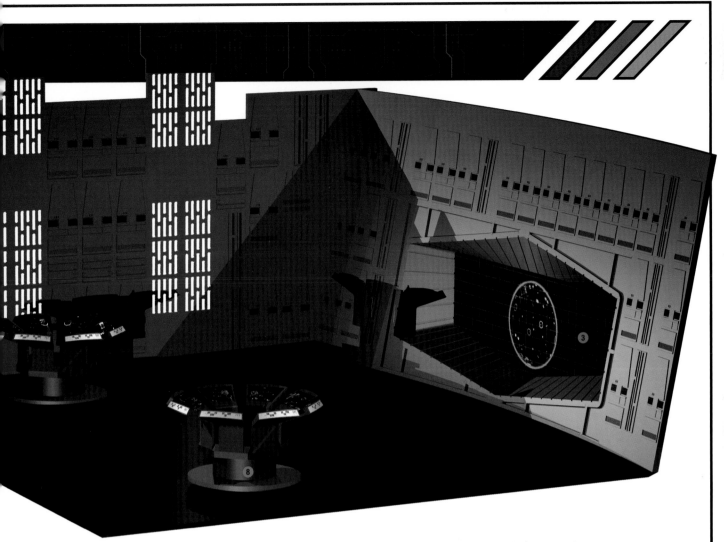

1. Conference room
2. To command staff offices
3. Viewscreens
4. Command sanctum
5. Secure holo booth
6. Grand Moff's office
7. Battle station operation's office
8. Duty posts
9. Security post
10. Command platform
11. Stormtrooper officer post
12. General's command station
13. Grand Moff's command station
14. Admiral's command station
15. Army operations chief
16. Battle station operations chief
17. Navy operations chief
18. Duty crew pit
19. Main viewscreen
20. Strategic holo display
21. Navy operation's office
22. Army operation's office

zone bridges or the throne room to assume control of the station. Only the Emperor's throne room could supersede the overbridge.

In addition to the operating officers and crew, 12 security officers and guards maintained posts on the overbridge to monitor the safety of the triumvirate. Sixteen stormtroopers were permanently assigned to the overbridge to maintain order and remind officers as well as crew that they all served the Emperor's will.

↑ The fortified command sanctum could be accessed only by the highest ranking officers during major station operations.

↓ Grand Moff Tarkin, Admiral Motti, Darth Vader, and General Tagge conferred on the Death Star's overbridge.

CONFERENCE ROOM

Adjacent to the Death Star's overbridge was a conference room with nearby offices for the command triumvirate and their aides. The conference room was used by the commanders to discuss daily operations as well as classified information. To ensure privacy, the rooms and offices were riddled with concealed sensors, sound dampeners, and frequency jammers that allowed conversation but effectively crippled any unauthorized transmissions or recordings.

To reach the conference room, one had to pass through four security points, each one requiring an increasing level of security clearance. Two guards remained in the room throughout meetings, quietly serving to remind delegates of the Imperial authority in charge.

Twelve seats ringed the room's large, circular table, which held embedded computer terminals and data displays. The terminals were used to brief commanders on battle tactics, and were linked to the Death Star's central command computers. A spherical holoprojector was located at the center of the table, and was used to display three-dimensional models of targets, planets, and enemy fleet formations.

Although a circular table in a conference room generally implies a degree of democracy, the Death Star's conference table had a strict seating hierarchy. The senior Imperial official, Grand Moff Tarkin, occupied a seat with an extended back. Those next in the chain of command would sit on either side of Tarkin, with the most junior officer seated opposite Tarkin at the bottom of the table. When Darth Vader attended such meetings, he rarely took a seat, and apparently preferred to remain standing.

A team of senior staff officers served as conference-room attendants. Responsible for preparing the room for meetings and keeping it spotless, they primed the terminals with necessary briefing notes, checked programming of holomodels, and executed thorough security sweeps prior to each meeting. During meetings, the attendants were stationed in a nearby room, ready to respond if summoned.

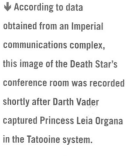

⬇ **According to data obtained from an Imperial communications complex, this image of the Death Star's conference room was recorded shortly after Darth Vader captured Princess Leia Organa in the Tatooine system.**

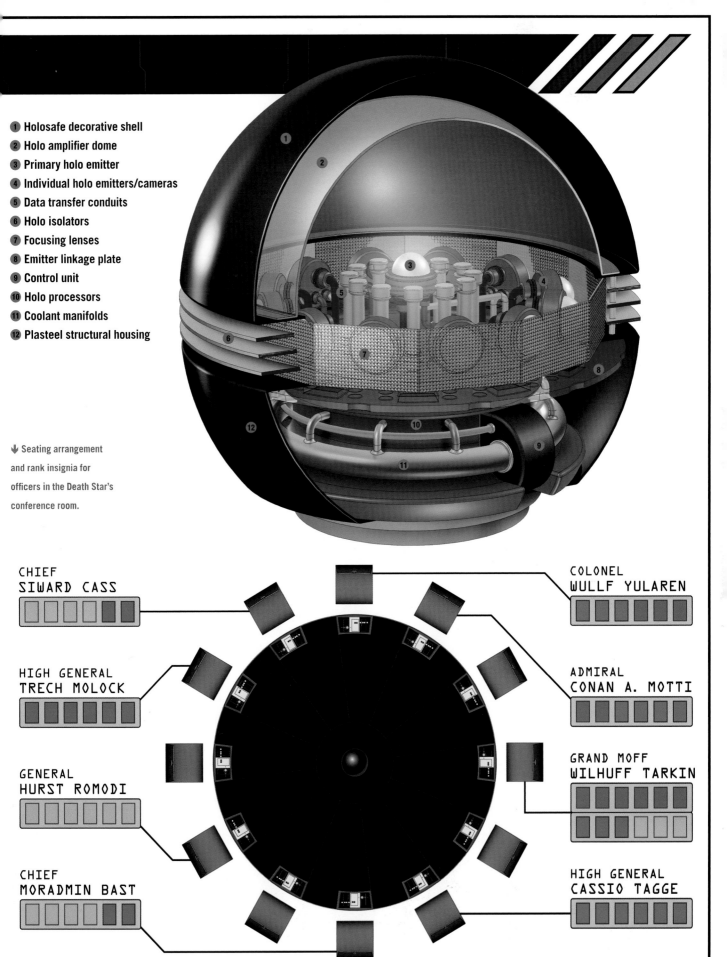

1. Holosafe decorative shell
2. Holo amplifier dome
3. Primary holo emitter
4. Individual holo emitters/cameras
5. Data transfer conduits
6. Holo isolators
7. Focusing lenses
8. Emitter linkage plate
9. Control unit
10. Holo processors
11. Coolant manifolds
12. Plasteel structural housing

⬇ Seating arrangement
and rank insignia for
officers in the Death Star's
conference room.

CHIEF
SIWARD CASS

HIGH GENERAL
TRECH MOLOCK

GENERAL
HURST ROMODI

CHIEF
MORADMIN BAST

COLONEL
WULLF YULAREN

ADMIRAL
CONAN A. MOTTI

GRAND MOFF
WILHUFF TARKIN

HIGH GENERAL
CASSIO TAGGE

COMMAND SECTOR DUTY POSTS

➡ Imperial records confirmed the identity of Sergeant Jad Bean at a duty post in the Death Star's command center.

On the Death Star, any supervision station operated by an Imperial lieutenant or higher-ranking officer was designated a command sector duty post. A single duty post served as a "mini-bridge" for the commanding officer, the primary place from which he supervised his command and issued orders to his crew.

Each duty post console contained up to eight control boards, with four boards dedicated to the particular tasks assigned to the post. The remaining boards handled communications, damage and diagnostics, computer access, and a direct feed to the post's controlling bridge. Duty posts with eight control boards were designed with partially extendible frames that slid selected console modules aside to create a gap between modules, which enabled commanding officers to step in and out of their posts with ease.

Two to four security guards were stationed at typical command sector duty posts. Using the post's communications console, the commanding officer could summon additional guards, stormtroopers, and even Death Star troopers if the need arose.

➡ Sergeant Derek Torent, the senior watch trooper at the Death Star's command center, monitored external sensor data and scanned for Rebel Alliance activity.

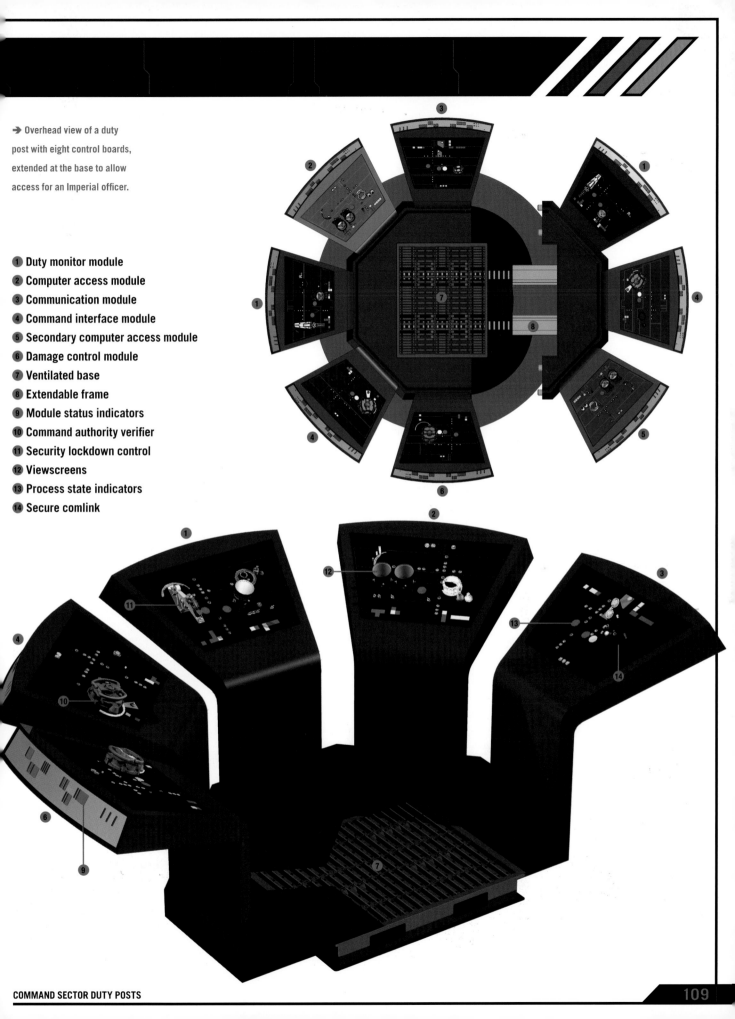

→ Overhead view of a duty post with eight control boards, extended at the base to allow access for an Imperial officer.

1. Duty monitor module
2. Computer access module
3. Communication module
4. Command interface module
5. Secondary computer access module
6. Damage control module
7. Ventilated base
8. Extendable frame
9. Module status indicators
10. Command authority verifier
11. Security lockdown control
12. Viewscreens
13. Process state indicators
14. Secure comlink

DEATH STAR II

Declassified message to Rebel Alliance leader Princess Leia Organa, delivered via messenger droid from Koth Melan, Assistant Consul General for the Bothan Trade Mission:

"Greetings, Princess Leia. Koth Melan here, speaking to you from my homeworld of Bothawui. Our spy network has uncovered information vital to the Alliance, and the nature of these data are of such significance as to justify sending this messenger droid. You must come to Bothawui immediately. I cannot overemphasize the importance of this information, or the urgency. Time is of the essence. I will be at the Intergalactic Trade Mission for five days. The Alliance must act in that time or the information may be lost."

Excerpt from Princess Leia Organa's address to fellow leaders of the Rebel Alliance:

"Koth Melan's Bothan agents discovered that the Empire has begun work on a new military project. The exact details are unknown, but according to Melan, the Emperor is diverting huge amounts of money, material, and men for this project. Unfortunately, the Bothans have been unable to pierce the cloud of secrecy that surrounds this matter.

"However, the agents have ascertained that the plans for this project are kept in the Emperor's computer vault on Coruscant, and that these plans will be copied onto another computer and transferred to Bothawui for dissemination to key personnel within the Imperial Intelligence community stationed there. If the Bothans can obtain this computer and crack its security codes, the Imperial secret will be laid bare.

"In case you're wondering, Koth Melan has not requested a fee for this information. Evidently, the Bothans are on our side."

← In its unfinished state in the remote Endor system, the second Death Star did not appear to be an immediate threat to the Rebel Alliance. However, both the construction status and location of the Death Star were part of an elaborate trap conceived by the Emperor himself.

After the destruction of the Death Star at Yavin, Emperor Palpatine ordered designer Bevel Lemelisk to produce an even more advanced battle station, with a hypermatter reactor able to generate power equivalent to hundreds of super-giant stars. The Emperor also demanded a faster hyperdrive for the new station.

Lemelisk immediately corrected the egregious flaws in the original design to leave no weak spots in the station's armor. Instead of relying on thermal exhaust ports to vent the reactor's incredible excess heat, the new station would instead funnel the waste energy through a series of millions of millimeter-wide heat dispersion ducts, which carried excess heat from the reactor core to the station's surface. If the ducts were hit during an attack, they were equipped with emergency baffles that were designed to muffle any high pulse of energy before it reached the core.

Lemelisk was also tasked with redesigning the station so its superlaser would deliver a more devastating blast, and have an increased rate of fire and greater accuracy.

While the first Death Star's superlaser required a recharge period of twenty-four hours, the second Death Star featured a superlaser that could be recharged in a matter of minutes. The superlaser's targeting and power-control systems were also refined so the weapon could be directed at relatively small moving targets such as capital ships.

The new superlaser and drive systems required larger power generators, which necessitated that the station would be much larger than its predecessor. When finished, the second Death Star would have over twice the volume of the original at 160 kilometers in diameter. To repel attacks from starfighters and capital ships, Lemelisk's plans included over 30,000 turbolasers, 7,500 laser cannons, and 5,000 ion cannons.

The second Death Star was constructed in orbit of the Forest Moon of Endor. Despite the improvements in the station's design, one flaw remained: the Emperor's hubris. His overconfidence allowed the forces of the Rebel Alliance to destroy the station, signaling a death knell for the Empire.

SPECIFICATIONS

CRAFT: Death Star II battlestation
MANUFACTURER: Imperial Department
  of Military Research
DIAMETER: 160km (99.4 miles)
HYPERDRIVE: Class 3.0
HYPERDRIVE BACKUP: 20
SHIELDING: Equipped
NAVIGATION SYSTEM: Navicomputer

ARMAMENT: Superlaser, 15,000 turbolaser batteries, 15,000
  heavy turbolasers, 7,500 laser cannons, 5,000 ion cannons,
  and 1,500 tractor-beam emplacements
CREW: 485,560; 152,275 gunners; 1,295,950 troops; 127,570
  infantry; 75,860 technical personnel; 334,432 support ship
  pilots and crew
CARGO CAPACITY: Over one million kilotons
CONSUMABLES: 3 years
COST: Unknown

Based on the design of Geonosian masticators used for the construction of Trade Federation battleships, Imperial Masticators are spherical vessels engineered to capture asteroids, break the asteroids down into raw materials, and prepare the processed materials for hull-plate extruders.

Each Imperial Masticator was equipped with tractor beam generators and projectors to draw asteroids into the maws of fusion-powered masticators. Masticators had maws with whirling durasteel teeth, which chewed the asteroid to tiny bits, and mixed the bits with alloy ores, including quadanium that had been mined and imported from the planet Despayre. Water was added to the resulting gravel, which was put under high pressure to form a semiliquid mixture that fed into pipelines that led to the smelters. Essentially huge melting pots that refined the mix, the smelters burned off impurities before the resulting scarified ore was conveyed to extruders that pressed out the hull plates. Leftover slag was gathered, then ejected toward the solar system's central star.

⬇ **After gathering and processing raw materials from an asteroid belt, Imperial Masticators worked in tandem with hull-plate extruders to construct the battle station.**

Imperial Masticators not only processed materials, but were also equipped with large utility arms and docking arms, enabling them to work directly on the Death Star's superstructure.

Determined to fully utilize the Masticators, Bevel Lemelisk engineered them so that they could be relatively easily dismantled, and then separated into components that could be reformed and incorporated into the Death Star during the battle station's final stages of construction.

IMPERIAL HULL-PLATE EXTRUDERS (HPES)

Equipped with sublight engines, Imperial hull-plate extruders were orbital manufacturing facilites that created complex cross-sectional materials for Imperial Star Destroyers and other large spacecraft. The Death Star's designers programmed the extruders to produce broad, curved durasteel plating that would simultaneously support the station's surface structures and protect the subsurface levels.

AT-CT
(ALL TERRAIN CONSTRUCTION TRANSPORT)

Used for large-scale construction projects on distant worlds, single-pilot All Terrain Construction Transports have advanced tractor beam technology that can lift, manipulate, and move heavy objects with ease. Death Star construction crews used the vehicles to move girders, crates, and other pieces of heavy equipment to precise locations.

↘ Manufactured by Kuat Drive Yards under the direction of the Imperial Department of Military Research, the All Terrain Construction Transport incorporated technology and parts from the Imperial All Terrain Scout Transport. The pressurized cockpit allowed pilots to operate in airless environments.

→ The large opening in the Death Star's superstructure allowed access for vehicles and droids during the battle station's construction.

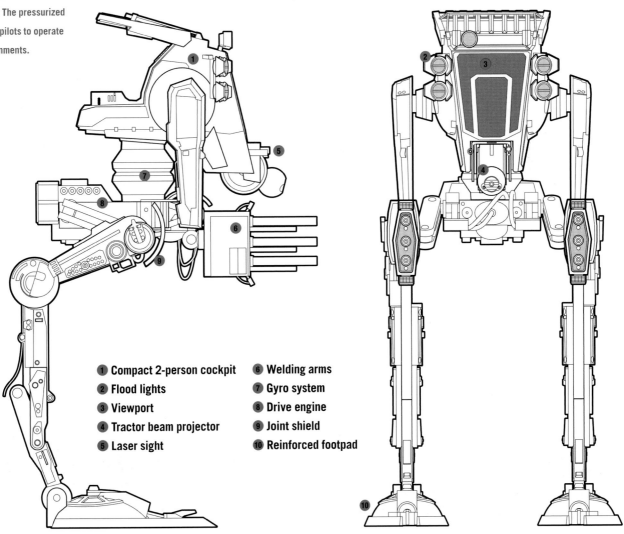

1. Compact 2-person cockpit
2. Flood lights
3. Viewport
4. Tractor beam projector
5. Laser sight
6. Welding arms
7. Gyro system
8. Drive engine
9. Joint shield
10. Reinforced footpad

PLANETARY SHIELD GENERATOR

Although the second Death Star, during its construction in orbit of the Forest Moon of Endor, was guarded by Imperial star destroyers and other warships, its most significant defense was a massive CoMar SLD-26 planetary shield generator. More powerful than any standard deflector shield system, a planetary shield is a force field that nullifies both physical and energy attacks. It uses layers of charged energy that are capable of not only dissipating turbolaser blasts and destroying space debris on contact, but is impervious to concussion missiles, asteroids, comet strikes, and enemy starships of any size. In fact, a collision with a planetary shield will reduce any starship to space dust.

Built on the forest moon's surface, the SLD-26 planetary shield generator consisted of a dish network, an underground generator, and an above-ground shield projector complex that spanned an area of 70km (43 miles) in diameter. The planetary shield generator projected an energy screen that completely enveloped the orbital Death Star II, and could be easily defended by anti-infantry and anti-vehicle turrets. The only

weapon capable of penetrating the energy screen was a superlaser.

Because the planetary shield generator's projected energy screen has great destructive power and is virtually invisible, it can be used as an offensive weapon. Enemy pilots are forced to rely on sensor readings to avoid contact with the energy screen, but technicians can jam or block enemy sensors to effectively conceal the planetary shield's presence. The Empire used this tactic at the Battle of Endor, and nearly destroyed numerous rebel starfighters.

⬇ **Constructed by Imperial forces on Endor, an elevated landing platform was the touchdown deck for Imperial shuttles and other spacecraft. The platform's columnar legs housed turbo lifts that led to corridors and catwalks that terminated at loading gantries for All Terrain Armored Transports (AT-ATs).**

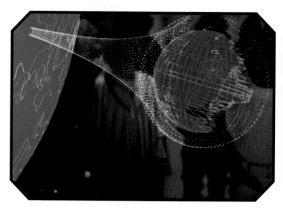

1. **Emitter antenna**
2. **Amplification projector**
3. **Projection focusers**
4. **Shield projectors**
5. **Focus dish**
6. **Projector relay**
7. **Amplification grid**
8. **Project adjust**
9. **Capacitor banks**
10. **Power core**
11. **Turbine generator**

← Stolen holographic schematics of the Imperial planetary shield generator allowed the Rebel Alliance to form a plan to destroy the second Death Star.

↓ Guarded by scout troopers, a reinforced durasteel-plated bunker served as a back door to the shield generator's control room and power generator.

↓ Located beneath Endor's surface, the Imperial installation's primary and back-up generators supplied power to the massive defensive shield projector.

Built within an armored sphere on the uppermost level of a high tower on the Death Star, the Imperial throne room was a fully functional command center that allowed the Emperor to control, monitor, and communicate with all areas of the battle station. The throne used technologies tuned to the Emperor's unique physical and mental patterns, and responded only to his commands. Large windows offered expansive views of the station and surrounding space. The tower was the most heavily shielded portion of the entire battle station, and its hull was doubly reinforced to protect against incoming artillery, making the tower virtually impenetrable from the outside. In the event that the tower ever suffered structural damage, an emergency throne room was located within the armored sphere, just below the tower.

The main area of the throne room was split into three levels. A narrow overseer gantry stretched above the central floor , and was connected to a single turbolift

shaft that ran the length of the tower. The lift shaft was situated inside a larger, open well that plunged for many kilometers, and led directly to the Death Star's main reactor core.

The royal living quarters and quarters for the Emperor's personal body guards were located below the throne room. When the throne room and royal apartment were unoccupied, four squads of stormtroopers guarded it in the Emperor's absence. When the Emperor was present, the stormtroopers were replaced by four squads of the Imperial Royal Guard.

To deter unwanted visitors, all corridors leading to the throne room and royal apartments were loaded with traps and security measures. Anyone approaching the corridor that led to the tower's restricted turbolift was required to punch in an identifying code before entering the trap-filled passageway. Those who failed to identify themselves properly were subject to either immediate capture or death by laserfire.

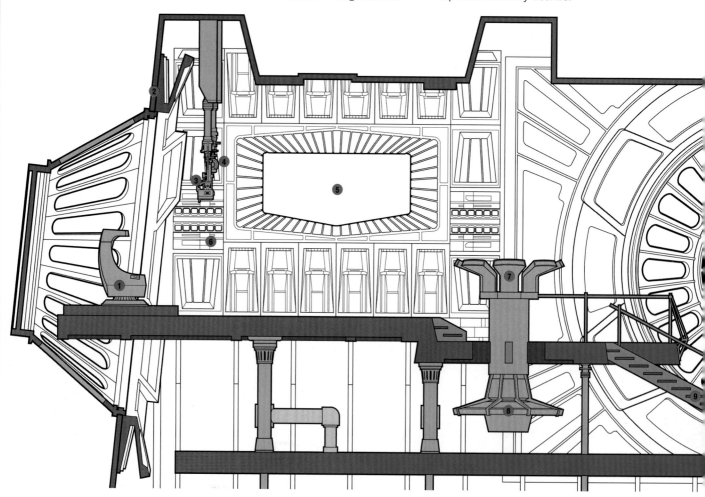

COMMAND SEAT

The Emperor's throne concealed a personal deflector shield generator and layers of ultra-dense alloyed armor. A panel on one of the armrests had controls that allowed the Emperor to turn the massive throne, and also light-beam secure communication links to summon members of the Imperial Guard, Darth Vader, the Death Star's commander, or the Emperor's advisors. Control consoles throughout the upper and lower levels of the throne room were engineered to allow a small staff of officers to override and operate all of the battle station's functions from the tower.

1. **Throne**
2. **Reinforced hull**
3. **Targeting viewer**
4. **Holocam/projector**
5. **Viewscreen**
6. **Display controls**
7. **Duty post**
8. **Lower console**
9. **Staircase**
10. **Catwalk**
11. **Transparasteel viewport**
12. **Bridge to turbolift**

⬆ Emperor Palpatine surveyed his throne room from a swivel-mounted seat.

⬇ Inside the shielded tower, the Emperor's Royal Guards were stationed by a turbolift.

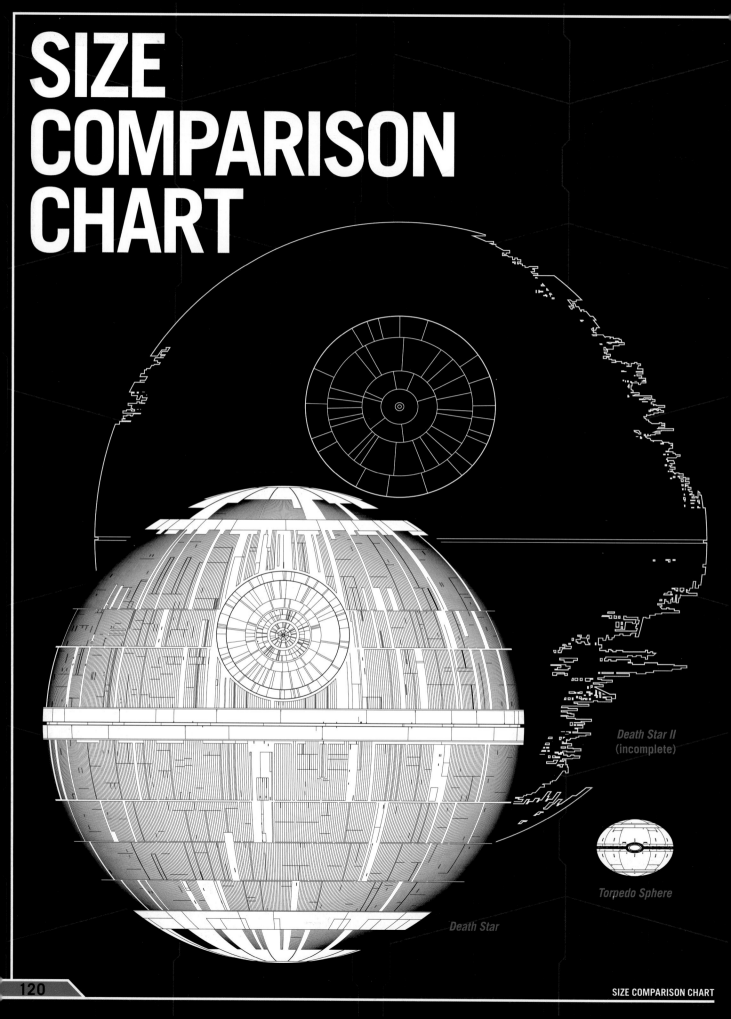

SIZE COMPARISON CHART

Death Star II
(incomplete)

Torpedo Sphere

Death Star

120

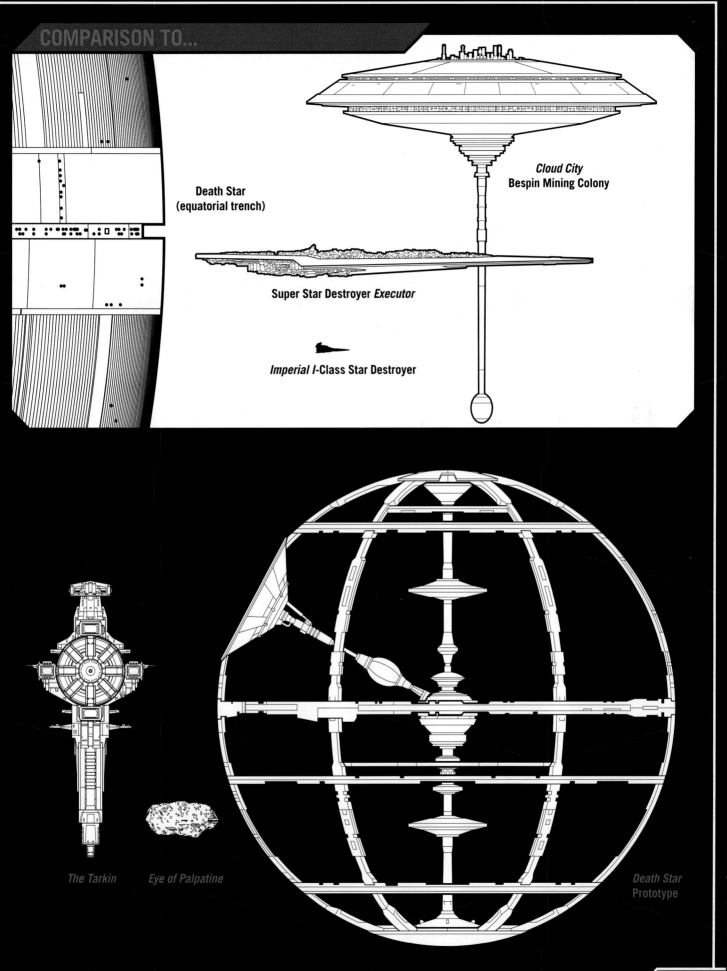

Death Star
(equatorial trench)

Cloud City
Bespin Mining Colony

Super Star Destroyer *Executor*

Imperial I-**Class Star Destroyer**

The Tarkin

Eye of Palpatine

Death Star
Prototype

ACKNOWLEDGMENTS

The author and artists of the *Death Star Owner's Workshop Manual* incorporated information about the Death Star from previously published *Star Wars* technical guides, game books, sourcebooks, and novels. We are especially indebted to Bill Slavicsek for his work on the invaluable *Star Wars: Death Star Technical Companion*. Other notable sources of reference include *The Star Wars Sourcebook* by Bill Slavicsek and Curtis Smith; *Star Wars Galaxy Guide 1: A New Hope* by Michael Stern and Paul Sudlow; *Star Wars Galaxy Guide 5: Return of the Jedi* by Michael Stern and George Strayton; *Star Wars: Imperial Sourcebook* by Greg Gorden; *Star Wars: The New Essential Guide to Characters* by Daniel Wallace; *Star Wars: The Essential Guide to Vehicles and Vessels* and *Star Wars: The Essential Guide to Weapons and Technology* by Bill Smith and Troy Vigil; *Star Wars Technical Journal* by Shane Johnson; *Star Wars: Incredible Cross-Sections: The Classic Trilogy* by David West Reynolds, Hans Jenssen, and Richard Chasemore; *The Complete Star Wars Encyclopedia* by Stephen J. Sansweet and Pablo Hidalgo with contributions from Bob Vitas, Daniel Wallace, Chris Cassidy, Mary Franklin, and Josh Kushins; *Star Wars: Death Star* by Michael Reeves and Steve Perry; and *Star Wars: The Blueprints* by J.W. Rinzler.

Special thanks to the following people for their help with reference for this project: Gus Lopez, Philip Wise, Michael Erwin, Daren Murrer, Cole Horton, Tiny Panganiban, Guy Vardaman, Zach Spencer, Marcus Thompson, Jean-François Boivin, and our friends at Lucasfilm including Leland Chee, Pablo Hidalgo, Stacey Leong, and Jonathan Rinzler.

We also gratefully acknowledge George Lucas, John Barry, Joe Johnston, Ralph McQuarrie, Lorne Peterson, Norman Reynolds, and their colleagues for their significant contributions to the Death Star in the *Star Wars* movies.

RYDER WINDHAM

A former editor for Dark Horse Comics, Ryder Windham is the author of more than fifty *Star Wars* books. His previous collaborations with artists Chris Trevas and Chris Reiff include *Star Wars Blueprints: The Ultimate Collection*, *Star Wars Blueprints: Rebel Edition*, *Star Wars: Millennium Falcon—A 3-D Owner's Guide* and the Haynes *Millennium Falcon Owner's Workshop Manual*. He resides with his family in Providence, Rhode Island.

CHRIS REIFF

Chris Reiff is an illustrator, toy designer, and inventor with more than 17 years experience working on official *Star Wars* projects and with licenses from companies like Marvel and Disney. Some of his latest illustration works include *The Bounty Hunter Code*, and *Star Wars Lightsaber Thumb Wrestling*. He lives in Cincinnati, Ohio with his dog named Dog and the full-size R2-D2 replica he built for himself.
www.chrisreiff.com

CHRIS TREVAS

Chris Trevas has been working professionally in the *Star Wars* universe since 1995 illustrating everything from limited edition fine art prints to floaty pens. His numerous book projects include *Star Wars: The Essential Reader's Companion* and *Darth Vader: A 3-D Reconstruction Log*. Chris works from his home studio in Beverly Hills, Michigan where he lives with his wife and three daughters.
www.christrevas.com

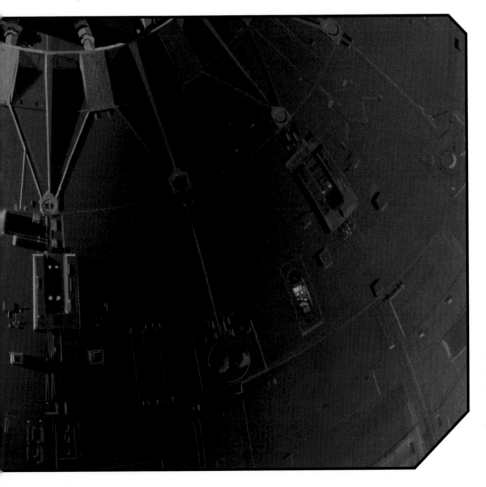

← **"Battle for Death Star (fighters dive on sphere)" (1975) was artist Ralph McQuarrie's first concept painting of the Death Star for *Star Wars*. Although the painting is frequently inverted for publication, McQuarrie intended it to be viewed with this orientation.**